The Highly Hypnotizable Person

It is commonly known that some individuals are more easily hypnotized than others. What is less clear is why, and what can be learnt from these individual differences for hypnosis as a whole. In recent years, the scientific study of hypnosis has become increasingly detailed and sophisticated. *The Highly Hypnotizable Person* examines these findings and provides an up-to-date, comprehensive overview of what evidence there is for the existence and features of highly hypnotizable people.

The Highly Hypnotizable Person draws on research findings from cognitive, developmental and clinical psychology and from neuropsychology and neurophysiology. With contributions from leading authorities in this field, this book presents a thorough account of what is known and understood about this phenomenon and treatment procedure, and in particular, the nature and implications of high susceptibility.

Michael Heap, Department of Psychology, Wathwood Hospital Medium Secure Unit, Rotherham.
Richard J. Brown, School of Psychiatry and Behavioural Sciences, University of Manchester.
David A. Oakley, Hypnosis Unit, Department of Psychology, University College London.

The Highly Hypnotizable Person

Theoretical, experimental and clinical issues

Edited by Michael Heap,
Richard J. Brown and
David A. Oakley

Routledge
Taylor & Francis Group

LONDON AND NEW YORK

First published 2004 by Brunner-Routledge
27 Church Road, Hove, East Sussex BN3 2FA

Simultaneously published in the USA and Canada
by Brunner-Routledge
29 West 35th Street, New York NY 10001

Brunner-Routledge is an imprint of the Taylor & Francis Group

© 2004 selection and editorial matter, Michael Heap, Richard J.
Brown and David A. Oakley; individual chapters, the contributors.

Typeset in Times by RefineCatch Ltd, Bungay, Suffolk
Printed and bound in Great Britain by
TJ International Ltd, Padstow, Cornwall
Cover design by Hybert Design

This publication has been produced with paper manufactured to
strict environmental standards and with pulp derived from
sustainable forests.

British Library Cataloguing in Publication Data
A catalogue record for this book is available from the British Library

Library of Congress Cataloging-in-Publication Data
The highly hypnotizable person : theoretical, experimental, and
clinical issues / edited by Michael Heap, Richard J. Brown, and David
A. Oakley.
      p. cm.
    Includes bibliographical references and index.
    ISBN 1-58391-171-5 (alk. paper) – ISBN 1-58391-172-3
(pbk. : alk. paper)
    1. Hypnotic susceptibility. I. Heap, Michael. II. Brown, Richard J.,
1974– . III. Oakley, David A. IV. Title.

    BF1156.S83H47   2004   2004002157
    154.7'6 – dc22

ISBN 1–58391–171–5 (Hbk)
ISBN 1–58391–172–3 (Pbk)

Contents

Contributors

Dr Amanda J. Barnier, School of Psychology, University of New South Wales, Sydney, NSW 2052, Australia.

Dr Richard J. Brown, Academic Division of Clinical Psychology, School of Psychiatry and Behavioural Sciences, University of Manchester, 2nd Floor ERC, Wythenshawe Hospital, Manchester, M23 9LT, UK.

Prof. Helen J. Crawford, Department of Psychology, Virginia Polytechnic Institute and State University, Blacksburg, VA 24060, USA.

Dr Donald R. Gorassini, Department of Psychology, King's College, 266 Epworth Avenue, London ON, N6A 2M3, Canada.

Dr Michael Heap, Department of Psychology, Wathwood Hospital Medium Secure Unit, Gipsy Green Lane, Wath-upon-Dearne, Rotherham, S63 7TQ, UK.

Dr James E. Horton, Department of Social and Behavioral Sciences, The University of Virginia's College at Wise, Wise, VA 24293, USA.

Prof. Steven Jay Lynn, Department of Psychology, State University of New York at Binghamton, Binghamton, NY 13902, USA.

Prof. Kevin M. McConkey, Department of Psychology, University of New South Wales, Sydney, NSW 2052, Australia.

Dr Eric Meyer, Department of Psychology, State University of New York at Binghamton, Binghamton, NY 13902, USA.

Dr David A. Oakley, Hypnosis Unit, Department of Psychology, University College London, Gower Street, London WC1E 6BT, UK.

Prof. Judith Rhue, College of Osteopathic Medicine, Ohio University, Athens, OH 45701, USA.

Dr Kelley Shindler, Department of Psychology, State University of New York at Binghamton, Binghamton, NY 13902, USA.

Prof. Graham Turpin, Clinical Psychology Unit, University of Sheffield, Western Bank, Sheffield, S10 2TP, UK.

Dr Graham F. Wagstaff, Department of Psychology, Eleanor Rathbone Building, Bedford Street South, University of Liverpool, L69 7ZA, UK

Introduction

This book presents a comprehensive account of theoretical and experimental work on hypnotizability, with particular reference to the characteristics of those people who are very responsive to hypnotic suggestions.

It has long been acknowledged that individuals vary in their capacity to respond to hypnosis, but it is only in relatively recent times that this responsiveness has been reliably measured by agreed criteria. The outcome of laboratory research on hypnotic responsiveness has confirmed that it is a characteristic that varies between extremes in the population around a central tendency and that an individual's score is very stable over a period of many years. Given the long history of scepticism, not infrequently expressed by the question 'Does hypnosis really exist?', these fundamental findings are very significant for the status of hypnosis as an important psychological phenomenon for scientific investigation.

Despite this, numerous important questions remain the focus of scientific exploration, not least amongst them being what it is that scales of hypnotic susceptibility are actually measuring. It has been the tradition in the history of hypnosis from its earliest modern foundations in mesmerism to conceive of high hypnotizability as the capacity to enter a profound 'state' of hypnosis or 'trance'. That is, hypnotizability is the depth of trance into which any individual is capable of entering. This is probably the popular contemporary view. However, research over the last 50 years has made it clear that the assumptions upon which this understanding of hypnosis is made have only very weak support. Consequently, the reader unfamiliar with hypnosis will soon discover as he or she embarks on this book that the hypnotizability scales currently in use are not designed in any direct manner to assess the traditional notion of 'trance capacity'.

This is immediately apparent when we consider the construction of the typical hypnotic susceptibility scale. This consists of a number of suggestions whereby the hypnotist directs the subject's imagination, with the intention of eliciting changes in the way that he or she is behaving, thinking and feeling. The extent to which the subject responds to each suggestion can be rated subjectively and objectively and these ratings can be summed over all the suggestions in the scale to give a total score.

What we derive from these tests then is a measure of the subject's 'suggestibility' (bearing in mind that there are different types of suggestibility, some of which are unrelated to suggestibility as measured by the scales in question). If we were to make the claim that these scales are measuring the subject's capacity for 'depth of trance', we would have to assume that in order to respond more profoundly to the suggestions in the scale, the subject must enter deeper levels of the hypnotic state or trance. This question is extensively discussed in various sections of this book, particularly in Chapters 1 and 4.

The most widely used hypnotizability scales for research purposes include a hypnotic induction, the purpose of which is the subject of controversy. It is clear, however, that by the term 'the highly hypnotizable person' we are referring to somebody who is highly suggestible after undergoing a hypnotic induction. This is currently the accepted meaning of the term in the learned literature.

What characteristics are required to be highly hypnotizable, according to the above definition? Given the stability of hypnotic susceptibility scores over time, reliable indicators of hypnotic susceptibility have proved unusually elusive and often account for only a small proportion of the total variation in hypnotic susceptibility scores. Hence, a reliable profile of the highly hypnotizable person has been very slow to emerge. Nevertheless, the evidence has accumulated and one thing that now suggests itself is that highly hypnotizable people constitute a very interesting population. We can summarize this research by referring to the following questions.

What are the personal characteristics that determine whether a person is highly hypnotizable? A number of authors in this book turn their attention to this question (e.g. Chapters 3, 5 and 8). Clear indications are now emerging, in fact, that hypnotizability is not a unitary trait and people may be highly hypnotizable for different reasons. This particular issue is the focus of Chapter 3, and in Chapter 7 a theoretical model is presented that allows for different routes to high hypnotizability.

To what extent are the determinants of high hypnotizability invariant for any given individual? Are they determined by heredity or very early learning experiences, hence the seemingly high stability of hypnotic susceptibility? Chapter 5 presents evidence for the genetic and developmental substrates of high hypnotizability. On the other hand, we can ask whether people can be trained to develop the characteristics that predispose to high hypnotizability. Chapters 4 and 9 present the case that high hypnotizability may arise in large measure from characteristics that can be easily modified – for example, one's attitude and expectations about hypnosis and the degree to which one is actively involved in creating the intended effects. Chapter 9, in particular, surveys the evidence that coaching people to adopt the 'right' approach to hypnosis may permanently increase their measured susceptibility, and that one can therefore train people to be highly susceptible.

At odds with the aforementioned stance are research findings that highly hypnotizable people, even when they are not experiencing hypnosis, are neurophysiologically and neuropsychologically different from those of lower susceptibility. Evidence in support of this is presented in Chapter 6.

Much scientific evidence has now accumulated on the nature of hypnosis and hypnotic suggestibility. The authors of Chapter 7 draw upon this knowledge and from current theory and research findings in mainstream cognitive science to construct a comprehensive theory of hypnosis that integrates the two major approaches, namely state, or special process, and non-state, or sociocognitive.

What are the clinical implications of high hypnotizability? We can ask this question with reference to the vulnerability or otherwise of highly susceptible people to different psychological or psychophysiological disorders. We also consider the consequences of high hypnotizability for the psychological treatment of these disorders both with and without hypnosis. This area is the focus of Chapter 8.

In order to seek answers to these questions, it is essential that the theoretical framework and the research undertaken be informed by reference to modern scientific psychology and its related disciplines. Knowledge and understanding of hypnosis by the general public and by academics and professionals who are only marginally acquainted with the subject has suffered because much of what is written is not grounded in mainstream academic and applied disciplines. Fortunately, over the last 50 years, the application of scientific enquiry to hypnosis has proceeded apace. The results of this in turn provide knowledge and insights that are of significance for other areas of academic and applied psychology.

We therefore believe that the theories and research findings presented in this book will be of interest to individuals from a wide range of academic and clinical fields for whom the scientific study of hypnosis may be unknown territory. To assist such readers, the opening chapter of this book is an overview of the nature of hypnosis and current theoretical controversies. Also, Chapter 2 of this book introduces the reader to procedures for assessing hypnotizability. We believe that the newcomer to hypnosis, armed with this knowledge, will find the remaining chapters interesting, provocative and useful for his or her own field of study and expertise. With this in mind, and somewhat unusually for an academic textbook, we have as our final chapter an overview of the contents of the book by Professor Graham Turpin of the University of Sheffield. Professor Turpin is distinguished both in the field of academic psychology, notably psychophysiology, and in clinical psychology. Hitherto relatively unfamiliar with the field of hypnosis, and therefore approaching the subject in an unbiased manner, he is well qualified to provide an informed commentary on and evaluation of the material presented in this book.

Chapter I

High hypnotizability

Key issues

*Michael Heap, Richard J. Brown and
David A. Oakley*

Introduction

The purpose of this chapter is to provide an overview of hypnosis for
the reader who is unfamiliar with the subject. We will not review
theories of hypnosis in any great depth, but sufficiently so to highlight
the main theoretical controversies. We state the case that those
people who score high on hypnotic susceptibility scales may be an
interesting population for study both within and outside of the
hypnotic context, by social, cognitive, developmental and clinical
psychologists and, in recent years, neuropsychologists. Many of the
themes that we cover in this chapter will be taken up in depth by the
other contributors to this book.

The nature of hypnosis

A consideration of the meaning of the term 'hypnosis' requires us to
acknowledge at least two ways in which it is commonly used. One
way is by reference to the actions of the hypnotist. This is typified by
the definition given by Heap et al. (2001) in a report on hypnosis
commissioned by the British Psychological Society.

> The term 'hypnosis' denotes an interaction between one person,
> the 'hypnotist', and another person or other people, the 'subject'
> or 'subjects'. In this interaction the hypnotist attempts to influ-
> ence the subjects' perceptions, feelings, thinking and behaviour
> by asking them to concentrate on ideas and images that may
> evoke the intended effects. The verbal communications that the
> hypnotist uses to achieve these effects are termed 'suggestions'.
>
> (p. 3)

It will be seen that this definition says nothing about whether or not the subject actually responds in the intended ways. Other definitions of hypnosis have the experience of the subject as their focus, and in fact the above report goes on to refer this. We shall return to this matter in due course. To begin with, we will describe some of the features that characterize a 'typical' hypnotic interaction.

The hypnotic induction

A session of hypnosis usually begins with a 'hypnotic induction', which may involve one or more of a considerable range of procedures. Although most theorists (with the notable exception of Edmonston, 1981, 1991) do not consider that relaxation is an essential property of hypnosis, the most commonly used methods consist of suggestions that direct the subjects to relax and to become absorbed in their thoughts, imagery and feelings. Examples are progressive muscular relaxation, relaxed breathing, pleasant and calming imagery, and suggestions of relaxation coupled with an ideosensory or ideomotor response (see below), the most popular being eyelid heaviness and arm levitation. Typically there will be a series of two, three or four such procedures, the later ones in the sequence being designated as 'deepening' methods.

Traditionally, the role of the hypnotic induction and deepening routine is conceived as a means by which the subject is guided into a special altered state of consciousness or 'hypnotic trance', one of the major properties of which is hyper-suggestibility. We return to this issue below.

Hypnotic suggestion

Following the induction and deepening procedures, the hypnotist typically makes suggestions for the subject to experience a range of phenomena, depending on the purposes of the hypnotic interaction, be it research, therapy or entertainment.

One common type of suggestion is 'ideomotor suggestion' in which the idea is conveyed of a simple, automatic movement of a part of the body, such as a finger or arm. This kind of suggestion often also includes the idea of some alteration in perceptual experience, say, in the case of arm levitation, a feeling of lightness in the arm. This exemplifies an 'ideosensory suggestion', others being suggestions of coldness, numbness, warmth or heaviness in a part of the body.

Inhibition of a movement may also be suggested, such as arm immobility or eye catalepsy. Suggestions of this sort are commonly described as 'challenge' suggestions in the experimental literature, to convey the idea that the subject is unable to perform a movement (e.g. move their arm, open their eyes) even when challenged to do so.

Very often suggestions are augmented by descriptions of appropriate imagery, such as a helium-filled balloon in the case of arm levitation, or immersion of the hand in icy water in the case of suggested hand numbness (glove anaesthesia).

Visual experiences may be the target of the suggestion (e.g. 'When you open your eyes you will see your best friend standing in front of you'), likewise auditory, olfactory or gustatory. In the literature, responses to these kinds of suggestions are sometimes termed 'hallucinations' to convey the quality of realness that the responsive subject often reports. The suggestion may also be expressed in the negative sense, as in the example 'When you open your eyes you will not see the chair in front of you' or 'You will hear nothing but the sound of my voice'.

Finally, some suggestions call for rather complex experiences and enactments, as in the case of the suggestion of reliving an early memory ('age regression') or progressing in time to some future event. Others include amnesia for all or some of the events during the hypnotic session, and time distortion (the idea that time is slowing down or speeding up).

In the experimental literature, suggestions that call for significant alterations in experience (e.g. hallucinations, amnesia, analgesia) are collectively described as 'cognitive' suggestions.

With most of the above suggestions it is sometimes stipulated that the response is to take place *after* the conclusion of hypnosis, in which case we use the term 'posthypnotic suggestion'. For example, the subjects may be told that at some stage after they have opened their eyes, the hypnotist will take out his or her handkerchief and they will immediately remove their left shoe.

Some people may wish to define hypnosis in terms of the subject's response. It can be seen that for many of the above examples of suggestion, such as arm levitation, whether the subject does respond will be immediately apparent to the hypnotist. For some, however, amnesia being an example, we may have to rely on the subject's own report. In fact, in most cases there are objective signs that we can look for. For example, a suggestion of drinking water may be accompanied by the subject's licking his or her lips and swallowing.

Likewise, the effectiveness of suggesting an exciting experience may be assessed by observing the subject's emotional reactions. With a suggestion such as hand warming or physical relaxation we can measure any physiological change if we are more interested in the *actual* rather than *perceived* effect. There is, however, one important characteristic of a successful suggested response. As Heap et al. (2001) state: 'Suggestions differ from everyday kinds of instructions in that they imply that a "successful" response is experienced by the subject as having a quality of involuntariness or effortlessness' (p. 3).

This characteristic is often called 'the classic suggestion effect'. In contrast, a subject may objectively show a good response to the suggestion of arm levitation, the arm rising high in the air, but he or she may simply be deliberately lifting the arm. Or, another subject may show a diminished pain response in the hand following the suggestion of glove anaesthesia, but may be consciously employing a strategy such as self-distraction. Although this distinction, as the reader will discover later in this book, is not without controversy, in neither case are these subjects said to be responding in the classic manner to the hypnotist's suggestion.

The measurement of hypnotic suggestion and individual differences in responsiveness

Clearly, a subject's response to a given suggestion can be measured, sometimes in several different ways. This fact paved the way for the development of standardized scales for the systematic assessment of subject responsivity to hypnotic suggestions in the 1950s and 1960s. These scales typically comprise a hypnotic induction followed by a series of test suggestions and an assessment of the subject's responsiveness to each. The number of suggestions successfully responded to is summed, yielding a total score denoting the subject's responsivity. Within the general population, scores on these instruments have a broad distribution and a clear central tendency. In this book, the term *hypnotizability* is defined operationally as the number of suggestions that an individual responds to on standard scales of this sort. The terms *hypnotizability, hypnotic susceptibility, hypnotic suggestibility* and *hypnotic responsivity* are used interchangeably throughout.

Further discussion of hypnotic susceptibility scales will be deferred until Chapter 2. For the time being, it is instructive to note that hypnotizability research has yielded the following important findings.

1   There are significant and reliable differences between hypnotic
    suggestions in the proportion of subjects who respond to (i.e.
    'pass') them. On the Stanford Hypnotic Susceptibility Scale
    Form C (SHSS:C; Weitzenhoffer and Hilgard, 1962), for example,
    92 per cent of subjects in the normative group passed the 'hand
    lowering' suggestion, 43 per cent passed 'age regression' and
    only 9 per cent passed 'negative visual hallucination'. In this
    sense, it is meaningful to talk about some suggestions being more
    'difficult' than others. Broadly speaking, ideomotor suggestions
    tend to be the easiest suggestions to pass, challenge suggestions
    are somewhat more difficult, and cognitive suggestions are the
    most difficult of all.

2   Most hypnotizability measures have high internal consistency,
    demonstrating that responsivity to one hypnotic suggestion is
    highly correlated with responsivity to others on the scale.

3   A person's score on any of these scales tends to remain
    unchanged over time, suggesting that hypnotic susceptibility is a
    stable individual characteristic or trait. Thus Piccione et al.
    (1989), have found that hypnotizability has high test–retest reli-
    ability over a period of 25 years, while a twin study by Morgan
    (1973) suggests that hypnotizability may be partly inherited.
    Some authorities have challenged the trait conception of hyp-
    notic responsiveness and this point will be taken up again below
    and in Chapter 9.

Hypnotizability has been found to correlate with a range of
attributes such as trait 'absorption', dissociative capacity, and fantasy-proneness (see below and, in particular, Chapter 2), although in
the first two cases the correlations are neither high nor stable across
different studies. This theme will be taken up in later chapters but
it is worth noting here that one explanation for this is that the population defined as highly susceptible may not be homogeneous (see
e.g. Barber, 1999). A discussion of typology will be deferred until
Chapter 3.

Current theoretical approaches to hypnosis

The requirement of any theory of hypnosis is that it provides explanations of the phenomena we observe. In addition we must be able
to assess the validity of these explanations, by testing the predictions
that they generate, modifying or abandoning the theory if the

predictions are not supported. For example, if we explain suggested amnesia as being due to subject compliance, we would predict that more compliant subjects would be more likely to pass this suggestion.

However, we first must decide what it is we are trying to explain. A good answer to this is the 'counter-expectational' nature of the subject's behaviour and experience (Coe and Sarbin, 1991). For instance, we do not expect that people will immediately forget something when we tell them to do so, and remember it again when we tell them that they can, likewise that they will not feel pain, that they will see their best friend greeting them, that they will smell a foul odour, that they will not see a chair that is in front of them, and so on. Here we note once again the importance of the *involuntariness* of the subjective and objective responses. That is, none of the aforementioned observations would be considered 'counter-expectational' if they were achieved by some kind of deliberate strategy on the subject's part, such as distraction of attention in the case of suggested analgesia or amnesia. Another possibility is that the 'responsive' subject is simply reporting that he or she is having the suggested experiences when such is not the case, and voluntarily enacting the appropriate responses. In other words, he or she is being compliant. We shall take up these themes again in due course.

Hence a theory will have to explain the occurrence of these phenomena, but it will also have to account for why some people do not respond in the suggested manner, whereas some respond very markedly, why responsiveness is so consistent, and why it is distributed in the way it is.

The concept of 'altered state' or 'trance'

The classic approach to these questions is that the 'counter-expectational' nature of suggested phenomena is explained by the properties of an altered state of consciousness or 'trance', which the subject enters as a result of the hypnotic induction procedure, and leaves following alerting instructions at the end of the session. The idea of a trance state that endows the subject with unusual characteristics and abilities has a long history outside of hypnosis and is common to many religious and quasi-religious practices.

Modern hypnosis (see e.g. Gauld, 1992) itself can be traced directly back to the ideas and practices of Franz Anton Mesmer (1734–1815), in response to whose ministrations, notably passes made by the hand over the patient's body, patients would experience 'crises' (swooning, convulsing, shaking, crying, laughing hysterically, and so on) and then a stuporous state. Later on, his student the Marquis de Puységur (1751–1825) dispensed with the crises, preferring in his patients a relaxed, quiet state of mind that he termed 'artificial somnambulism'. The Abbé de Faria (1756–1819) described as 'lucid sleep' this state, which was achieved by the subject's concentrating on the idea of sleep rather than responding to mesmeric passes. Later, James Braid (1795–1860) postulated that hypnosis was a physiological state, characterized by a fixed stare, complete body relaxation, suppressed breathing and fixed attention on the words of the hypnotist. He later introduced the concept of 'monoideism', proposing that hypnosis is characterized by a state of heightened concentration on a single idea suggested by the hypnotist. In this state, imagination, belief and expectancy are purported to be more intense than in the normal waking state.

In this understanding of hypnosis, people are said to vary in the 'depth' of trance that they can attain. Trance depth and capacity (in both cases often designated as 'light', 'medium', or 'deep') are much more controversial concepts than hypnotic suggestion and hypnotizability. These two sets of concepts are traditionally related by the idea that the fewer the number of subjects passing a given suggestion, the deeper the required depth of trance. So, for example, a suggestion of arm levitation is said to require only a 'light trance', whereas to respond to a suggestion of a negative hallucination or profound analgesia requires a 'deep trance'.

Absorption

The 'level of trance' idea is problematic because no stable physiological marker has been found that will reliably identify the 'trance state' and its putative 'depth' across different conditions of responding to suggestion. However, the idea is commonly used in a weaker sense, particularly by clinicians, to describe the state of absorption and detachment from one's immediate surroundings and concerns, characteristic of the hypnotic subject when he or she is responding successfully to different kinds of suggestion, including those comprising the induction and deepening. In this respect, 'trance' resembles everyday experiences when one is so absorbed in something – a book, a film, some music or one's own daydreams – that one may not even respond to one's name when it is called. Tellegen and Atkinson

(1974, p. 5) have described this state of absorption as one in which there is 'almost total immersion in the [imaginal] activity, with indifference to distracting stimuli in the environment'.

There is some evidence that hypnosis is characterized by a state of focused attention (Crawford, 1994), although reliable objective markers for this state have yet to be identified. Moreover, despite evidence showing that a tendency to experience similar states in everyday life (so-called 'trait' absorption – Tellegen and Atkinson, 1974) is the most consistent personality correlate of hypnotic susceptibility (Roche and McConkey, 1990), the correlation between hypnotizability and trait absorption is typically quite low and may even be a methodological artefact.

Ego-psychological theory

Despite the absence of objective markers for the hypnotic 'state', there exist modern theoretical approaches based on the idea that hypnosis involves some 'special' process, and that this has a physiological basis. An early model of hypnosis that incorporated this idea was proposed by Shor (1959, 1962). According to Shor, the depth of a hypnotic trance corresponds to the degree to which the subject loses awareness of the distinction between imagination and reality – the so-called 'generalized reality orientation' that characterizes normal psychological functioning. This idea was subsequently extended in Fromm's (1979, 1992) ego-psychological model of hypnosis. Originating in the work of Freud (e.g. Freud, 1961), ego-psychology draws a basic distinction between primary and secondary mental processes. The primary processes are emotional, holistic, illogical, unconscious and developmentally immature forms of mental processing, which are primitive but thought to be the source of creativity. Secondary processes, in contrast, are affect-free, analytic, logical, conscious and developmentally mature, and are said to be the seat of reason. Normal adult functioning is biased towards secondary processing. According to Fromm's model, the induction of hypnosis causes the subject to relinquish a degree of secondary process activity, biasing them towards primary processing. This psychological 'regression' (Gill and Brenman, 1959) from sophisticated, logical thought towards more primitive and illogical mental activity is said to account for the increased suggestibility associated with hypnosis, and the apparent involuntariness of suggested phenomena.

Support for ego-psychological theory in the experimental literature has been mixed (Fromm et al., 1970; Hammer et al., 1978; Levin and Harrison, 1976; Lynn and Sivec, 1992; Orne, 1959; Sheehan, 1979). It is fair to say that it has not been as influential as other theories amongst cognitive psychologists, as readers will discover for themselves as they progress through this book.

Although the ego-psychological model does not provide a detailed account of what makes some individuals more responsive to hypnotic procedures than others, it seems likely that high hypnotizability from this perspective would be observed in individuals who have a well-developed ability or tendency to inhibit secondary process activity and engage in primary processing.

Dissociated control theory

The idea that hypnosis involves the inhibition of high-level mental processes and a subsequent bias towards simpler forms of processing is also central to dissociated control theory (Bowers, 1990, 1992; Woody and Bowers, 1994). Dissociated control theory is based on the model of action control proposed by Norman and Shallice (1986), which is widely respected and supported by a growing literature within cognitive neuroscience. According to Norman and Shallice (1986), the cognitive system consists of a large, distributed set of specialized processing structures operating under the guidance of a two-tiered control system. In routine situations, behaviours can be controlled exclusively by low-level cognitive control representations or 'schemata', each describing the sequence of processing operations involved in the execution of a given act. These schemata are triggered automatically by cues from the internal and external environment in accordance with a competitive scheduling mechanism ('contention scheduling'). In the case of non-routine situations, however, where schemata are inappropriate or their triggering conditions are not present, a high-level supervisory attentional system (SAS) may intervene to excite or inhibit schemata by means of contention scheduling. The SAS is a limited-capacity executive structure associated with a sense of mental effort and volition. In contrast, actions controlled exclusively at the level of contention scheduling require neither awareness nor volition for their operation.

According to dissociated control theory, hypnosis represents one situation where executive control is inhibited, leading to an over-reliance on situational cues for the control of behaviour. By this view, the resulting dissociation between higher and lower levels of control allows for the automatic activation of suggestion-related schemata by the words of the hypnotist, at the level of contention scheduling. In this sense, dissociated control theory proposes that hypnotic behaviours are akin to everyday 'action-slips' (Reason, 1979), in which unplanned or inappropriate actions (e.g. dialling an out-of-date telephone number) are triggered by situational cues following a lack of monitoring by the SAS. In this sense, Woody and Bowers (1994) liken the highly hypnotizable individual to frontal-lobe-damaged patients who often produce unintended actions that are initiated by cues in the external environment. According to this account, hypnotic involuntariness is a reflection of the fact that the SAS – the seat of volition in the Norman and Shallice model – has not been involved in the generation of the suggested effect.

A small number of studies have provided evidence that is consistent with predictions derived from dissociated control theory (Bowers and Woody, 1996; Miller and Bowers, 1993). That notwithstanding, not all of the available evidence is consistent with the theory and a number of conceptual problems with this approach have been identified (see Brown, 1999a; Kirsch and Lynn, 1998).

According to dissociated control theorists (e.g. Balthazard and Woody, 1992; Hargadon et al., 1995; Woody et al., 1997), not all hypnotic suggestions are generated by the same mechanisms. By this view, the easier suggestions on traditional hypnotic susceptibility scales (e.g. ideomotor responses) may be controlled by simple social mechanisms, whereas the more difficult cognitive items (e.g. amnesia and analgesia) are mediated by the processes described in dissociated control theory. In support of this view, Woody et al. (1997) found that a measure of social suggestibility correlated significantly with the easier but not the more difficult items on the Harvard Group Scale of Hypnotic Susceptibility, Form A (Shor and Orne, 1962; see also Chapter 2). Conversely, a study by Balthazard and Woody (1992) using similar analytic techniques found that the difficult items on two commonly used susceptibility scales are more strongly associated with scores on the Tellegen Absorption Scale (Tellegen and Atkinson, 1974) than are the easier items. These findings are particularly important as they indicate that hypnotic susceptibility scales may not be unidimensional measures as is often assumed. This idea will be taken up again in Chapters 2 and 3.

Dissociated control theorists have yet to provide a detailed account of the nature of hypnotizability. Nevertheless, it seems plausible that the ability to inhibit executive functioning – or a tendency to experience such inhibition spontaneously – would be associated with hypnotic responsivity. A small number of studies have yielded findings that are consistent with this proposal (Dixon et al., 1990; Dixon and Laurence, 1992).

Neodissociation theory

Dissociated control theory assumes that hypnotic responses are the product of a dissociation between high- and low-level cognitive control processes. Hilgard's neodissociation theory (e.g. Hilgard, 1979, 1986) also assumes that hypnotic phenomena are brought about through a process of dissociation. In this case, however, the dissociation is not between higher and lower levels of control, but within high-level control systems themselves. By this view, the hypnotic induction serves to inhibit high-level functioning, causing a fractionation within executive systems. Although part of the executive continues to function as normal during hypnosis, a second, dissociated, part is concealed from awareness by the formation of an amnesic barrier. This part of the executive can exert control in the usual fashion but such control is prevented from representing itself in consciousness by the amnesic barrier. The hypnotist's suggestions operate by influencing the dissociated part of the executive to initiate actions or changes in cognitive processing. As the individual is aware only of the resultant changes in behaviour and experience, and not the cognitive activity by which such changes are brought about, they experience the execution of suggestions as occurring involuntarily.

The concept of executive fractionation that is central to neodissociation theory was inspired by Hilgard's discovery of the now well-documented 'hidden observer' phenomenon. The classic demonstration of the hidden observer (see Hilgard, 1979, 1986) involves the elicitation of 'true' ratings of ischaemic pain by highly hypnotizable subjects who are responsive to suggestions of profound analgesia. During hypnotic analgesia the experimenter suggests that there is a hidden or 'unhypnotized' part of the mind that can give the pain ratings 'out of awareness', for example in writing or by pressing numbered keys.

The hidden observer has been the subject of much empirical and theoretical scrutiny (see e.g. Hilgard et al., 1975, 1978; Laurence and Perry, 1981; Nogrady et al., 1983; Spanos, 1986; Spanos and Hewitt, 1980; Spanos et al., 1983, 1984) with much of the debate focusing on the most appropriate explanation for the phenomenon. At present, the idea that the hidden observer effect reveals the co-existence of conscious and unconscious executive systems during hypnosis remains controversial (see e.g. Kirsch and Lynn, 1998).

Nevertheless, the hidden observer aside, there is some evidence in support of the neodissociation account of hypnosis. A number of studies have shown, for example, that hypnotic suggestions tend to affect explicit but not implicit perceptual and memorial processes (see e.g. Kihlstrom, 1992, 1998). Data from certain dual-task interference studies have also been interpreted as evidence for neodissociation theory (e.g. Green and Lynn, 1995; Knox et al., 1975; Stevenson, 1976), although this interpretation is controversial (see e.g. Kihlstrom, 1998; Kirsch and Lynn, 1998; Ruehle and Zamansky, 1997).

According to neodissociation theory, hypnotizability is a stable cognitive trait related to an individual's ability to experience dissociative phenomena. Evidence for a relationship between hypnotizability and dissociative capacity has been obtained in a number of studies investigating the hypnotic capacity of patients with dissociative psychopathology. Pettinati et al. (1985), for example, found that individuals suffering from bulimia nervosa tend to display unusually high levels of hypnotic susceptibility. A similar pattern of results has been found with individuals suffering from dissociative identity disorder (Bliss, 1980, 1983) and post-traumatic stress disorder (e.g. Spiegel et al., 1988; see also Chapter 8). In each of these cases, it has been suggested that the individual's ability to dissociate material from consciousness is used as an adaptive mechanism to protect him or her from overwhelming negative affect at times of extreme stress or trauma. It has been argued that such dissociative abilities are reflected in the high hypnotizability of these individuals.

Regarding less pathological forms of dissociation, however, results have been less conclusive. Although some studies (e.g. Butler and Bryant, 1997; Frischholz et al., 1992) have found a significant correlation between the Dissociative Experiences Scale (DES; Bernstein and Putnam, 1986) and standard measures of hypnotic susceptibility, others have not (e.g. DiTomasso and Routh, 1993; Faith and Ray, 1994). In addition, it has been argued that any such significant correlations can be accounted for by a context effect (Kirsch and Council, 1992). One study attempting to investigate the relationship between hypnotizability and dissociative ability using more objective measures of dissociation (Stava and Jaffa, 1988) also failed to provide evidence for neodissociation theory.

Gruzelier's neurophysiological theory

Despite their differences, the ego-psychological, dissociated control and neodissociation theories are united in their assumption that hypnotic responding is facilitated by the inhibition of high-level cognitive processes. A similar view has been proposed by Gruzelier (e.g. 1998), based on the results of an extensive series of neurophysiological studies using traditional hypnotic relaxation induction procedures. According to the Gruzelier model, hypnosis is characterized by three discrete stages, each with a different neurophysiological signature. In the first instance, the hypnotic subject concentrates carefully on the words of the induction, as evidenced by increase activity in left fronto-limbic brain areas associated with focused attention. In the second stage, the hypnotic subject 'lets go' of deliberate attentional functions and cedes executive control to the hypnotist; this is accompanied by an inhibition of activity in left frontal brain regions. Finally, there is increased activation of right-sided temporo-posterior systems, as the subject becomes engaged in passive imagery and dreaming. According to the theory, this inhibition of deliberate executive control renders the individual more responsive to suggestions, which operate via the reallocation of attention according to the nature of the given suggestion.

Gruzelier's model is well supported by neurophysiological and behavioural evidence (see Gruzelier, 1998, for a review), and clearly converges with other state-oriented accounts of hypnosis such as dissociated control theory. According to this approach, hypnotic susceptibility is underpinned by superior attentional abilities that allow subjects to switch, focus and sustain their attention to relevant material during the hypnotic procedure. A number of studies have found evidence in support of this proposal (for reviews see Crawford, 1994; Gruzelier, 1998). However, not all studies have found a relationship between susceptibility and attentional processing (e.g. Jamieson and Sheehan, 2002). Wagstaff, in Chapter 4 of this volume, provides further critical analysis of the neurophysiological evidence.

Sociocognitive theories

The absorption concept is often cited by state-oriented theorists as an important element in hypnotic responding, be it as the mechanism responsible for a shift from primary to secondary processing or as a marker of high-level executive inhibition. Despite this, it is unclear whether the phenomenon of absorption is sufficiently unusual to constitute a 'special' phenomenon or 'altered' state of consciousness. Indeed, many theorists from the 'sociocognitive' tradition have embraced the existence of absorption while rejecting the idea that the hypnotic state is a useful explanatory construct (Spanos and Barber, 1974). Rather than citing altered states or special processes, such theorists attempt to account for hypnotic phenomena by reference to normal psychological processes and influences.

According to the sociocognitive approach, the role of the hypnotic induction is not to encourage the subject to enter a 'trance state', but to enhance the subject's sense of expectation and his or her motivation to engage in the process of responding to suggestion. So long as the induction procedure fulfils these aims (and defines the context as 'hypnosis') then the content of the induction procedure is less important, at least so far as enhancing the subject's responsiveness to suggestion is concerned.

There is strong support for this assertion. For example, laboratory subjects who are presented with instructions designed to increase their motivation respond well to hypnotic suggestions even in the absence of an induction and deepening routine (Barber and Calverley, 1963a, 1963b). Moreover, induction procedures comprising suggestions calling for greater awareness and increased energy, conducted while the subject is engaged in an energetic activity, lead to virtually the same increases in hypnotic suggestibility as a traditional induction comprising suggestions for relaxation and drowsiness, conducted with the subject lying passively (Bányai and Hilgard, 1976). Likewise there is evidence that 'dummy' procedures presented as 'genuine' induction methods (e.g. inhaling an inert gas or swallowing a pill bearing the word 'hypnosis') have the same effect on suggestibility as a traditional induction (Kirsch, 1991). This casts doubt on the idea that traditional procedures put subjects into a unique or special state characterized by extreme suggestibility. Indeed, the gains in responsiveness due to prior administration of a hypnotic induction are, in the psychological laboratory at least, quite modest and not present for all individuals (Kirsch, 1997).

Sociocognitive processes in hypnosis

Despite their obvious similarities, there are important differences between specific sociocognitive models, typically in the emphasis that they place on particular psychological processes in their account of hypnotic phenomena. The most commonly cited sociocognitive processes identified in the hypnosis literature are described below.

Imagination

One obvious candidate for understanding hypnosis is imagination. One of the major figures in the 'non-state' approach to hypnosis over the last half-century, T.X. Barber, made imagination (or the ability to fantasize realistically) one of the central features of his understanding of hypnosis (see Barber et al., 1974). In support of this is the higher-than-average hypnotizability of individuals who have a propensity for vivid fantasy. This important finding is taken up in a number of chapters in this book. However, hypnosis is not *equivalent* to imagery as such, since the capacity for vivid imagery is at most only weakly related to hypnotic ability (Kogon et al., 1998; Sheehan, 1979).

Response expectancy

Another contender is response expectancy: the idea that the hypnotist creates the expectancy that the subject will have certain experiences and responses and, in a motivated subject, this is sufficient for those experiences to occur. Kirsch (1991) considers that response expectancy is the essence of hypnosis and not simply a by-product. He and his colleagues have demonstrated experimentally how responsiveness to hypnotic suggestion can be modified by manipulating expectancy on the subject's part.

Strategic enactment

In the main, sociocognitive theorists do not regard the hypnotic subject as a *passive* participant in the hypnotic interaction, that is, someone who just 'lets things happen'. Instead, he or she is actively striving to deploy his or her cognitive skills to create the responses and experiences suggested by the hypnotist. When these are experienced by the subject as 'automatic' or involuntary', sociocognitive theorists view this as an attribution on the subject's part that arises from the expectations generated by the hypnotic context.

As an example, when attending to the arm levitation suggestion, the responsive subject may not be the one who just waits for the arm to rise but he or she actually lifts the arm, attempting to create, through imagination, the feeling that it is being pulled up. Similarly, when given the suggestion of analgesia, he or she may adopt a cognitive strategy (e.g. self-distraction) instead of simply waiting for the suggestion to take effect. And when a responsive subject is tested for suggested posthypnotic amnesia, he or she is not struggling to recall the lost information, but is adopting a strategy, such as attention switching, that inhibits recall. Thus the influential cognitive theorist Spanos (Spanos, 1991) conceived of hypnotic responding as involving a process of 'strategic enactment'.

Compliance and role-playing

One possibility, of course, is that the responsive hypnotic subject is just knowingly pretending. That is, he or she is simply lifting the arm in the normal way, or denying that he or she feels pain when the pain is consciously felt (and suppressing any pain behaviour), falsely insisting that he or she cannot recall the targeted information, and so on. In other words, the subject is 'compliant', that is overtly responding in the required manner while privately experiencing the opposite. At least one theorist, Wagstaff (1981, 1991; also see Chapter 4), considers that compliance is a major component of hypnotic responding. Coming from the standpoint of role theory, Sarbin and Coe (Coe and Sarbin, 1991; Sarbin and Coe, 1972) have presented a similar thesis: 'susceptible' individuals are motivated to play the role of the good hypnotic subject and will, where necessary, engage in deception (and this occasionally includes self-deception) to fulfil that role.

Hypnotic susceptibility and sociocognitive theories

It is a challenge for sociocognitive approaches to account for the fact that there are variations within the general population in hypnotic responsiveness, roughly normally distributed between two extremes, likewise that susceptibility tends to be very stable over time for any individual. Whereas imaginative abilities and fantasy-proneness may be relatively stable characteristics of any given individual, likewise to some extent role-playing ability, others, such as expectation effects, strategic enactment and compliance do not necessarily involve the deployment of skills which are either inherited or plateau at an early developmental stage. Consequently, according to some of these theories, hypnotic susceptibility is modifiable and a low-susceptible individual can be trained to become highly susceptible as defined by a standard hypnotic susceptibility scale. For example, at least some people who respond poorly to hypnotic suggestions may have the wrong attitude. They may have misgivings about 'being hypnotized' or come to the hypnotic session with the conviction that they are not going to be responsive. Such negative expectations are known to inhibit subjects' responding to suggestion (Spanos, 1991; see also Chapter 9); in the words of Barber (1999) they are less likely to 'go with the flow' when attending to the hypnotist's suggestion. Importantly for sociocognitive theory, they may adopt a passive role, not allowing themselves to be *actively* engaged in utilizing their cognitive skills to make the suggested responses happen, as is the case with more 'hypnotizable' people.

If this is true it should be possible to train such subjects to adopt the correct approach and thus increase their hypnotic susceptibility. But even if this were possible, would this training have a permanent effect? These questions define a major project that Spanos and his colleagues and students engaged in from the early 1980s onwards. They developed a training programme called the Carleton Skills Training Program (CSTP), which is now available in published form (Gorassini and Spanos, 1999). Gorassini presents an account of this research in Chapter 9 of the present book. Advocates of this approach claim that it leads to a permanent increase in hypnotic suggestibility (see Chapter 9). Others remain unconvinced (Bowers and Davidson, 1991; see also Chapter 2), their contention being that 'naturally' highly susceptible subjects owe their high scores on susceptibility scales to cognitive processes that are different from those operating in subjects who have been trained to be highly susceptible. This is a matter of ongoing controversy.

Hypnotizability as change in suggestibility due to hypnosis

Kirsch (1997) has gone further than most sociocognitive theorists in challenging traditional ideas about hypnotizability. He argues that it is inappropriate to identify the traditional scales as measures of hypnotizability, citing evidence showing that most individuals who respond to suggestions following a hypnotic induction will respond almost as well in the absence of this procedure. According to Kirsch, this evidence indicates that these measures actually assess responsivity to 'hypnotic-like' suggestions *per se* (i.e. responsivity to these kinds of suggestions in all contexts, hypnotic and otherwise) rather than hypnotizability. Kirsch terms this capacity 'imaginative suggestibility', preferring this term to the more commonly used 'non-hypnotic suggestibility' to differentiate this capacity from other types of suggestibility not associated with hypnosis (e.g. interrogative suggestibility; Gudjonsson, 1989). From this perspective, hypnotizability should be conceptualized as any *change* in suggestibility associated with the hypnotic context. Although highly controversial, Kirsch's perspective is particularly important as it demonstrates that there are other ways of defining hypnotizability than those traditionally espoused. Nevertheless, for the sake of continuity this book follows the traditional definition of hypnotizability.

Summary of theories

For many years hypnotic theorizing was dominated by the idea that hypnosis involves an alteration in consciousness or 'trance'. Although the altered state construct has in many cases been replaced by a watered-down version based on the concept of absorption, many theorists continue to assert that hypnotic phenomena involve the operation of special psychological processes. A common theme spanning these approaches is that hypnosis involves the inhibition of high-level cognitive processes, with the ability to experience such inhibition being an important and stable component of hypnotizability. Other theorists have rejected the altered state and special process assumptions, and attempted to identify normal social and cognitive processes involved in the generation of hypnotic phenomena. According to this approach, hypnotizability is related to individual differences in imagination, expectation, role-playing ability and strategy choice that are essentially modifiable.

This distinction between 'state' or 'special process' theories on the one hand, and 'non-state' or 'sociocognitive' theories on the other, is not as clear-cut as much of the literature suggests (Kirsch and Lynn, 1995). Indeed, a number of recent commentators have suggested that these accounts are not mutually exclusive, and that a comprehensive explanation of hypnotic phenomena must embrace concepts from both schools of thought (e.g. Brown, 1999a, 1999b; Nadon, 1997; see also Chapter 7).

Conclusions

It may be clear from this chapter that individuals who are naturally highly susceptible may constitute an interesting and important group, both within and outside the hypnotic context. However, it is apparent that high susceptibles are by no means a homogeneous group and it is of interest to study the various factors that may contribute to a high score on a hypnotic susceptibility scale.

It may be partly owing to the heterogeneous nature of the highly susceptible population that it has proved such a challenge to find robust differences between high- and low-susceptible subjects on important dimensions of personality and cognitive style. For example, recent research has failed to find evidence of any important relationships between hypnotic susceptibility and the 'big five' personality factors (Nordenstrom et al., 2002). Nevertheless, much work has now been undertaken and a fascinating and complex picture is emerging. It will be seen from this brief survey of theoretical and research controversies that modern accounts of hypnosis, unlike earlier explanations, rely less on speculations about special processes or unusual or pathological states and more on concepts and models drawn from contemporary cognitive psychology and the neurosciences. It is our contention that sufficient acknowledgement has yet to be given to the reciprocal nature of this process, notably the potential contribution of the growing scientific literature on hypnosis and, in particular, hypnotic susceptibility, to mainstream psychology and related disciplines. Similarly, as the reader will discover in later chapters of this book, our growing understanding of hypnotic susceptibility is of relevance to the more general study of human personality and clinical psychology. For these reasons we are confident that readers who do not themselves use hypnosis in their work will nevertheless find the contents of this volume essential reading for their own fields of study and practice.

References

Balthazard, C.G. and Woody, E.Z. (1992) 'The spectral analysis of hypnotic performance with respect to "absorption" ', *International Journal of Clinical and Experimental Hypnosis*, 40:21–43.

Bányai, E.I. and Hilgard, E.R. (1976) 'A comparison of active-alert hypnotic induction with traditional relaxation induction', *Journal of Abnormal Psychology*, 85:218–24.

Barber, T.X. (1999) 'A comprehensive three-dimensional theory of hypnosis', in I. Kirsch, A. Capafons, E. Cardeña-Buelna, and S. Amigó (eds), *Clinical Hypnosis and Self-regulation: Cognitive-behavioral Perspectives* (pp. 21–48), Washington, DC: American Psychological Association.

Barber, T.X. and Calverley, D.S. (1963a) 'The relative effectiveness of task motivating instructions and trance induction procedure in the production of "hypnotic like" behavior', *Journal of Nervous and Mental Disease*, 137:107–16.

—— and Calverley, D.S. (1963b) 'Toward a theory of hypnotic behavior: Effects on suggestibility of task motivating instructions and attitudes toward hypnosis', *Journal of Abnormal and Social Psychology*, 67:557–65.

—— Spanos, N.P. and Chaves, J.F. (1974) *Hypnosis: Imagination and Human Potentialities*, New York: Pergamon.

Bernstein, E. and Putnam, F.W. (1986) 'Development, reliability and validity of a dissociation scale', *Journal of Nervous and Mental Disease*, 174:727–35.

Bliss, E.L. (1980) 'Multiple personalities: A report of 14 cases with implications for schizophrenia and hysteria', *Archives of General Psychiatry*, 37:1388–97.

—— (1983) 'Multiple personalities, related disorders and hypnosis', *American Journal of Clinical Hypnosis*, 26:114–23.

Bowers, K.S. (1990) 'Unconscious influences and hypnosis', in J.L. Singer (ed.), *Repression and Dissociation: Implications for Personality Theory, Psychopathology and Health* (pp. 143–79), Chicago: University of Chicago Press.

—— (1992) 'Imagination and dissociation in hypnotic responding', *International Journal of Clinical and Experimental Hypnosis*, 40:253–75.

—— and Davidson, T.M. (1991) 'A neodissociative critique of Spanos's social-psychological model of hypnosis', in S.J. Lynn and J.W. Rhue (eds), *Theories of Hypnosis: Current Models and Perspectives* (pp. 105–43), New York: Guilford Press.

—— and Woody, E.Z. (1996) 'Hypnotic amnesia and the paradox of intentional forgetting', *Journal of Abnormal Psychology*, 105:381–90.

Brown, R.J. (1999a) *An Integrative Cognitive Theory of Suggestion and Hypnosis*, Unpublished doctoral dissertation, University College London.

—— (1999b) 'Three dimensions of hypnosis or multiple routes to suggested responding?', *Contemporary Hypnosis*, 16:128–31.

Butler, P.V. and Bryant, R.A. (1997) 'Assessing hypnotizability and dissociation in different contexts', *Contemporary Hypnosis*, 14:167–72.

Coe, W.C. and Sarbin, T.R. (1991) 'Role theory: Hypnosis from a dramaturgical and narrational perspective', in S.J. Lynn and J.W. Rhue (eds), *Theories of Hypnosis: Current Models and Perspectives* (pp. 303–23), New York: Guilford Press.

Crawford, H.J. (1994) 'Brain dynamics and hypnosis: Attentional and disattentional processes', *International Journal of Clinical and Experimental Hypnosis*, 42:204–32.

DiTomasso, M.J. and Routh, D.K. (1993) 'Recall of abuse in childhood and three measures of dissociation', *Child Abuse and Neglect*, 17:477–85.

Dixon, M. and Laurence, J.-R. (1992) 'Hypnotic susceptibility and verbal automaticity: Automatic and strategic processing differences in the Stroop color-naming task', *Journal of Abnormal Psychology*, 101:344–7.

—— Brunet, A. and Laurence, J.-R. (1990) 'Hypnotizability and automaticity: Toward a parallel distributed processing model of hypnotic responding', *Journal of Abnormal Psychology*, 99:336–43.

Edmonston, W.E. (1981) *Hypnosis and Relaxation: Modern Verification of an Old Equation*, New York: Wiley,

—— (1991) 'Anesis', in S.J. Lynn and J.W. Rhue (eds), *Theories of Hypnosis: Current Models and Perspectives* (pp. 197–240), New York: Guilford Press.

Faith, M. and Ray, W.J. (1994) 'Hypnotizability and dissociation in a college age population: Orthogonal individual differences', *Personality and Individual Differences*, 17:211–16.

Freud, S. (1961) 'The ego and the id', in J. Strachey (ed. and trans.) *The Standard Edition of the Complete Psychological Works of Sigmund Freud*, vol. 19 (pp. 12–59), London: Hogarth Press (Original work published 1923).

Frischholz, E.J., Braun, B.G., Sachs, R.G., Schwartz, D.R. et al. (1992) 'Construct validity of the Dissociative Experiences Scale: II. Its relationship to hypnotizability', *American Journal of Clinical Hypnosis*, 35:145–52.

Fromm, E. (1979) 'The nature of hypnosis and other altered states of consciousness: An ego-psychological theory', in E. Fromm and R. Shor (eds), *Hypnosis: Developments in Research and New Perspectives* (pp. 81–103), New York: Aldine.

—— (1992) 'An ego-psychological theory of hypnosis', in E. Fromm and M.R. Nash (eds), *Contemporary Hypnosis Research* (pp. 131–48), London: Guilford Press.

—— Oberlander, M.I. and Gruenewald, D. (1970) 'Perceptual and cognitive processes in different states of consciousness: The waking state and hypnosis', *Journal of Projective Techniques and Personality Assessment*, 34:375–87.

Gauld, A. (1992) *A History of Hypnotism*, Cambridge: Cambridge University Press.

Gill, M.M. and Brenman, M. (1959) *Hypnosis and Related States: Psychoanalytic Studies in Regression*, New York: International Universities Press.

Gorassini, D.R. and Spanos, N.P. (1999) 'The Carleton Skill Training Program for modifying hypnotic suggestibility: Original version and variations', in I. Kirsch, A. Capafons, S. Amigó and E. Cardeña-Buelna (eds), *Clinical Hypnosis and Self-regulation Therapy: A Cognitive-behavioral Perspective* (pp. 141–77), Washington, DC: American Psychological Association Books.

Green, J.P. and Lynn, S.J. (1995) 'Hypnosis, dissociation, and simultaneous-task performance', *Journal of Personality and Social Psychology*, 69:728–35.

Gruzelier, J.H. (1998) 'A working model of the neuropsychophysiology of hypnosis: A review of evidence', *Contemporary Hypnosis*, 15:5–23.

Gudjonsson, G.H. (1989) 'Compliance in an interrogative situation: A new scale', *Personality and Individual Differences*, 10:535–40.

Hammer, A.G., Walker, W. and Diment, A.D. (1978) 'A nonsuggested effect of trance induction', in F.H. Frankel and H.S. Zamansky (eds), *Hypnosis at its Bicentennial: Selected Papers* (pp. 91–100), New York: Plenum.

Hargadon, R., Bowers, K.S. and Woody, E.Z. (1995) 'Does counterpain imagery mediate hypnotic analgesia?', *Journal of Abnormal Psychology*, 104:508–16.

Heap, M., Alden, P., Brown, R.J., Naish, P.L.N., Oakley, D.A., Wagstaff, G.F. and Walker, L.J. (2001) 'The nature of hypnosis: Report prepared by a working party at the request of the Professional Affairs Board of the British Psychological Society', Leicester: British Psychological Society.

Hilgard, E.R. (1979) 'Divided consciousness in hypnosis: The implications of the hidden observer', in E. Fromm and R.E. Shor (eds), *Hypnosis: Developments in Research and New Perspectives, 2nd Edition* (pp. 45–79), New York: Aldine.

—— (1986) *Divided Consciousness: Multiple Controls in Human Thought and Action: Expanded Edition*, New York: Wiley.

—— Morgan, A.H. and Macdonald, H. (1975) 'Pain and dissociation in the cold-pressor test: A study of hypnotic analgesia with "hidden reports" through automatic key-pressing and automatic talking', *Journal of Abnormal Psychology*, 84:280–9.

—— Hilgard, J.R., Macdonald, H., Morgan, A.H. and Johnson, L.S. (1978) 'Covert pain in hypnotic analgesia: Its reality as tested by the real-simulator design', *Journal of Abnormal Psychology*, 84:280–9.

Jamieson, G.A. and Sheehan, P.W. (2002) 'A critical evaluation of the relationship between sustained attentional abilities and hypnotic susceptibility', *Contemporary Hypnosis*, 19:62–74.

Kihlstrom, J.F. (1992) 'Dissociative and conversion disorders', in D.J. Stein and J. Young (eds), *Cognitive Science and Clinical Disorders* (pp. 247–70), San Diego: Academic Press.

—— (1998) 'Dissociations and dissociation theory in hypnosis: Comment on Kirsch and Lynn (1998)', *Psychological Bulletin*, 123:186–91.

Kirsch, I. (1991) 'The social learning theory of hypnosis', in S.J. Lynn and J.W. Rhue (eds), *Theories of Hypnosis: Current Models and Perspectives* (pp. 439–66), New York: Guilford Press.

—— (1997) 'Suggestibility or hypnosis: What do our scales really measure?', *International Journal of Clinical and Experimental Hypnosis*, 45:212–25.

—— and Council, J.R. (1992) 'Situational and personality correlates of hypnotic responsiveness', in E. Fromm and M.R. Nash (eds), *Contemporary Hypnosis Research* (pp. 267–91), London: Guilford Press.

—— and Lynn, S.J. (1995) 'The altered state of hypnosis', *American Psychologist*, 50:846–58.

—— and Lynn, S.J. (1998) 'Dissociation theories of hypnosis', *Psychological Bulletin*, 123:100–15.

Knox, V.J., Crutchfield, L. and Hilgard, E.R. (1975) 'The nature of task interference in hypnotic dissociation: An investigation of hypnotic behaviour', *International Journal of Clinical and Experimental Hypnosis*, 30:305–23.

Kogon, M.M., Jasiukatis, P., Berardi, A., Gupta, M., Kosslyn, S.M. and Spiegel, D. (1998) 'Imagery and hypnotizability revisited', *International Journal of Clinical and Experimental Hypnosis*, 46:363–70.

Laurence, J.-R. and Perry, C. (1981) 'The "hidden observer" phenomenon in hypnosis: Some additional findings', *Journal of Abnormal Psychology*, 90:334–44.

Levin, L.A. and Harrison, R.H. (1976) 'Hypnosis and regression in the service of the ego', *International Journal of Clinical and Experimental Hypnosis*, 24:400–18.

Lynn, S.J. and Sivec, H. (1992) 'The hypnotizable subject as a creative problem solving agent', in E. Fromm and M.R. Nash (eds), *Contemporary Hypnosis Research* (pp. 292–333), New York: Guilford Press.

Miller, M.E. and Bowers, K.S. (1993) 'Hypnotic analgesia: Dissociated experience or dissociated control?', *Journal of Abnormal Psychology*, 102:29–38.

Morgan, A.H. (1973) 'The heritability of hypnotic susceptibility in twins', *Journal of Abnormal Psychology*, 82:55–61.

Nadon, R. (1997) 'What this field needs is a good nomological network', *International Journal of Clinical and Experimental Hypnosis*, 45:314–23.

Nogrady, H., McConkey, K.M., Laurence, J.-R. and Perry, C. (1983) 'Dissociation, duality and demand characteristics in hypnosis', *Journal of Abnormal Psychology*, 92:223–35.

Nordenstrom, B.K., Council, J.R. and Meier, B.P. (2002) 'The "big five" and hypnotic suggestibility', *International Journal of Clinical and Experimental Hypnosis*, 50:276–81.

Norman, D.A and Shallice, T. (1986) 'Attention to action: Willed control of behavior', in R.J. Davidson, G.E. Schwartz and D. Shapiro (eds), *Consciousness and Self-regulation* (vol. 4, pp. 1–18), New York: Plenum.

Orne, M.T. (1959) 'The nature of hypnosis: Artifact and essence', *Journal of Abnormal Psychology*, 58:277–99.

Pettinati, H.M., Horne, R.L. and Staats, J.M. (1985) 'Hypnotizability in patients with anorexia nervosa and bulimia', *Archives of General Psychiatry*, 42:1014–16.

Piccione, C., Hilgard, E.R. and Zimbardo, P.G. (1989) 'On the degree of stability of measured hypnotizability over a 25-year period', *Journal of Personality and Social Psychology*, 56:289–95.

Reason, J.T. (1979) 'Actions not as planned', in G. Underwood and R. Stevens (eds), *Aspects of Consciousness, Vol. 1: Psychological Issues* (pp. 67–89), London: Academic Press.

Roche, S.M. and McConkey, K.M. (1990) 'Absorption: Nature, assessment and correlates', *Journal of Personality and Social Psychology*, 59:91–101.

Ruehle, B.L. and Zamansky, H.S. (1997) 'The experience of effortlessness in hypnosis: Perceived or real?', *International Journal of Clinical and Experimental Hypnosis*, 45:144–57.

Sarbin, T.R. and Coe, W.C. (1972) *Hypnosis: A Social Psychological Analysis of Influence Communication*, New York: Holt, Rinehart and Winston.

Sheehan, P.W. (1979) 'Hypnosis and the process of imagination', in E. Fromm and R.E. Shor (eds), *Hypnosis: Developments and New Perspectives, 2nd Edition* (pp. 381–411), New York: Aldine.

Shor, R.E. (1959) 'Hypnosis and the concept of the generalized reality-orientation', *American Journal of Psychotherapy*, 13:582–602.

—— (1962) 'Three dimensions of hypnotic depth', *International Journal of Clinical and Experimental Hypnosis*, 10:23–38.

—— and Orne, E.C. (1962) *The Harvard Group Scale of Hypnotic Susceptibility*, Palo Alto, CA: Consulting Psychologists Press.

Spanos, N.P. (1986) 'Hypnotic behavior: A social psychological interpretation of amnesia, analgesia, and "trance logic" ', *Behavioral and Brain Sciences*, 9:449–67.

—— (1991) 'A sociocognitive approach to hypnosis', in S.J. Lynn and J.W. Rhue (eds), *Theories of Hypnosis: Current Models and Perspectives* (pp. 324–63), New York: Guilford Press.

—— and Barber, T.X. (1974) 'Towards a convergence in hypnosis research', *American Psychologist*, 29:500–19.

—— and Hewitt, E.C. (1980) 'The hidden observer in hypnotic analgesia: Discovery or experimental creation?', *Journal of Personality and Social Psychology*, 39:1201–14.

—— Gwynn, M.I. and Stam, H.J. (1983) 'Instructional demands and ratings of overt and hidden pain during hypnotic analgesia', *Journal of Abnormal Psychology*, 92:479–88.

—— Radtke, H.L. and Bertrand, L.D. (1984) 'Hypnotic amnesia as a strategic enactment: Breaching amnesia in highly susceptible subjects', *Journal of Personality and Social Psychology*, 47:1155–69.

Spiegel, D., Hunt, T. and Dondershine, H.E. (1988) 'Dissociation and hypnotizability in posttraumatic stress disorder', *American Journal of Psychiatry*, 145:301–5.

Stava, L.J. and Jaffa, M. (1988) 'Some operationalizations of the neodissociation concept and their relationship to hypnotic susceptibility', *Journal of Personality and Social Psychology*, 54:989–96.

Stevenson, J.H. (1976) 'The effect of posthypnotic dissociation on the performance of interfering tasks', *Journal of Abnormal Psychology*, 85:398–407.

Tellegen, A. and Atkinson, G. (1974) 'Openness to absorbing and self-altering experiences ("absorption"), a trait related to hypnotic susceptibility', *Journal of Abnormal Psychology*, 83:268–77.

Wagstaff, G.F. (1981) *Hypnosis, Compliance and Belief*, Brighton: Harvester Press.

—— (1991) 'Compliance, belief and semantics in hypnosis: A non-state, sociocognitive perspective', in S.J. Lynn and J.W. Rhue (eds), *Theories of Hypnosis: Current Models and Perspectives* (pp. 362–96), New York: Guilford Press.

Weitzenhoffer, A.M. and Hilgard, E.R. (1962) *Stanford Hypnotic Susceptibility Scale: Form C (SHSS: C)*, Palo Alto, CA: Consulting Psychologists Press.

Woody, E.Z. and Bowers, K.S. (1994) 'A frontal assault on dissociated control', in S.J. Lynn and J.W. Rhue (eds) *Dissociation: Clinical and Theoretical Perspectives*, (pp. 52–9), New York: Guilford Press.

—— Drugovic, M. and Oakman, J.M. (1997) 'A reexamination of the role of nonhypnotic suggestibility in hypnotic responding', *Journal of Personality and Social Psychology*, 72:399–407.

Chapter 2

Defining and identifying the highly hypnotizable person

Amanda J. Barnier and Kevin M. McConkey

Introduction

Highly hypnotizable people have particular personal characteristics, and they differ in substantial ways from their less hypnotizable counterparts. They often become deeply absorbed in experiences, are highly imaginative and use vivid imagery, respond to suggestions across situations, process information more automatically, and show distinct patterns of brain activity (e.g. Crawford and Gruzelier, 1992; Dixon and Laurence, 1992; Hilgard, 1974; Kirsch and Braffman, 2001; Ray, 1997; Roche and McConkey, 1990; Tellegen and Atkinson, 1974). However, not all highly hypnotizable people show all of these characteristics all of the time or across all situations.

Hypnotizability has been defined operationally as 'the capacity to produce those effects generally considered to be "hypnotic"' (Weitzenhoffer, 1997, p. 128). It has been measured by taking 'samples of hypnotic performance under standard conditions of induction and testing' (Hilgard, 1965, p. 69). Thus, a 'hypnotizability measure' typically involves administering a standard induction procedure, suggesting a number of hypnotic experiences, and scoring responses according to predetermined pass/fail criteria. High hypnotizability is defined as a high score on such a measure.

The first major contemporary measures of hypnotizability were developed in the 1950s. The drive to develop standardized measures was motivated by two important views. First, capturing and understanding individual differences in response to hypnotic suggestion is fundamental to understanding hypnosis (Hilgard, 1965; Kirsch and Lynn, 1995; Sheehan and McConkey, 1982). Second, good measurement is essential for scientific advance (Weitzenhoffer, 1997). Methods of measuring hypnotic experience have been discussed since the late 19th century (e.g. Bernheim, 1888; Liébeault, 1889), and formal scales first appeared in the 1930s (e.g. Davis and Husband, 1931; Friedlander and Sarbin, 1938). However, psychometrically sound measurement began with the Stanford Scales of Hypnotic Susceptibility (Weitzenhoffer and Hilgard, 1959, 1962), which were sophisticated measures that encompassed the entire 'domain' of hypnosis (Hilgard, 1973, 1991). Notably, the move to valid and reliable measurement of hypnotic ability was consistent with advances in measurement in other areas of psychology at that time.

The impact of standardized measures on understanding the highly hypnotizable person cannot be overstated. The availability of a procedure that incorporates induction, suggestion, and scoring protocol, meant that hypnotizability could be assessed and compared across both time and space. So a hypnotizability score obtained in 1959 in Palo Alto, USA could be compared with one obtained in 2004 in Sydney, Australia. This equivalence of measurement not only enabled the growth of hypnosis research, but also gave the endeavour scientific tools and credibility. In addition, these first hypnotizability scales stimulated the development of other scales that measured hypnotizability in childhood, alone or in groups, when hypnotized by another or by oneself, with or without a formal induction, and in the clinical context (e.g. Barber, 1965; Morgan and Hilgard, 1978–9a, 1978–9b; Shor, 1978; Shor and Orne, 1962; Weitzenhoffer and Hilgard, 1962).

In this chapter, we review the measurement of hypnotizability and we discuss some investigations of hypnotizability. We begin by describing selected measures of hypnotizability, and we discuss the role of theory and research in the design and use of these measures. Measurement is never atheoretical (Woody, 1997) and many hypnotizability measures can be understood in terms of the conceptual approach or research agenda of the developers. We consider the empirical literature on hypnotizability, and we focus on hypnotizability across scales, time, and cultures, modification of hypnotizability, correlates of hypnotizability, and the relationship between hypnotizability and subjective experience.

Before turning to this discussion, it is worth noting that terms such as hypnotizability, suggestibility, hypnotic responsivity, hypnotic susceptibility, hypnotic preparedness, hypnotic suggestibility, hypnotic responding, and hypnotic depth have been used interchangeably at various times and by various investigators. Weitzenhoffer (1997) commented that although the measures he developed with

E.R. Hilgard were labelled 'hypnotic susceptibility scales', this choice of term was unintentional (at that time) and might just as easily have been hypnotic responsiveness, hypnotizability, or hypnotic depth. These terms are not all interchangeable, however (Council, 1999; Kirsch and Braffman, 2001), because they carry different implications. Hypnotic susceptibility and hypnotic suggestibility, for instance, imply stable characteristics of the individual, whereas hypnotic responsivity and hypnotic responding refer more to the individual's behaviour in a given situation. We consider some of these issues later in this chapter, but we use the term 'hypnotizability' specifically to refer to an individual's responses to test suggestions after a formal induction procedure.

Contemporary measurement of hypnotizability

Major measures

Early investigators realized that people experienced hypnosis to varying degrees, and that people could be classified according to these differences (for a review of 19th-century views of hypnotizability, see Hilgard, 1965). Some early measures focused on subjective depth of experience. Liébeault (1889; see also Bernheim, 1888) categorized hypnotic depth on a 6-point scale from 'drowsiness' to 'profound somnambulistic sleep'. Davis and Husband (1931) categorized individuals from 'insusceptible' to 'somnambulistic trance'. On this scale, people were assigned scores across classes of suggestions, which were considered symptomatic of different stages of hypnotic depth. Although these categories were yoked to particular responses (e.g. somnambulists were expected to be amnesic and to show positive and negative hallucinations), there was little emphasis on standard induction procedures, a standard set of items, or precise response criteria. Friedlander and Sarbin (1938) developed a scale that was the major precursor to contemporary measures; in fact, the first Stanford scales were essentially a revision of this measure (Hilgard, 1965). Although this scale drew heavily on the items of earlier scales (e.g. Barry et al., 1931; Davis and Husband, 1931), it included a standardized induction and defined scoring criteria. Friedlander and Sarbin (1938) indexed observable hypnotic behaviour because it was assumed to reflect an underlying experience. This choice has been repeated in many contemporary measures of hypnotizability.

Table 2.1 lists in chronological order 13 selected measures of hypnotizability: (1) the Stanford Hypnotic Susceptibility Scales, Forms A and B (SHSS:A and B); (2) the Stanford Hypnotic Susceptibility Scale, Form C (SHSS:C); (3) the Harvard Group Scale of Hypnotic Susceptibility, Form A (HGSHS:A); (4) the Stanford Profile Scales, Forms I and II (SPS:I and II; and Revised Stanford Profile Scales, Forms I and II; RSPS:I and II); (5) the Barber Suggestibility Scale (BSS); (6) the Diagnostic Rating Scale (DRS); (7) the Hypnotic Induction Profile (HIP); (8) the Creative Imagination Scale (CIS); (9) the Stanford Hypnotic Clinical Scale, Adults (SHCS:A); (10) the Stanford Hypnotic Clinical Scale, Children (SHCS:C); (11) the Stanford Hypnotic Arm Levitation Induction and Test (SHALIT); (12) the Carleton University Responsiveness to Suggestion Scale (CURSS); and (13) the Waterloo–Stanford Group Scale of Hypnotic Susceptibility, Form C (WSGC). Sheehan and McConkey (1982) provide a detailed description of most of these scales. This table identifies the type, design, and purpose of each scale, as well as the number of items, induction procedure (if any), and method of scoring.

Of these thirteen measures, six were constructed and normed during the 1960s – the heyday of hypnotic test development; five, mostly clinical, scales were developed in the late 1970s; and, two, which owe much to previous scales, were introduced in 1983 and 1998. Only a handful of these measures are in wide use today, as indexed by their citation in the major journal of the field. Table 2.2 presents a summary of the use of these scales across 1992–2003, as reflected in empirical experimental and clinical articles published in the *International Journal of Clinical and Experimental Hypnosis*. We counted articles if they used a full or modified version of the scale, rather than just the induction procedure or a single item. Of 137 empirical articles published in this period, 120 reported formal assessment of hypnotizability. In these 120 articles, 164 uses of formal scales were reported; the larger number of scales than articles reflects the inclusion of multiple scales in some articles (either for comparison purposes or to confirm hypnotizability levels). The HGSHS:A and SHSS:C were the most widely used scales; some investigators used both of these scales to confirm hypnotizability. Those who did not employ both measures generally opted for the HGSHS:A, which is less resource-intensive and less demanding of participants than the SHSS:C. Fourteen of the seventeen articles that did not use formal assessment involved clinical research. When a scale was used in this

Table 2.1 Selected measures of hypnotizability

Scale	Year	Author	Type	Design	Purpose	Items	Induction	Scoring
SHSS:A&B	1959	Weitzenhoffer & Hilgard	Behavioural hypnotic	Individual	Assessment/ Selection	12 in each form	Yes, standard	Behaviour
SHSS:C	1962	Weitzenhoffer & Hilgard	Behavioural hypnotic	Individual	Assessment	12	Yes, standard	Behaviour
HGSHS:A	1962	Shor & Orne	Behavioural hypnotic	Group	Assessment/ Selection	12	Yes, standard	Behaviour
SPS:I&II (RSPS:I&II)	1963 (1967)	Weitzenhoffer & Hilgard	Behavioural hypnotic	Individual	Assessment/ Selection	9 in each form	Yes, standard	Behaviour
BSS	1965	Barber	Behavioural suggestibility	Individual	Assessment/ Selection	8	No, but may be added	Behaviour/ subjective
DRS	1967	Orne & O'Connell	Clinical assessment	Individual	Assessment/ Selection/ Clinical	Any no. from item categories	Yes, any clinically appropriate	Behaviour/ subjective
HIP	1978	Spiegel & Spiegel	Clinical assessment	Individual	Clinical	6	Yes, part of test	Behaviour
CIS	1978	Wilson & Barber	Behavioural suggestibility	Individual/ Group	Assessment/ Clinical	10	Not formally associated with test	Subjective
SHCS:A	1978– 9a	Morgan & Hilgard	Clinical	Individual	Clinical	5	Yes, relaxation	Behaviour/ subjective
SHCS:C	1978– 9b	Morgan & Hilgard	Clinical assessment	Individual (children)	Clinical	7 or 6	Relaxation or imagination	Behaviour/ subjective
SHALIT	1979	Hilgard, Crawford & Wert	Behavioural hypnotic	Individual	Assessment/ Selection/ Clinical	1	Yes, standard	Behaviour/ subjective
CURSS	1983	Spanos	Behavioural hypnotic	Group	Assessment/ Selection	7	Yes, standard	Behaviour/ subjective
WSGC	1993, 1998	Bowers	Behavioural hypnotic	Group	Assessment/ Selection	12	Yes, standard	Behaviour

Table 2.2 Current use of hypnotizability measures

Hypnotizability Scale	Laboratory Research	Clinical Research	Total Use
Stanford Hypnotic Susceptibility Scale, Forms A & B	4	0	4 (2.8%)
Stanford Hypnotic Susceptibility Scale, Form C	38	3	**41 (25.0%)**
Harvard Group Scale of Hypnotic Susceptibility, Form A	74	2	**76 (46.3%)**
Stanford Profile Scales, Forms I & II	0	0	0 (0.0%)
Barber Suggestibility Scale	4	0	4 (2.8%)
Diagnostic Rating Scale	0	0	0 (0.0%)
Hypnotic Induction Profile	2	2	4 (2.4%)
Creative Imagination Scale	2	0	2 (1.4%)
Stanford Hypnotic Clinical Scale, Adults	4	6	10 (6.1%)
Stanford Hypnotic Clinical Scale, Children	2	3	5 (3.0%)
Stanford Hypnotic Arm Levitation Induction & Test	0	0	0 (0.0%)
Carleton University Responsiveness to Suggestion Scale	7	0	7 (4.3%)
Waterloo–Stanford Group Scale	9	0	9 (5.5%)
Other scale	2	0	2 (1.4%)
	148 (90.2%)	**16 (9.8%)**	**164 (100.0%)**

Note. These numbers represent the instances of reported use of each scale in empirical articles in the *International Journal of Clinical and Experimental Hypnosis* (1992–2003). Multiple scales were used in some articles.

context, the SHCS:A was the measure of choice. The formal assessment of hypnotizability in the majority of empirical articles in this period reinforces the importance of standardized measurement in the field of hypnosis.

This pattern of usage can be understood partly in terms of the design and administration of the scales and partly in terms of the needs and interests of the investigators. Some measures were never intended for widespread use when they were first developed. For instance, the SPS:I and II were designed to map aptitude among highly hypnotizable individuals (Sheehan and McConkey, 1982), and it is not surprising that it is uncommon in research that uses scales for the general assessment or selection of research participants. Also, the literature does not necessarily reflect the clinical use of scales. For example, although the 10-minute HIP appears in only two articles during this period (and has been controversial at times; Orne et al., 1979; Perry et al., 1992), it meets clinicians' needs for a brief hypnotizability scale in the clinical context (Spiegel and Spiegel, 1978).

In addition to differences in use, the scales differ in their theoretical orientation and development, design, and purpose, as well as in what it means to be highly hypnotizable on them. Following Sheehan and McConkey (1982), the scales can be categorized into: (1) behavioural hypnotic scales, which are labelled 'hypnotic', involve a standard induction procedure, and emphasize behaviour over experience; (2) behavioural scales of suggestibility, which measure responsiveness to suggestion with or without an induction procedure; and (3) clinical scales, which index 'clinically useable hypnotic capacity' (Stern et al., 1978–9). Differences across these categories reflect underlying theoretical orientation as well as design. In essence, the scales were the direct work, or intellectual offspring, of four major groups: E.R. Hilgard, A.M. Weitzenhoffer and colleagues at Stanford University; M.T. Orne, E.C. Orne and colleagues at Harvard University and then at the University of Pennsylvania; T.X. Barber and colleagues at the Medfield Foundation; and H. and D. Spiegel in New York and at Stanford University, respectively. Six scales were the product of Hilgard and Weitzenhoffer's group, including the SHSS:A, B, and C, the original and revised Profile Scales, the adult and children's versions of the Clinical Scale, and the SHALIT; also, Bower's WSGC is a group adaptation of the SHSS:C. Although these measures differ in many ways, they share assumptions about the nature of hypnosis and hypnotizability.

In terms of design and purpose, whereas the majority of scales were developed with an interaction between the hypnotist and subject in mind, some were constructed or adapted for group administration. Some evaluate hypnotizability in terms of strict behavioural criteria, some consider both behavioural and subjective responses, and one focuses on experience alone. Overall, the scales have three major uses: (1) formal assessment of hypnotizability in the laboratory, (2) selection of particular individuals for further testing or research, and (3) assessment of clinically relevant hypnotic ability. Some scales meet more than one of these uses. For instance, the SHALIT, a brief, single-item measure intended for clinical use as well as assessment and selection, was developed after the HIP and was partly a political response to the controversial HIP (for comment on the 'politics of hypnosis', see Coe, 1989).

The design and purpose of the scales is reflected in the choice and configuration of the test items. For instance, the SHSS:A and B, and its group adaptation, the HGSHS:A, is appropriate for screening because it includes a series of relatively easy and simple suggestions across item types, and it estimates responsiveness under standard conditions; it is a 'general-purpose' or 'work sample' scale. In contrast, the SHSS:C is useful for individual assessment because it includes a series of increasingly difficult and complex items that index maximum performance. Often it is administered after practice on an initial scale, such as the HGSHS:A, and after performance reaches asymptotic or plateau hypnotizability; it is a 'graded difficulty' or 'achievement after practice' scale (Hilgard, 1965; see also Orne and O'Connell, 1967, for the DRS). The SPS:I and II (and RSPS:I and II; Weitzenhoffer and Hilgard, 1963, 1967) profiles the abilities of the most talented hypnotic participants, and it is an interesting combination of work sample and achievement test. Based on the assumption that individuals have different, rather than uniform, areas of susceptibility (e.g. age regression but not hallucination; Hilgard, 1965), the SPS:I and II involves complex suggestions across classes of items; even for a highly hypnotizable person, some items are more difficult and/or complex than others. Also, the skills that the hypnotist needs in order to properly administer these different scales increases as the complexity of the scale increases. Whereas administering the HGSHS:A is relatively simple, administering the SPS:I and II is relatively complex.

What does it mean to be highly hypnotizable on these measures? On behavioural hypnotic scales, such as the SHSS:A and B, SHSS:C, HGSHS:A, and the WSGC, a highly hypnotizable person passes the majority of items according to clear behavioural criteria. On these scales, normative data indicate that 5–7 per cent of individuals pass 11–12 of the 12 items (and are labelled 'very high' or 'virtuoso') and 17–34 per cent pass 8–10 items (and are labelled 'high'; Bowers, 1993, 1998; McConkey et al., 1996; Sheehan and McConkey, 1979; Shor and Orne, 1963; Weitzenhoffer and Hilgard, 1959, 1962). On measures that combine both behavioural and subjective assessment, such as the CURSS, a highly hypnotizable person responds behaviourally to the majority of suggestions and also reports that their experiences were compelling and involuntary. Spanos et al. (1983a) analysed CURSS data for 400 students and reported that 16 per cent passed 5–7 of the 7 items according to objective behavioural criteria, but only 6–7 per cent of them rated their responses as strong and involuntary (for further discussion of mismatches between observable behaviour and subjective experience, see Bowers, 1981; Kirsch et al., 1990, 1998; Weitzenhoffer, 1974).

A high score on the behavioural scales of suggestibility (BSS and CIS) indicates an ability to respond to suggestion across contexts. In other words, the highly hypnotizable (or highly suggestible) person responds without the situation being labelled as hypnotic and without the suggestions being preceded by an induction. Barber (1965) reported that 18 per cent and 15 per cent of individuals who had been given a hypnotic induction or task-motivational instructions (see Chapter 1), respectively, passed the eight items of the BSS according to behavioural criteria; 10 per cent and 13 per cent, respectively, passed all items according to subjective criteria. These percentages of 'highs' are not only similar across hypnotic and non-hypnotic conditions, but also similar to the behavioural hypnotic scales (for similar CIS data, see Wilson and Barber, 1978).

In the clinical domain, hypnotizability is often thought of in terms of practical treatment criteria. For instance, what level of hypnotic ability will maximize treatment success? Thus, according to clinical scales, a highly hypnotizable person possesses cognitive abilities and achieves levels of responsiveness that are benchmarked to clinical utility (J. Barber, 1993). For example, in terms of the DRS, medium hypnotizable individuals become subjectively involved in suggestions (a score of 3 out of 5), and high hypnotizable individuals experience reversible amnesia (a score of 5; Orne and O'Connell, 1967). Similarly, those who score high on the SHCS:A show therapeutically relevant responses, including strong imagery, enjoyment of age regression, and posthypnotic responding (Hilgard, 1965; Morgan and Hilgard, 1978–9a). High hypnotizability on the HIP (Grades 4 and 5) is interpreted somewhat differently – in terms of broad personality styles ('dionysians', 'apollonians', 'odysseans'), patterns of psychopathology, and a biologically based potential to experience a clinically useful 'trance' (Orne et al., 1979; Spiegel and Spiegel, 1978).

Despite differences in orientation, contemporary scales identify the highly hypnotizable individual in a relatively clear and meaningful way.

Theory and research in hypnotizability assessment

Psychological measures are never theory-free instruments. In terms of hypnotizability scales, they reflect particular theoretical frameworks, were often developed to meet pragmatic goals, and are often used to test and shape different accounts of hypnosis. A link between theory and assessment can be seen in the maturation of the Stanford scales. The major scales (SHSS:A and B, SHSS:C, SPS:I and II, RSPS:I and II) were developed from 1959 to 1967 and they became increasingly cognitive in focus. For instance, SHSS:A and B predominantly contain ideomotor items, whereas SHSS:C and SPS:I and II are skewed towards cognitive items. This change in emphasis reflected E.R. Hilgard's increasing interest in the types of responses that he would later label as 'dissociative' (Hilgard, 1973, 1974). The role of (changing) theory can also be seen in T.X. Barber's shift from the strongly behavioural and operational BSS to the more permissive, individualistic, and introspective CIS (Barber, 1999; see also, Sheehan and Perry, 1976). E.R. Hilgard designed the Stanford scales to include hypnotic induction as an integral component, whereas T.X. Barber designed the BSS and CIS to be used with or without an induction. These choices were consistent with their distinct theoretical and methodological approaches.

Many scales were developed for pragmatic reasons. The HGSHS:A and the WSGC are both adaptations of individually administered scales and were constructed to allow the efficient testing of large numbers of participants. Testing 100 people individually on a screening measure is vastly more resource-consuming (over say 100–150 hours) than testing 4 groups of 25 people (over say 4–6 hours). The development and validation of such group measures has ensured the viability and cost-effectiveness of large-scale hypnosis research programmes around the world. Other scales addressed the need to assess certain types of individuals or to include certain types of items. The SPS:I and II can be used to select people who have skills that are of particular interest to the researchers. Similarly, a tailored version of the SHSS:C, developed and normed by Hilgard et al. (1979b), allows the researchers to replace one of the original items within the standard protocol with a specific-purpose item.

In addition to these theory–instrument and research–instrument links in scale development, investigators have focused on aspects of the scales to comment on broader issues. Coe and Sarbin (1971) interpreted item difficulty within their dramaturgical perspective. They argued that hypnotic items differed mainly in terms of the level of the 'role-relevant skill' that was needed to perform them. Council and Kirsch (Council, 1993; Kirsch and Council, 1992) used 'context effects', which they defined as a shift in the correlation between HGSHS:A scores and personality measures across hypnotic and nonhypnotic testing contexts, to argue that hypnotic responding is a function of expectancies activated by the way in which a situation is defined, such as 'hypnotic'. And Bowers's (1981) long-held view that behavioural scoring criteria alone do not tap the essential experience of hypnosis (the 'classic suggestion effect'; Weitzenhoffer, 1974) led to the group adaptation of the SHSS:C, the WSGC (Bowers, 1993, 1998), being accompanied by a subjective scoring system (Kirsch et al., 1998).

Psychometric issues in hypnotizability assessment

Consistent with modern test development, hypnotizability measures are psychometrically sound, as indexed by internal consistency, split-half reliability, test–retest reliability, and so on (Barber, 1965; Bowers, 1993, 1998; Hilgard, 1965; Spanos et al., 1983b; Wilson and Barber, 1978). Perhaps the most interesting psychometric data come from longitudinal test–retest studies, which have assessed hypnotizability across the life span. Piccione et al. (1989; see also Spanos et al., 1994) compared SHSS:A performance across 10-, 15-, and 25-year intervals: 60 per cent and 62 per cent of people were categorized similarly after 10 and 25 years, respectively, and test–retest correlations ranged from 0.64 to 0.82. These findings highlight strong consistency in hypnotic ability across time.

Individuals not only differ quantitatively in their hypnotizability, but also may differ qualitatively. In other words, a highly hypnotizable person may be a different 'type' of person (Balthazard and Woody, 1989; Oakman and Woody, 1996). The dimensional (rather than typological) assumption of contemporary scales is challenged to some degree by the bimodal distribution of scale scores (e.g. Balthazard and Woody, 1989; Hilgard, 1965). It is also challenged by evidence that very hypnotizable people (hypnotic virtuosos) typically use strategies of involvement and response that are quite different from those that are used by their less hypnotizable counterparts to experience hypnotic suggestions, particularly when those suggestions are complex and demanding (e.g. Barnier and McConkey, 1999a; Burn et al., 2001; Noble and McConkey, 1995).

Although it is often assumed that the single construct of 'hypnotizability' accounts for all levels of performance on standardized scales, this assumption may not be warranted (Balthazard, 1993). The major hypnotizability scales, such as the HGSHS:A and SHSS:C, yield at least three distinct factors that reflect responses to ideomotor, challenge, and cognitive test items (for a review of factor-analytic work, see Balthazard and Woody, 1985; see also Chapter 1). Ideomotor items involve 'thoughts becoming action' and include suggestions that lead to particular motor responses, such as feeling your arm getting heavier and being pulled down. Challenge items involve the inhibition of motor responses, such as trying to open your eyes when you have been told they are tightly shut. Cognitive items involve alterations in perceptual or cognitive functioning, such as visual or auditory hallucinations, age regression, and posthypnotic amnesia. Some commentators have argued that the three-factor solution is an artefact of item difficulty (i.e. cognitive items are generally more difficult and passed by fewer participants than ideomotor items). However, the factorial structure has been confirmed by recent research that matched item difficulty across suggestion types by revising scoring criteria to equate pass percentages (Kihlstrom, 1999). Although ideomotor, challenge, and cognitive items are distinct in many ways, they all fall within Hilgard's (1973) domain of hypnotic behaviour and experiencing them depends upon the capacity of hypnotizability.

Woody et al. (1992) proposed that hypnotizability scales measure at least two major, discrete latent characteristics. They argued that easy (ideomotor) versus difficult (cognitive) items are correlated with different, independent underlying dimensions. The spectral analysis of scale scores has supported this interpretation. Balthazard and Woody (1992) reported that absorption, as measured by the Tellegen Absorption Scale (Tellegen and Atkinson, 1974), was correlated differentially with the most difficult items, whereas Woody et al. (1997) reported that nonhypnotic suggestibility was correlated differentially with the easiest items. Although other investigators have failed to replicate these differential relationships (e.g. Kirsch et al., 1995), the two-component model of hypnotizability raises the possibility that competing accounts of hypnosis may be due to a focus on different kinds of suggestions and across different levels of hypnotizability (Woody, 1997). This is one issue that needs to be explored further in research on hypnotizability, and we now turn to consider selected investigations of hypnotizability.

Contemporary investigations of hypnotizability

Hypnotizability across scales, time, and cultures

Is 'high' on one scale, high on other scales? Consistency in categorization across scales depends on the items used, the method of scoring, and the context in which the scales are used. In terms of items, a comparison of the HGSHS:A and the SHSS:C indicated that 46 per cent of highs and 34 per cent of very highs/virtuosos were confirmed within the same category across the two measures (Register and Kihlstrom, 1986; see also Perry et al., 1992); more people were categorized as highly hypnotizable on the HGSHS:A than on the SHSS:C. This is probably because the SHSS:C (2 ideomotor, 2 challenge, 8 cognitive) contains more difficult items than the HGSHS:A (4 ideomotor, 5 challenge, 3 cognitive). In terms of scoring, a comparison of the SHSS:C and the CURSS yielded strong concordance in categorizations when scoring focused on behaviour, but not when scoring focused on subjective experience (Spanos et al., 1983c). Across 102 participants, 64 per cent who were classified high on the SHSS:C (scores of 8–12) were classified high on CURSS objective scores (5–7), but only 39 per cent of participants who were classified high on the SHSS:C were classified high on CURSS subjective and involuntariness scores (Spanos et al., 1983c). In other words, behavioural responding overestimated subjective responding. In terms of context, a comparison between the HIP and the SHSS:C suggested that the clinically oriented HIP is more likely to confer high hypnotizability status than the behavioural measures of the SHSS:C (Orne et al., 1979). Across two studies, 100 per cent of participants who were categorized very high on the SHSS:C (11–12) and 77 per cent who were categorized high (8–10) were categorized high on the HIP induction score, which is based on subjective qualities of an arm levitation suggestion. However, 82 per cent of participants who were classified medium on the SHSS:C (5–7) and 54 per cent who were classified low (0–4) were categorized high on the HIP. In other words, 76 per cent of all participants were categorized high according to the HIP, a figure that far exceeds estimates of high hypnotizability on other scales. This overestimation may be due in part to the dichotomizing (high vs. low) of the HIP distribution in these studies and partly due to the reliance of the HIP on a relatively simple ideomotor item in addition to the 'eye roll sign' (Spiegel and Spiegel, 1978; see also Perry et al., 1992).

Test–retest reliability of contemporary measures of hypnotizability indicates that hypnotic performance is reasonably consistent over time, albeit with some changes in categorization (i.e. low, medium, or high). Normative samples, particularly for the HGSHS:A, offer insight into the stability of hypnotizability within populations across time. For instance, Australian normative data are available for the years 1973–5 ($N = 1944$; Sheehan and McConkey, 1979) and 1985–92 ($N = 4752$; McConkey et al., 1996). Although these data were collected 10–19 years apart, there is substantial consistency in item difficulty, pass percentages, and categorization of hypnotizability. There is consistency also from year to year; for instance, across the eight years of the later sample, the mean HGSHS:A score ranged from 5.9 to 6.9 (McConkey et al., 1996). In contrast, Benham et al.'s (2002) recent analysis of mean SHSS:C scores across four decades yielded a significant linear trend, with higher scores in more recent years. They speculated that the increase in average scores could be due to: (1) shifts in recruitment, administration, and population demographics; (2) changes in the social construction of 'hypnosis', and thus the demands of the hypnotic situation; and/or (3) a genuine upward swing in the underlying trait of hypnotizability.

HGSHS:A normative samples also allow cross-cultural comparisons of hypnotizability. In addition to the original American samples (Coe, 1964; Shor and Orne, 1963), there are samples from Australia (McConkey et al., 1996; Sheehan and McConkey, 1979), Canada (Laurence and Perry, 1982), Denmark (Zachariae et al., 1996), Finland (Kallio and Ihamuotila, 1999), Germany (Bongartz, 1985), Italy (De Pascalis et al., 2000), and Spain (Lamas et al., 1989). These samples cross geographic, national, cultural, and language barriers, and even cultural barriers within geographical or national regions (e.g. norms for African-American individuals; Sapp and Hitchcock, 2001). Using the HGSHS:A across contexts does not decrease its precision or substantially change its psychometric properties (e.g. McConkey et al., 1996). There are some discrepancies in the profile of pass percentages for the 12 suggestions on the scale. For instance, Canadian participants (15 per cent) are less likely to respond to a posthypnotic suggestion than are Spanish (29 per cent) or Australian (26 per cent) participants; nevertheless, the rank order of item difficulty is very similar across samples (Perry et al., 1992). Thus, at least for those (predominantly Western) countries that have provided norms, the HGSHS:A is generally not affected by cultural or language differences. It remains to be seen whether hypnotizability is a truly universal individual difference attribute, particularly since 'hypnotic-like' behaviour is common to many cultures (Spanos, 1996).

Hypnotizability crosses other boundaries as well. Researchers have compared signing deaf with hearing individuals by using a signed videotaped as against a standard version of the induction and suggestions, and reported that participants' behavioural responding, subjective experience, and involvement with the hypnotist are generally similar (e.g. Matthews and Isenberg, 1995; Repka and Nash, 1995). Other research has compared hypnotizability in response to a standard 'live' administration with a computer-assisted administration (Grant and Nash, 1995), and found no difference in hypnotic behaviour, experience, and involvement. Given the growth in 'on-line' cultures, communities, and professional practice, such findings have important implications for hypnotizability measurement in the 21st century.

Overall, the highly hypnotizable person is much the same whether they are tested on different scales, in 1974 or 2004, in person or via computer, are European, Australian, or African-American, speak English, Spanish, German, or Finnish, and communicate verbally or with sign language. In other words, high hypnotizability can be reliably indexed across scales, time, and cultures.

Modifying hypnotizability

Hypnotizability is generally thought of as a relatively stable personal trait, and the impressive longitudinal test–retest data support this view. However, some researchers have argued that hypnotizability can be substantially modified or enhanced (see Chapter 9 for a fuller discussion of this topic). Broadly speaking, this debate asks whether hypnotizability is a developmentally based, stable capacity (Bowers and Davidson, 1991) or the product of attitudes, expectations, and interpretations of test demands, which can be manipulated (Spanos,

1991; Spanos and Coe, 1992). This issue is important not only for understanding the phenomena and processes of hypnosis, but also for the application of hypnosis in various applied settings. Given that the addition of hypnotic techniques to some psychological or medical treatment programmes increases their efficacy (e.g. Montgomery et al., 2000; for review, see Lynn et al., 2000), the enhancement of hypnotizability could arguably extend treatment gains to more disorders and/or to more people.

The Carleton Skills Training Program (CSTP) was developed by Gorassini and Spanos (1986, 1999) to enhance hypnotizability, particularly amongst less responsive individuals (see Chapter 9). In the CSTP, low hypnotizable people receive information and training to: (1) enhance their attitudes and expectations concerning hypnosis; (2) become absorbed in their imaginings to experience suggested responses as involuntary; and (3) enact the hypnotic responses via appropriate imagery and interpret them as involuntary. Spanos and colleagues reported significant increases in hypnotizability scores as measured by the CURSS (for review, see Gorassini, 1999; Gorassini and Spanos, 1999); across these studies, at least 50 per cent of trained lows typically responded like 'natural highs' (Spanos et al., 1993).

Other researchers, however, failed to find these major changes in hypnotizability. They argued that the CSTP may not enhance hypnotizability, but it may simply promote behavioural compliance in the absence of an authentic subjective experience (Bates, 1992; Bowers and Davidson, 1991). Bates et al. (1988) tested low hypnotizables who received the CSTP and were told that subsequent testing on the CURSS was part of the same experiment, lows who received the training but were told that subsequent testing was unrelated, and lows who received no training. They found that training increased responsiveness in a very modest way. Also, lows who were told that training and testing were related showed the greatest gains; thus, the demands of this condition may have led to compliance and increased scores. Notably, hypnotizability gains were not maintained at a 4-month follow-up. Nevertheless, it is important to know if hypnotizability can be increased to a clinically useful extent (Gfeller, 1993). Also, it is important to know if training programmes can create highs who not only behave in the same way as natural highs, but experience the suggestions in the same way as natural highs (Barnier and McConkey, 1999a; Sheehan and McConkey, 1982).

There are characteristics of the highly hypnotizable person that may not be trainable, such as their strong cognitive commitment to the hypnotist and his or her communications (McConkey, 1991; Sheehan, 1991). Highly hypnotizable people become very involved in their experiences and they often process information selectively and/ or disregard conflicting information to maintain the integrity of that experience (e.g. Barnier and McConkey, 1999a; Burn et al., 2001). Moreover, highs often develop a very strong interpersonal relationship or rapport with the hypnotist (e.g. McConkey, 1983; Sheehan, 1971). One implication of this involvement is that highly hypnotizable people may not be able to suppress their hypnotic ability. Of course, the hypnotist can inhibit responding, perhaps unknowingly, by creating an interpersonal context that is uncomfortable and that does not allow the development of strong rapport. However, this failure to engage the individual's ability within the hypnotic relationship is different from highs deciding and being able to behaviourally and experientially resist the effects of suggestions.

Hilgard (1963) asked 12 highly hypnotizable individuals to resist suggestions for an item on which they had previously responded. They were instructed to try to resist on two of six trials, but were given no information about whether they were expected to succeed or fail. Six participants resisted both suggestions, five resisted one of two, and only one failed to resist either suggestion. Most indicated that they partially experienced the suggestions and that their trying to resist the suggestions took great effort and created feelings of conflict (see also Spanos et al., 1985). Austin et al. (1963) investigated the ability of five highly hypnotizable individuals to simulate or fake hypnosis without becoming hypnotized. Although most simulated successfully, they described it as a difficult, somewhat unpleasant, and very effortful task. Notably, at least one of the five responded compellingly (i.e. as a normal high) to many of the suggestions despite initially being very confident of his ability to simulate (see also Orne, 1971; Reyher, 1973). Overall, these data suggest that highly hypnotizable people can control and inhibit their level of response when actively resisting hypnotic suggestions. However, when they are passive, as it were, they are likely to experience suggestions inadvertently.

Correlates of hypnotizability

The highly hypnotizable person is thought to possess certain enduring characteristics that predict their successful responding.

Researchers have focused on selected attitude and aptitude components of hypnotizability (Hilgard, 1965). Attitudinal components include individuals' attitudes toward and expectancies about hypnosis. People with negative attitudes towards hypnosis almost always are low hypnotizable, and those with positive attitudes may be high, medium, or low (see also Chapter 9). Thus, positive attitudes are necessary but not sufficient for successful performance (Spanos et al., 1987). Individuals' attitudes can influence not only their susceptibility to hypnosis, but also their initial willingness to participate, whether in an experimental or a clinical setting.

Expectancies also influence hypnotizability. People develop expectations about the nature and degree of their experience, which can influence how they respond (Kirsch, 2001). Interestingly, whereas lows are relatively accurate in predicting how responsive they will be to a hypnotizability scale, mediums and highs often underestimate their responsiveness. Hypnotic participants also develop expectations about what a hypnotic interaction is like and what kinds of things the hypnotist will say to them. When these expectations are transgressed, responding may be inhibited. For example, Barnier and McConkey (1999a) asked highly hypnotizable participants a question ('Do you think it will rain tonight?') before, during, and after hypnosis. They also gave them a suggestion before, during, or after hypnosis to rub their ear lobe when they were asked this question. In this way, the experiment placed a question that required a verbal response in conflict with a suggestion that only sometimes required a behavioural response. Participants were less likely to respond, and their behaviour was less compelling and compulsive, when they received the suggestion at an unexpected time (e.g. before hypnosis) or when they weren't sure whether to answer the question or rub their ear. Notably, hypnotic virtuosos, the most hypnotizable individuals, were less concerned about these ambiguities and tended to respond to the suggestion at all times.

Aptitudinal components of hypnotizability include constructs drawn from general personality research (e.g. absorption) and phenomenological hypnosis research (e.g. imaginative involvement), as well as constructs that are relevant to particular accounts of hypnosis (e.g. fantasy-proneness, dissociation). Absorption involves an openness to experience emotional and cognitive alterations across a variety of situations (Tellegen, 1981; Tellegen and Atkinson, 1974; for review, see Roche and McConkey, 1990). Measured by the 34-item Tellegen Absorption Scale, absorption is related to 'openness to experience', a subscale of the NEO Personality Inventory (Costa and McCrae, 1985; Glisky et al., 1991; McCrae, 1993). Absorption correlates with hypnotizability generally (Roche and McConkey, 1990; Tellegen and Atkinson, 1974) as well as with response to particular hypnotic suggestions (Balthazard and Woody, 1992). Fantasy-proneness describes the capacity for deep involvement in a private world of fantasy, vivid daydreams, and paranormal experiences (see also Chapters 5 and 8). Wilson and Barber (1983) argued that a high level of fantasy-proneness drives exceptional hypnotic ability. When indexed by the Inventory of Childhood Memories and Imaginings (Wilson and Barber, 1983), fantasy-proneness is positively, albeit modestly, related to hypnotizability (for a summary of research, see Lynn and Rhue, 1988). Dissociation is another construct linked to a particular account of hypnosis. Broadly speaking, the Dissociative Experiences Scale (Bernstein and Putnam, 1986) measures pathological dissociation and correlates modestly with hypnotizability, although this may be an artefact (for a summary of relevant research, see Kirsch and Council, 1992).

Overall, differences in personality traits explain less variance in hypnotizability scores than one might expect. In addition, these relationships can be attenuated by contextual factors. Council et al. (1996) reported that the correlations between hypnotizability and absorption were smaller when absorption was measured in nonhypnotic than in hypnotic contexts. They argued that when individuals complete an absorption measure during a hypnosis session, they develop expectancies about their hypnosis responses on the basis of their absorption responses (or vice versa). Thus, any relationship is artefactual rather than genuine, and is determined by the context in which absorption is assessed (Council, 1993; Council et al., 1996; Kirsch and Council, 1992). This simple differentiation of hypnotic and nonhypnotic settings, however, ignores the original conceptualization of absorption as inherently interactive with the situation. Barnier and McConkey (1999b) assessed the relationship between hypnotizability and absorption when absorption was tested in two nonhypnotic settings: an imagination condition (with other imagery and imagination measures) and a classroom condition. We reported a significant correlation between hypnotizability and absorption in the imagination, but not the classroom, condition, and we argued that settings that elicit imaginative responses influence the expression of absorption and its relationship with hypnotizability. Personality variables, including those related to hypnotic ability, may be inherently contextual and only become apparent in settings that are consistent with and encourage their expression (Barnier and McConkey, 1999b; Bowers, 1973; Tellegen, 1981).

Hypnotizability and private experience

Most scales focus on observable responses, and they assume that behavioural responses reflect the underlying experience of the individual. Many early measures of hypnotizability, as well as measures developed concurrently with the behavioural measures, focused on the individual's 'depth of hypnosis' (e.g. LeCron Scale, LeCron, 1953; North Carolina Scale, Tart, 1970; Brief Stanford Scale, Hilgard and Tart, 1966; Long Stanford Scale, Tart, 1970; Harvard Discrete Scale, O'Connell, 1964; Harvard Continuous Scale, Cheek, 1959, Orne and Evans, 1966; Field's Inventory of Hypnotic Depth, Field, 1965; for review, see Sheehan and McConkey, 1982). The North Carolina Scale required individuals to rate their depth of hypnosis after each suggested experience on a scale from 0 ('waking') to 50+ ('mind sluggish'). Shor's (1979) Phenomenological Method also focused on experience rather than behaviour, but a person other than the subject made the judgements and ratings. According to Shor (1979), hypnosis involved a suspension of the 'generalized reality orientation', in the sense that ongoing experience became isolated from external reality and critical self-appraisal. These various measures of private experience recognized that hypnotic experiences may not always result in criterion-relevant behaviour of the kind indexed by standardized scales. They reflect the view that hypnotic experience is more general and more variable than response to specific suggestions, and can fluctuate in intensity from moment to moment (McConkey et al., 1999).

Investigations of the relationship between behavioural and experiential measures indicate not only substantial concordance, but also that experiential measures offer additional information. Pekala's (1991) comparisons of behavioural measures and his Phenomenology of Consciousness Inventory (PCI; Pekala, 1991) are a good illustration. The PCI indexes five factors associated with the hypnosis scale: dissociative control, positive affect, negative affect, visual imagery, and attention to internal processes. The PCI is a better predictor of SHSS:C scores than is the HGSHS:A (Hand et al., 1995; see also Forbes and Pekala, 1993) and higher behavioural scores on measures of hypnotizability are associated with greater feelings of dissociative control, positive affect, and attention to internal processes on the PCI (Kumar et al., 1996a).

The wish to understand more about the link between hypnotic behaviour and experience has encouraged methodological advances. These include not only the addition of subjective scales to standard behavioural measures, but also the development of the Experiential Analysis Technique (EAT; Sheehan and McConkey, 1982). In terms of subjective scales, individuals can respond to a hypnotic item for many reasons, and there can be a mismatch between the appearance of a complete hypnotic response and the experience of one. Alternatively, individuals may have the experience in a reasonably complete way, but this experience may not be expressed to a level that meets the behavioural criterion (Bowers, 1981; Kirsch et al., 1990, 1998; Kumar et al., 1996b). For example, the hallucination item in the HGSHS:A suggests that a fly is buzzing around the person's head. To receive a positive score, the individual must overtly indicate the presence of the fly by brushing it away. If he or she hears or feels the fly but make no behavioural response, then the behavioural scale alone does not reflect the experience; a subjective scale that asks for a rating of strength of experience would capture this.

Although subjective scales add useful information, they typically involve a retrospective and subjective averaging of an experience that is complex and variable. Moreover, they reveal nothing about the strategies individuals use to experience suggestions. The EAT was developed to explore these aspects and it has been used to investigate various phenomena including hypnotic blindness, hypnotic pseudo-memory, posthypnotic suggestion, and posthypnotic amnesia (e.g. Barnier and McConkey, 1992, 1999a; Bryant and McConkey, 1989a, 1989b; McConkey et al., 1980, 1989; McConkey and Sheehan, 1981). In this procedure, participants view a videotape record of their hypnosis session in the presence of an independent experimenter (the 'inquirer') and comment on their experiences as they watch. McConkey et al. (1989) used this procedure in a single-case comparison of two excellent hypnotic participants who were tested on difficult items such as positive and negative visual hallucination, circle anaesthesia, and posthypnotic amnesia. The EAT revealed that these two talented participants interpreted and processed the suggestions in very different ways; one was very passive cognitively ('concentrative'), whereas the other was very active cognitively ('constructive style'; Sheehan and McConkey, 1982). This difference between 'happenings' and 'doings' (Sarbin and Coe, 1972) could only have been revealed by an experientially focused method such as the EAT.

Summary and conclusions

It is almost 45 years since A.M. Weitzenhoffer and E.R. Hilgard developed the first major modern hypnotizability scale at Stanford University. This scale, and those that followed, met the two major goals of scale development: they allowed individual differences in hypnotic responding to be mapped and explored, and they placed the measurement of hypnotic ability, and the field of hypnosis, on a firm scientific footing. Subsequent advances in the domains of personality, psychometrics, and hypnosis have highlighted both the value and the limits of these scales. However, it is important to understand that the conceptualization and features of our major scales represent thoughtful theoretical, methodological, and practical choices on the part of their developers.

Work remains to be done, however, to develop a more complete measurement and understanding of hypnotizability. This work includes a consideration of the general and specific components of hypnotizability, a closer linking of development in the measurement of hypnotizability to development in psychometric theory and practice more broadly, and a wider investigation of hypnotizability in non-Western cultures. Also, the relationship between hypnotizability as expressed in the presence of a hypnotist and responsiveness to an induction and suggestions given to oneself, in the sense of self-hypnotizability, remains an important direction for further research. While recognizing the need to advance along these avenues of future inquiry, it is important to underscore that the highly hypnotizable person is well identified and well defined by current methods of measurement.

Acknowledgement

The writing of this chapter was supported in part by an Australian Research Council Queen Elizabeth II Fellowship to Amanda Barnier. We are grateful for that support.

References

Austin, M., Perry, C., Sutcliffe, J.P. and Yeomans, N. (1963) 'Can somnambulists successfully simulate hypnotic behavior without becoming entranced?', *International Journal of Clinical and Experimental Hypnosis*, 11:175–86.

Balthazard, C.G. (1993) 'The hypnosis scales at their centenary: Some fundamental issues still unresolved', *International Journal of Clinical and Experimental Hypnosis*, 41:47–73.

—— and Woody, E.Z. (1985) 'The "stuff" of hypnotic performance: A review of psychometric approaches', *Psychological Bulletin*, 98:283–96.

—— and Woody, E.Z. (1989) 'Bimodality, dimensionality, and the notion of hypnotic types', *International Journal of Clinical and Experimental Hypnosis*, 37:70–89.

—— and Woody, E.Z. (1992) 'The spectral analysis of hypnotic performance with respect to "absorption" ', *International Journal of Clinical and Experimental Hypnosis*, 40:21–43.

Barber, J. (1993) 'The clinical role of responsivity tests: A master class commentary', *International Journal of Clinical and Experimental Hypnosis*, 41:165–8.

Barber, T.X. (1965) 'Measuring "hypnotic-like" suggestibility with and without "hypnotic induction": Psychometric properties, norms, and variables influencing response to the Barber Suggestibility Scale (BSS)', *Psychological Reports*, 16:809–44.

—— (1999) 'Hypnosis: A mature view', *Contemporary Hypnosis*, 16:123–7.

Barnier, A.J. and McConkey, K.M. (1992) 'Reports of real and false memories: The relevance of hypnosis, hypnotizability, and context of memory test', *Journal of Abnormal Psychology*, 101:521–7.

—— and McConkey, K.M. (1999a) 'Hypnotic and posthypnotic suggestion: Finding meaning in the message of the hypnotist', *International Journal of Clinical and Experimental Hypnosis*, 47:192–208.

—— and McConkey, K.M. (1999b) 'Absorption, hypnotizability, and context: Nonhypnotic contexts are not all the same', *Contemporary Hypnosis*, 16:1–8.

Barry, H., MacKinnon, D.W. and Murray, H.A., Jr. (1931) 'Studies on personality: A. Hypnotizability as a personality trait and its typological relations', *Human Biology*, 13:1–36.

Bates, B.L. (1992) 'The effect of demands for honesty on the efficacy of the Carleton Skills Training Program', *International Journal of Clinical and Experimental Hypnosis*, 40:88–102.

—— Miller, R.J., Cross, H.J. and Brigham, T.A. (1988) 'Modifying hypnotic suggestibility with the Carleton Skills Training Program', *Journal of Personality and Social Psychology*, 55:120–7.

Benham, G., Smith, N. and Nash, M.R. (2002) 'Hypnotic susceptibility scales: Are the mean scores increasing?', *International Journal of Clinical and Experimental Hypnosis*, 50:5–16.

Bernheim, H. (1888) *Hypnosis and Suggestion in Psychotherapy*, New Hyde Park, NY: University Books (Reprinted 1964).

Bernstein, E.M. and Putnam, F.W. (1986) 'Development, reliability, and validity of a dissociation scale', *Journal of Nervous and Mental Disease*, 174:727–35.

Bongartz, W. (1985) 'German norms for the Harvard Group Scale of Hypnotic Susceptibility, Form A', *International Journal of Clinical and Experimental Hypnosis*, 33:131–40.

Bowers, K.S. (1973) 'Situationism in psychology', *Psychological Review*, 80:307–36.

—— (1981) 'Do the Stanford scales tap the "classic suggestion effect"?' *International Journal of Clinical and Experimental Hypnosis*, 29:42–53.

—— (1993) 'The Waterloo–Stanford Group C (WSGC) scale of hypnotic susceptibility: Normative and comparative data', *International Journal of Clinical and Experimental Hypnosis*, 41:35–46.

—— (1998) 'Waterloo–Stanford Group Scale of Hypnotic Susceptibility, Form C: Manual and response booklet', *International Journal of Clinical and Experimental Hypnosis*, 46:250–68.

—— and Davidson, T.M. (1991) 'A neodissociative critique of Spanos's social-psychological model of hypnosis', in S.J. Lynn and J.W. Rhue (eds), *Theories of Hypnosis: Current Models and Perspectives* (pp. 105–43), New York: Guilford Press.

Bryant, R.A. and McConkey, K.M. (1989a) 'Hypnotic blindness: A behavioural and experiential analysis', *Journal of Abnormal Psychology*, 98:71–7.

—— and McConkey, K.M. (1989b) 'Hypnotic blindness, awareness and attribution', *Journal of Abnormal Psychology*, 98:443–7.

Burn, C., Barnier, A.J. and McConkey, K.M. (2001) 'Information processing during hypnotically suggested sex change', *International Journal of Clinical and Experimental Hypnosis*, 49:231–42.

Cheek, D.B. (1959) 'Use of rebellion against coercion as mechanism for hypnotic trance deepening', *International Journal of Clinical and Experimental Hypnosis*, 7:223–7.

Coe, W.C. (1964) 'Further norms for the Harvard Group Scale of Hypnotic Susceptibility, Form A', *International Journal of Clinical and Experimental Hypnosis*, 12:184–90.

—— (1989) 'Hypnosis: The role of sociopolitical factors in a paradigm clash', in N.P. Spanos and J.F. Chaves (eds), *Hypnosis: The Cognitive-behavioral Perspective* (pp. 418–36), Amherst, NY: Prometheus Books.

—— and Sarbin, T.R. (1971) 'An alternative interpretation to the multiple composition of hypnotic scales: A single role relevant skill', *Journal of Personality and Social Psychology*, 18:1–8.

Costa, P.T. and McCrae, R.R. (1985) *The NEO Personality Inventory: Manual*, Odessa, FL: Psychological Assessment Resources.

Council, J.R. (1993) 'Context effects in personality research', *Current Directions in Psychological Science*, 2:31–4.

—— (1999) 'Measures of hypnotic responding', in I. Kirsch, A. Capafons, E. Cardeña-Buelna and S. Amigó (eds), *Clinical Hypnosis and Self-regulation: Cognitive-behavioral Perspectives* (pp. 119–40), Washington, DC: American Psychological Association.

—— Kirsch, I. and Grant, D.L. (1996) 'Imagination, expectancy, and hypnotic responding', in R.G. Kunzendorf, N.P. Spanos and B. Wallace (eds), *Hypnosis and Imagination* (pp. 41–65), New York: Baywood.

Crawford, H.J. and Gruzelier, J. (1992) 'A midstream view of the neuropsychophophysiology of hypnosis: Recent research and future directions', in E. Fromm and M.R. Nash (eds), *Contemporary Hypnosis Research* (pp. 227–66), New York: Guilford Press.

Davis, L.W. and Husband, R.W. (1931) 'A study of hypnotic susceptibility in relation to personality traits', *Journal of Abnormal and Social Psychology*, 26:175–82.

De Pascalis, V., Russo, P. and Marucci, F.S. (2000) 'Italian norms for the Harvard Group Scale of Hypnotic Susceptibility, Form A', *International Journal of Clinical and Experimental Hypnosis*, 48:44–55.

Dixon, M. and Laurence, J.-R. (1992) 'Hypnotic susceptibility and verbal automaticity: Automatic and strategic processing differences in the Stroop color-naming task', *Journal of Abnormal Psychology*, 101:344–7.

Field, P.B. (1965) 'An inventory scale of hypnotic depth', *International Journal of Clinical and Experimental Hypnosis*, 13:238–49.

Forbes, E.J. and Pekala, R.J. (1993) 'Predicting hypnotic susceptibility via a phenomenological approach', *Psychological Reports*, 73:1251–6.

Friedlander, J.W. and Sarbin, T.R. (1938) 'The depth of hypnosis', *Journal of Abnormal and Social Psychology*, 33:453–75.

Gfeller, J.D. (1993) 'Enhancing hypnotizability and treatment responsiveness', in J.W. Rhue, S.J. Lynn and I. Kirsch (eds), *Handbook of Clinical Hypnosis* (pp. 235–50), Washington DC: American Psychological Association.

Glisky, M.L., Tataryn, D.J., Tobias, B.A., Kihlstrom, J.F. and McConkey, K.M. (1991) 'Absorption, openness to experience, and hypnotizability', *Journal of Personality and Social Psychology*, 60:263–72.

Gorassini, D.R. (1999) 'Hypnotic responding: A cognitive-behavioral analysis of self-deception', in I. Kirsch, A. Capafons, E. Cardeña-Buelna and S. Amigó (eds), *Clinical Hypnosis and Self-regulation: Cognitive-behavioral Perspectives* (pp. 73–103), Washington, DC: American Psychological Association.

—— and Spanos, N.P. (1986) 'A cognitive–social skills approach to the successful modification of hypnotic susceptibility', *Journal of Personality and Social Psychology*, 50:1004–12.

—— and Spanos, N.P. (1999) 'The Carleton Skill Training Program for Modifying Hypnotic Suggestibility: Original version and variations', in I. Kirsch, A. Capafons, E. Cardeña-Buelna and S. Amigó (eds), *Clinical Hypnosis and Self-regulation: Cognitive-behavioral Perspectives* (pp. 141–77), Washington, DC: American Psychological Association.

Grant, C.D. and Nash, M.R. (1995) 'The Computer-Assisted Hypnosis Scale: Standardization and norming of a computer-administered measure of hypnotic ability', *Psychological Assessment*, 7:49–58.

Hand, J., Pekala, R.J. and Kumar, V.K. (1995) 'Prediction of Harvard and Stanford Scale scores with a phenomenological instrument', *Australian Journal of Clinical and Experimental Hypnosis*, 23:124–34.

Hilgard, E.R. (1963) 'Ability to resist suggestions within the hypnotic state: Responsiveness to conflicting communications', *Psychological Reports*, 12:3–13.

—— (1965) *Hypnotic Susceptibility*, New York: Harcourt, Brace and World.

—— (1973) 'The domain of hypnosis, with some comments on alternative paradigms', *American Psychologist*, 28:972–82.

—— (1974) 'Toward a neodissociation theory: Multiple cognitive controls in human functioning', *Perspectives in Biology and Medicine*, 17:301–16.

—— (1991) 'A neodissociation interpretation of hypnosis', in S.J. Lynn and J.W. Rhue (eds), *Theories of Hypnosis: Current Models and Perspectives* (pp. 83–104), New York: Guilford Press.

—— and Tart, C.T. (1966) 'Responsiveness to suggestions following waking and imagination instructions and following induction of hypnosis', *Journal of Abnormal Psychology*, 71:196–208.

—— Crawford, H.J. and Wert, A. (1979a) 'The Stanford Hypnotic Arm Levitation Induction and Test (SHALIT): A six minute hypnotic induction and measurement scale', *International Journal of Clinical and Experimental Hypnosis*, 27:111–24.

—— Crawford, H.J., Bowers, P.G. and Kihlstrom, J.F. (1979b) 'A tailored SHSS:C, permitting user modification for special purposes', *International Journal of Clinical and Experimental Hypnosis*, 27:125–33.

Kallio, S.P. and Ihamuotila, M.J. (1999) 'Finnish norms for the Harvard Group Scale of Hypnotic Susceptibility, Form A', *International Journal of Clinical and Experimental Hypnosis*, 47:227–35.

Kihlstrom, J.F. (1999) 'The fox, the hedgehog, and hypnosis', Invited Address to the 50th Annual Meeting of the Society for Clinical and Experimental Hypnosis, New Orleans, USA, September.

Kirsch, I. (2001) 'The response set theory of hypnosis: Expectancy and physiology', *American Journal of Clinical Hypnosis*, 44:69–73.

—— and Braffman, W. (2001) 'Imaginative suggestibility and hypnotizability', *Current Directions in Psychological Science*, 10:57–61.

—— and Council, J.R. (1992) 'Situational and personality correlates of suggestibility', in E. Fromm and M.R. Nash (eds), *Contemporary Hypnosis Research* (pp. 267–91), New York: Guilford Press.

—— and Lynn, S.J. (1995) 'The altered state of hypnosis: Changes in the theoretical landscape', *American Psychologist*, 50:846–58.

Kirsch, I., Council, J.R. and Wickless, C. (1990) 'Subjective scoring for the Harvard Group Scale of Hypnotic Susceptibility, Form A', *International Journal of Clinical and Experimental Hypnosis*, 38:112–24.

—— Silva, C.E., Comey, G. and Reed, S. (1995) 'A spectral analysis of cognitive and personality variable in hypnosis: Empirical disconfirmation of the two-factor model of hypnotic responding', *Journal of Personality and Social Psychology*, 69:167–75.

—— Milling, L.S. and Burgess, C.A. (1998) 'Experiential scoring for the Waterloo–Stanford Group C Scale', *International Journal of Clinical and Experimental Hypnosis*, 46:269–79.

Kumar, V.K., Pekala, R.J. and Cummings, J. (1996a) 'Trait factors, state effects, and hypnotizability', *International Journal of Clinical and Experimental Hypnosis*, 44:232–49.

—— Marcano, G. and Pekala, R.J. (1996b) 'Behavioral and subjective scoring of the Harvard Group Scale of Hypnotic Susceptibility: Further data and extension', *American Journal of Clinical Hypnosis*, 38:191–209.

Lamas, J.E., del Valle-Inclan, F., Blanco, M.J. and Diaz, A.A. (1989) 'Spanish norms for the Harvard Group Scale of Hypnotic Susceptibility, Form A', *International Journal of Clinical and Experimental Hypnosis*, 37:264–73.

Laurence, J.-R. and Perry, C. (1982) 'Montréal norms for the Harvard Group Scale of Hypnotic Susceptibility, Form A', *International Journal of Clinical and Experimental Hypnosis*, 30:167–76.

LeCron, L.M. (1953) 'A method of measuring the depth of hypnosis, and the experience of nonvolition', *International Journal of Clinical and Experimental Hypnosis*, 31:293–308.

Liébeault, A.A. (1889) *Le Sommeil Provoqué et les États Analogues* [Induced Sleep and Analogous States], Paris: Doin.

Lynn, S.J. and Rhue, J.W. (1988) 'Fantasy-proneness: Hypnosis, developmental antecedents, and psychopathology', *American Psychologist*, 43:35–44.

—— Kirsch, I., Barabasz, A., Cardeña, E. and Patterson, D. (2000) 'Hypnosis as an empirically supported clinical intervention: The state of the evidence and a look to the future', *International Journal of Clinical and Experimental Hypnosis*, 48:239–59.

Matthews, W.J. and Isenberg, G.L. (1995) 'A comparison of the hypnotic experience between signing deaf and hearing participants', *International Journal of Clinical and Experimental Hypnosis*, 43:375–85.

McConkey, K.M. (1983) 'The impact of conflicting communications on response to hypnotic suggestions', *Journal of Abnormal Psychology*, 92:351–8.

—— (1991) 'The construction and resolution of experience and behavior in hypnosis', in S.J. Lynn and J.W. Rhue (eds), *Theories of Hypnosis: Current Models and Perspectives* (pp. 542–63), New York: Guilford Press.

—— and Sheehan, P.W. (1981) 'The impact of videotape playback of hypnotic events on posthypnotic amnesia', *Journal of Abnormal Psychology*, 90:46–54.

—— Sheehan, P.W. and Cross, D.G. (1980) 'Posthypnotic amnesia: Seeing is not remembering', *British Journal of Social and Clinical Psychology*, 19:99–107.

—— Glisky, M.L. and Kihlstrom, J.F. (1989) 'Individual differences among hypnotic virtuosos: A case comparison', *Australian Journal of Clinical and Experimental Hypnosis*, 17:131–40.

—— Barnier, A.J., Maccallum, F.L. and Bishop, K. (1996) 'A normative and structural analysis of the HGSHS:A with a large Australian sample', *Australian Journal of Clinical and Experimental Hypnosis*, 24:1–11.

—— Wende, V. and Barnier, A.J. (1999) 'Measuring change in the subjective experience of hypnosis', *International Journal of Clinical and Experimental Hypnosis*, 47:23–39.

McCrae, R.R. (1993) 'Openness to experience as a basic dimension of personality', *Imagination, Cognition and Personality*, 13:39–55.

Montgomery, G.H., DuHamel, K.N. and Redd, W.H. (2000) 'A meta-analysis of hypnotically-induced analgesia: How effective is hypnosis?', *International Journal of Clinical and Experimental Hypnosis*, 48:138–53.

Morgan, E. and Hilgard, J.R. (1978–9a) 'The Stanford Hypnotic Clinical Scale for Adults', *American Journal of Clinical Hypnosis*, 21:134–47.

—— and Hilgard, J.R. (1978–9b) 'The Stanford Hypnotic Clinical Scale for Children', *American Journal of Clinical Hypnosis*, 21:148–69.

Noble, J. and McConkey, K.M. (1995) 'Hypnotic sex change: Creating and challenging a delusion in the laboratory', *Journal of Abnormal Psychology*, 104:69–74.

Oakman, J.M. and Woody, E.Z. (1996) 'A taxometric analysis of hypnotic susceptibility', *Journal of Personality and Social Psychology*, 72:981–91.

O'Connell, D.N. (1964) 'An experimental comparison of hypnotic depth measured by self-ratings and by an objective scale', *International Journal of Clinical and Experimental Hypnosis*, 12:34–46.

Orne, M.T. (1971) 'The simulation of hypnosis: Why, how, and what it means', *International Journal of Clinical and Experimental Hypnosis*, 19:183–210.

—— and Evans, F.J. (1966) 'Inadvertent termination of hypnosis with hypnotized and simulating subjects', *International Journal of Clinical and Experimental Hypnosis*, 14:61–78.

—— and O'Connell, D.N. (1967) 'Diagnostic ratings of hypnotizability', *International Journal of Clinical and Experimental Hypnosis*, 15:125–33.

—— Hilgard, E.R., Spiegel, H., Spiegel, D., Crawford, H.J., Evans, F.J., Orne, E.C. and Frischholz, E.J. (1979) 'The relation between the Hypnotic Induction Profile and the Stanford Hypnotic Susceptibility Scales, Forms A and C', *International Journal of Clinical and Experimental Hypnosis*, 27:85–102.

58 Barnier and McConkey

Pekala, R.J. (1991) *The Phenomenology of Consciousness Inventory (PCI)*, West Chester, PA: Mid-Atlantic Educational Institute. (Original work published 1982).

Perry, C., Nadon, R. and Button, J. (1992) 'The measurement of hypnotic ability', in E. Fromm and M.R. Nash (eds), *Contemporary Hypnosis Research* (pp. 459–90), New York: Guilford Press.

Piccione, C., Hilgard, E.R. and Zimbardo, P.G. (1989) 'On the degree of stability of measured hypnotizability over a 25-year period', *Journal of Personality and Social Psychology*, 56:289–95.

Ray, W.J. (1997) 'EEG concomitants of hypnotic susceptibility', *International Journal of Clinical and Experimental Hypnosis*, 45:301–13.

Register, P.A. and Kihlstrom, J.F. (1986) 'Finding the hypnotic virtuoso', *International Journal of Clinical and Experimental Hypnosis*, 34:84–97.

Repka, R.J. and Nash, M.R. (1995) 'Hypnotic responsivity of the deaf: The development of the University of Tennessee Hypnotic Susceptibility Scale for the Deaf', *International Journal of Clinical and Experimental Hypnosis*, 43:316–31.

Reyher, J. (1973) 'Can hypnotized subjects simulate waking behavior?', *American Journal of Clinical Hypnosis*, 16:31–6.

Roche, S. and McConkey, K.M. (1990) 'Absorption: Nature, assessment and correlated', *Journal of Personality and Social Psychology*, 59:91–101.

Sapp, M. and Hitchcock, K. (2001) 'Harvard Group Scale with African American college students', *Sleep and Hypnosis*, 3:120–6.

Sarbin, T.R. and Coe, W.C. (1972) *Hypnosis: A Social Psychological Analysis of Influence Communication*, New York: Holt, Rinehart and Winston.

Sheehan, P.W. (1971) 'Countering preconceptions about hypnosis: An objective index of involvement with the hypnotist' [Monograph], *Journal of Abnormal Psychology*, 78:299–322.

—— (1991) 'Hypnosis, context, and commitment', in S.J. Lynn and J.W. Rhue (eds), *Theories of Hypnosis: Current Models and Perspectives* (pp. 520–41), New York: Guilford Press.

—— and McConkey, K.M. (1979) 'Australian norms for the Harvard Group Scale of Hypnotic Susceptibility, Form A', *International Journal of Clinical and Experimental Hypnosis*, 27:294–304.

—— and McConkey, K.M. (1982) *Hypnosis and Experience: The Exploration of Phenomena and Process*, Hillsdale, NJ: Erlbaum.

—— and Perry, C. (1976) *Methodologies of Hypnosis: A Critical Appraisal of Contemporary Paradigms of Hypnosis*, Hillsdale, NJ: Erlbaum.

Shor, R.E. (1978) *Inventory of Self-Hypnosis, Form A*. Palo Alto, CA: Consulting Psychologists Press.

—— (1979) 'A phenomenological method for the measurement of variables important to an understanding of the nature of hypnosis', in E. Fromm and R.E. Shor (eds), *Hypnosis: Developments in Research and New Perspectives*, 2nd edn (pp. 105–35), Hawthorne, NY: Aldine.

—— and Orne, E.C. (1962) *The Harvard Group Scale of Hypnotic Suscepti-bility, Form A*, Palo Alto, CA: Consulting Psychologists Press.

—— and Orne, E.C. (1963) 'Norms on the Harvard Group Scale of Hypnotic Susceptibility, Form A', *International Journal of Clinical and Experimental Hypnosis*, 11:39–47.

Spanos, N.P. (1983) *The Carleton University Responsiveness to Suggestion Scale (Group Administration)*, Unpublished manuscript, Carleton University: Ottawa, Ontario, Canada.

—— (1991) 'A sociocognitive approach to hypnosis', in S.J. Lynn and J.W. Rhue (eds), *Theories of Hypnosis: Current Models and Perspectives* (pp. 324–61), New York: Guilford Press.

—— (1996) *Multiple Identities and False Memories: A Sociocognitive Per-spective*, Washington, DC: American Psychological Association.

—— and Coe, W.C. (1992) 'A social-psychological approach to hypnosis', in E. Fromm and M.R. Nash (eds), *Contemporary Hypnosis Research* (pp. 102–30), New York: Guilford Press.

—— Radtke, H.L., Hodgins, D.C., Bertrand, L.D., Stam, H.J. and Dubreuil, D.L. (1983a) 'The Carleton University Responsiveness to Suggestion Scale: Stability, reliability, and relationships with expectancy and "hypnotic experiences" ', *Psychological Reports*, 53:555–63.

—— Radtke, H.L., Hodgins, D.C., Bertrand, L.D., Stam, H.J. and Moretti, P. (1983b) 'The Carleton University Responsiveness to Suggestion Scale: Relationship with other measures of hypnotic susceptibility, expectan-cies, and absorption', *Psychological Reports*, 53:723–34.

—— Radtke, H.L., Hodgins, D.C., Stam, H.J. and Bertrand, L.D. (1983c) 'The Carleton University Responsiveness to Suggestion Scale: Normative data and psychometric properties', *Psychological Reports*, 53:523–35.

—— Cobb, P.C. and Gorassini, D.R. (1985) 'Failing to resist hypnotic test suggestions: A strategy for self-presenting as deeply hypnotized', *Psy-chiatry*, 48:282–92.

—— Brett, P.J., Menary, E.P. and Cross, W.P. (1987) 'A measure of attitudes toward hypnosis: Relationships with absorption and hypnotic susceptibil-ity', *American Journal of Clinical Hypnosis*, 30:139–50.

—— Flynn, D.M. and Gabora, N.J. (1993) 'The effects of cognitive skill training on the Stanford Profile Scale: Form I', *Contemporary Hypnosis*, 10:29–33.

—— Liddy, S.J., Baxter, C.E. and Burgess, C.A. (1994) 'Long-term and short-term stability of behavioral and subjective indexes of hypnotiz-ability', *Journal of Research in Personality*, 28:301–13.

Spiegel, H. and Spiegel, D. (1978) *Trance and Treatment: Clinical Uses of Hypnosis*, New York: Basic Books.

Stern, D.B., Spiegel, H. and Nee, J.C.M. (1978–9) 'The Hypnotic Induction Profile: Normative observations, reliability and validity', *American Journal of Clinical Hypnosis*, 21:109–33.

Tart, C.T. (1970) 'Self-report scales of hypnotic depth', *International Journal of Clinical and Experimental Hypnosis*, 18:105–25.

Tellegen, A. (1981) 'Practicing the two disciplines for relaxation and enlightenment: Comment on "Role of the feedback signal in electromyograph biofeedback: The relevance of attention" by Qualls and Sheehan', *Journal of Experimental Psychology: General*, 110:217–26.

—— and Atkinson, G. (1974) 'Openness to absorbing and self-altering experiences ("absorption"), a trait related to hypnotic susceptibility', *Journal of Abnormal Psychology*, 83:268–77.

Weitzenhoffer, A.M. (1974) 'When is an "instruction" an "instruction"?', *International Journal of Clinical and Experimental Hypnosis*, 22:258–69.

—— (1997) 'Hypnotic susceptibility: A personal and historical note regarding the development and naming of the Stanford scales', *International Journal of Clinical and Experimental Hypnosis*, 45:126–43.

—— and Hilgard, E.R. (1959) *Stanford Hypnotic Susceptibility Scales, Forms A and B*. Palo Alto, CA: Consulting Psychologists Press.

—— and Hilgard, E.R. (1962) *Stanford Hypnotic Susceptibility Scales, Form C*, Palo Alto, CA: Consulting Psychologists Press.

—— and Hilgard, E.R. (1963) *Stanford Profile Scales Hypnotic Susceptibility Scales: Forms I and II*, Palo Alto, CA: Consulting Psychologists Press.

—— and Hilgard, E.R. (1967) *Revised Stanford Profile Scales Hypnotic Susceptibility Scales: Forms I and II*, Palo Alto, CA: Consulting Psychologists Press.

Wilson, S.C. and Barber, T.X. (1978) 'The Creative Imagination Scale as a measure of hypnotic responsiveness: Applications to experimental and clinical hypnosis', *American Journal of Clinical Hypnosis*, 20:235–49.

—— and Barber, T.X. (1983) *Inventory of Childhood Memories and Imaginings*, Framingham, MA: Cushing Hospital.

Woody, E.Z. (1997) 'Have the hypnotic susceptibility scales outlived their usefulness?', *International Journal of Clinical and Experimental Hypnosis*, 45:226–38.

—— Bowers, K.S. and Oakman, J.M. (1992) 'A conceptual analysis of hypnotic responsiveness: Experience, individual differences, and context', in E. Fromm and M.R. Nash (eds), *Contemporary Perspectives in Hypnosis Research* (pp. 3–33), New York: Guilford Press.

—— Drugovic, M. and Oakman, J.M. (1997) 'A re-examination of the role of nonhypnotic suggestibility in hypnotic responding', *Journal of Personality and Social Psychology*, 72:399–407.

Zachariae, R., Sommerlund, B. and Molay, F. (1996) 'Danish norms for the Harvard Group Scale of Hypnotic Susceptibility, Form A', *International Journal of Clinical and Experimental Hypnosis*, 44:140–52.

Chapter 3

High hypnotizability
Unity and diversity in behaviour and experience

Kevin M. McConkey and Amanda J. Barnier

Introduction

The highly hypnotizable person is 'better at hypnosis' than is the low or medium hypnotizable person. But this does not mean that all high hypnotizables have the same experience or show the same behaviour during hypnosis. Let's turn to swimming to better appreciate the issue we seek to address in this chapter. Good swimmers are 'better at swimming' than are poor swimmers. Whereas poor swimmers are probably equally poor at freestyle, breaststroke, backstroke, and butterfly, good swimmers are unlikely to be equally good at each of those styles and even when excellent at one they are unlikely to be equally good over 100, 400, or 1500 metres because they will have different natural abilities and preferences and will have been exposed to different training programmes. Let's turn back to hypnotizability and hypnosis. Highs are better at hypnosis than lows. Whereas lows are probably equally unresponsive to suggestions for visual hallucination, age regression, anaesthesia, and posthypnotic amnesia, highs are unlikely to be equally responsive to each of those suggestions and even when strongly responsive to them, different highs are unlikely to bring the same processes to bear on achieving those strong responses.

The unity and the diversity in the behaviour and experience of the high hypnotizable person can be seen in historical reports of hypnosis, clinical anecdotes and analyses of hypnosis, laboratory investigations of various hypnotic phenomena, and emphases and speculations in some theories and models of hypnosis. In this chapter, we focus on the similarities and dissimilarities within the group of people typically labelled as 'high hypnotizable', and we point to the work that is needed to help fill the gaps in knowledge in the field.

Those gaps need to be filled not only because of the inherent value in advancing knowledge of hypnotizability and hypnosis, but also because of the implications that further knowledge will carry for the sensible and effective use of hypnosis clinically.

In this chapter, we consider profiles of the high hypnotizable in terms of their assessment and their place within selected theories of hypnosis. Then, we look at the performance patterns of high hypnotizables in terms of selected hypnotic phenomena and on different types and phases of hypnotic suggestion. Finally, we summarize our perspective on unity and diversity within high hypnotizability and attempt to integrate theoretical views and empirical findings.

Profiles of the highly hypnotizable person

Assessment of profiles

Individuals differ in the degree to which they respond to hypnotic suggestions. Because of this, the measurement of individual differences in hypnotic responsivity is central to the field, and there is a rich range of measures of hypnotizability (for review, see Barnier and McConkey in Chapter 2 of this book; Sheehan and McConkey, 1982; see also Balthazard and Woody, 1985, 1989; Oakman and Woody, 1996; Tellegen, 1978–9; Woody et al., 1992). The assessment of hypnotizability is likely to reflect the researcher's theoretical leanings or the clinician's therapeutic orientation. Moreover, it is likely to reflect the degree to which one needs to get an indication of the general level of hypnotizability (e.g. low, medium, high) or an indication of the specific responses of individuals to particular hypnotic suggestions (e.g. age regression, visual hallucination, posthypnotic amnesia). Although most measures of hypnotizability have been designed to assess response to hypnotic suggestion across the spectrum of ideomotor, challenge, and cognitive suggestions, some have been designed to assess the specific response profiles of individuals who are medium to high hypnotizable, typically across different types of cognitive suggestions. These measures include the Stanford Profile Scale of Hypnotic Susceptibility, Form I and Form II (SPS: I and II; Weitzenhoffer and Hilgard, 1963, 1967), and the Diagnostic Rating Scale (DRS; Orne and O'Connell, 1967).

The Stanford Profile Scale of Hypnotic Susceptibility, Form I and Form II (SPS: I and II; Weitzenhoffer and Hilgard, 1963, 1967; see also Chapter 2) was developed to differentiate hypnotic performance more precisely and thus to allow a diagnosis of particular profiles of high hypnotizability. These profile scales were developed as an explicit recognition that individuals who are high hypnotizable do not show a uniform pattern of response to hypnotic suggestions. SPS: I and II index the idiosyncratic responses of high hypnotizables by evaluating response to a series of hypnotic suggestions that are heavily cognitive in character. Following an induction procedure that involves arm levitation, the SPS: I tests individuals on nine items (hand analgesia, music hallucination, anosmia to ammonia, recall of meal, hallucinated light, dream, agnosia, arithmetic impairment, posthypnotic verbal compulsion), and each is scored on a 0–3 scale (maximum score = 27) that involves a mixture of behavioural and experiential criteria. Similarly, following an induction procedure that involves hand lowering, the SPS: II tests individuals on nine items (heat hallucination, selective deafness, hallucinated ammonia, regression to birthday, missing watch hand, dream, agnosia, personality alteration, posthypnotic automatic writing) and each is scored in a similar way to those on the SPS: I. The SPS: I and the SPS: II are complementary, rather than parallel, scales, and to get a complete indication of the profile of a high hypnotizable individual both forms should be used. Normative and standardization information is available for the scales (Weitzenhoffer and Hilgard, 1963, 1967) as are summary evaluations of their use and utility (Hilgard, 1965, 1978–9; Sheehan and McConkey, 1982). Notably, individuals who are high hypnotizable on scales such as the Stanford Hypnotic Susceptibility Scale, Form A, B, or C (SHSS:A and B, SHSS:C; Weitzenhoffer and Hilgard, 1959, 1962) show varying patterns of scores on the SPS: I and II (Hilgard, 1978–9). Although the SPS: I and II have been neither widely used nor systematically investigated, they nevertheless offer a sensitive and standardized way of measuring individual responses to demanding hypnotic suggestions.

The Diagnostic Rating Scale (DRS; Orne and O'Connell, 1967; see also Chapter 2) was developed to be used in either the laboratory or the clinical setting and to allow a detailed specification of particular hypnotic skills. The structure of the scale is similar to that of the much earlier Davis–Husband Scale in that it categorizes individuals based on clinical observations of responses to a flexible array of hypnotic suggestions (Davis and Husband, 1931; for summary, see Sheehan and McConkey, 1982). This flexibility of administration is both a strength and a weakness of the DRS, as is its requirement for a researcher or clinician who is trained to make an interpretative judgement about the response that the hypnotized person is showing. The scale is seen as 'an achievement test after practice, rather than a work sample under standard conditions' (Orne and O'Connell, 1967, p. 126). It involves categorizing individuals on a 5-point scale (1 – no response, 2 – ideomotor response, 3 – challenge response with subjective involvement, 4 – hallucinatory response, 5 – amnesia and posthypnotic response) in terms of their observed response and reported experience; the points on the scale are also rated + or – for degree of automaticity for a score of 2, and reality of experience for scores of 3, 4, and 5. Normative and standardization information is not available for this scale, but some approximate norms have been provided (Hilgard, 1978–9) and the relationship of the scale to the SHSS: A and B has been discussed (Shor et al., 1966). The DRS has not been widely used or systematically investigated. However, when it is used with individuals who have had previous experience of standardized testing and who have achieved a plateau level of high hypnotizability, the DRS allows an understanding of the nexus of involvement and response of the hypnotized individual across a range of hypnotic suggestions that have clinical relevance and that have been specifically chosen to index the profile of that individual (see Chapter 2).

The development and use of these measurement scales at the very least underscores the complexity of hypnotic responding overall and the variability of responding within individuals labelled as high hypnotizable. A different approach to the assessment of profiles of hypnotic experience and behaviour involves a focus on the subjective experience of the hypnotized individual as he or she experiences a range of hypnotic suggestions. This phenomenologically oriented approach aims to be especially attuned to the individual's experiential involvement in and behavioural response to hypnotic suggestions. This approach includes Shor's Phenomenological Method (Shor, 1979) and the Experiential Analysis Technique (Sheehan and McConkey, 1982).

Shor's Phenomenological Method (SPM; Shor, 1979) was developed to give primacy to the experience of the hypnotized individual. It involves a skilled investigator making interpretative judgements and applying specific rating scales to retrospective descriptions by an individual about their experience of hypnotic suggestions. Specifically, the SPM involves the investigator rating on a 6-point scale each of three primary dimensions (trance, non-conscious involvement, archaic involvement) and five secondary dimensions (drowsiness, relaxation, vividness of imagery, absorption, access to the unconscious), and the focus of this evaluation could be a single hypnotic suggestion, a set of suggestions, or the hypnotic session as a whole. This method is aligned closely to Shor's (1962) three-factor theory of hypnosis, which argues that the hypnotic experience involves a loss of generalized reality orientation, the unconscious involvement of the hypnotized individual in the suggestions of the hypnosis, and the closeness of the relationship between the hypnotized individual and the hypnotist. In emphasizing these primary dimensions of experience, this theory and the SPM highlight more than many other theories and methods the experiential diversity that is often masked by the behavioural unity of high hypnotizable individuals. The SPM has not been widely used or systematically investigated, although its influence can be seen strongly in the development and use of approaches such as the Phenomenology of Consciousness Inventory (PCI; Pekala, 1991a, 1991b; see also Kumar et al., 1995, 1996; Varga et al., 2001). Nevertheless, the emphasis of the SPM on the multidimensionality of the hypnotic experience and the importance of the 'profundity' (Shor, 1979, p. 131) of that experience underscores the importance of assessing and understanding different profiles of high hypnotizability.

The Experiential Analysis Technique (EAT; Sheehan and McConkey, 1982; see also McConkey, 1991; Sheehan, 1991; and Chapter 2 of this book) was developed as a method of inquiry into and assessment of the hypnotic experience and the processes that are involved in the determination and behavioural display of hypnotic effects. The EAT typically involves an individual watching a videotape of their just-completed hypnotic session and commenting about their experience and behaviour during that session to a person, the inquirer, other than the person who conducted the hypnotic session, the hypnotist. The inquirer probes the comments of the individual along various dimensions (cognitions, images, expectancies, image presentation, perceptions, emotions), and seeks to elicit an indication of how the individual believed they were functioning, both cognitively and socially, during the hypnotic interaction. The rating and analysis of individuals' comments are conducted after the EAT inquiry, and the quantitative and qualitative methods used depend upon the emphasis of the investigation. The focus of the EAT on the individuality and patterning of hypnotized individuals' subjective reactions to hypnotic suggestions is consistent with the

views of Orne (1972) that the 'hallmark of the hypnotic phenomena
. . . is the nature and quality of the concomitant subjective events'
(p. 421) and of Spanos and Barber (1974) that 'hypnotic phenomena
involve genuine changes in the subject's experience that cannot be
explained away in terms of faking or sham behavior' (p. 508). The
EAT has been used in a range of investigations of hypnotic
phenomena and processes, and the method has been evaluated
and extended by a variety of investigators (e.g. Bányai, 1991; Barnier
and McConkey, 1999; Bryant and Mallard, 2002; Bryant and
McConkey, 1989a; Laurence and Perry, 1981; Sheehan et al., 1978;
West and Fellows, 1996). The use of the EAT has highlighted that
together with the individual's actual hypnotic behaviour, strong
attention should be given to the essential diversity and variability
that exists in the way in which high hypnotizable individuals think
about, create, and explain their responding. There are real differences in how high hypnotizable individuals approach, experience,
and respond to hypnotic suggestions, and these differences can be
framed in part in terms of the cognitive styles that they bring to bear
on their processing of the communications of the hypnotist (Sheehan
and McConkey, 1982).

Profiles and theories of hypnosis

Differences between as well as within hypnotizability levels exist, and
some but not all hypnotic theories have sought to capture these variations. We turn now to consider the place of hypnotic profiles in
theories of hypnosis.

The behaviour and experience of the hypnotized person is motivated in part by their desire to respond in a socially appropriate way,
but active effort is needed on their part to fulfil that desire. The task
of responding during hypnosis can be seen as processing information
and solving problems in a complex social context that is defined and
regulated by rules that are mutually understood by the hypnotist and
the hypnotized person. This requires the active social and cognitive
involvement of them both, and there is substantial scope for individual differences to emerge in and influence the hypnotic interaction
and expression (Sheehan and McConkey, 1982; Spanos, 1981). Any
theory that attempts to explain the phenomena and processes of
hypnosis must address why individual differences occur in response
to hypnotic suggestion and why different profiles of response occur
within high hypnotizable persons.

Although most theories of hypnosis recognize and incorporate into their approach some comment on levels of hypnotizability (i.e. low, medium, high), only some theories have explicitly considered the response profiles of high hypnotizable individuals. Hilgard (1965) pointed clearly to this variation among high hypnotizable individuals, but there has been very little theoretical discussion of the variation itself or the processes that might underlie such differential responding across high hypnotizable individuals. Hilgard (1965) argued: 'Hypnosis is sufficiently a single domain to permit a strong general factor to emerge, but it is also varied enough in its manifestations to reflect individual idiosyncrasies' (p. 282). With empirical support from the use of the SPS: I and II, he argued that hypnotic suggestions varied in the degree to which they required, and high hypnotizable individuals varied in the degree to which they could meet the requirements of, distortion of meaning and value (agnosia and cognitive distortion), experiencing sensory and perceptual phenomena in the absence of appropriate stimuli (hallucination positive), lack of awareness of stimulation that would normally be perceived (hallucination negative), memory revival and fantasy production (dreams and regressions), behaviour suggested during hypnosis but carried out after hypnosis (amnesia and posthypnotic compulsions), and motor responses carried out automatically as a result of suggestion (loss of motor control).

These aspects are directly relevant to propositions in Hilgard's (1965) developmental–interactive theory of hypnosis. In this theory, the developmental aspects include what the individual brings to the hypnotic setting, and the interactive aspects include what happens between the hypnotist and the individual in that setting. For instance, Hilgard (1965) specified that 'Individualizing experiences of various kinds may produce selective responsiveness within hypnotic susceptibility' (p. 385), and 'The various dissociative experiences activated by hypnotic induction and by suggestions within hypnosis are correlated with specific developmental experiences' (p. 388). In other words, high hypnotizables may respond differently on hypnotic suggestions and differences within this group may be because of particular developmental experiences. When Hilgard (1973, 1977) turned to propose a neodissociation theory for the phenomena of hypnosis and for a variety of cognitive processing beyond the hypnotic setting, the main tenet of that theory was that mental functioning may be regulated by multiple cognitive control systems rather than by a single mental apparatus. In various experimental investigations of this notion (e.g. Hilgard et al., 1978; Knox et al., 1974; see also Nogrady et al., 1983), he used the metaphor of the 'hidden observer' to reflect the part of the hypnotized person that knows the reality of the situation rather than the situation as suggested by the hypnotist. Notably, not all high hypnotizable individuals demonstrate this hidden-observer effect, and this suggests that there may be distinctly different reactions by high hypnotizables to a hypnotic suggestion that seeks to tap dissociation. Indeed, Nogrady et al. (1983) reported that about half the high hypnotizable participants in their experiment displayed the hidden-observer response and half did not, and that this split could not be explained by hypnotizability level. Nogrady et al. (1983) considered this '50 per cent phenomenon' to be similar to the heterogeneity seen among high hypnotizable individuals in their responses to trance logic (Orne, 1959; McConkey et al., 1991), countering preconceptions in hypnosis (Sheehan, 1980), showing posthypnotic persistence of an uncancelled suggestion (Perry, 1977), and breaching posthypnotic amnesia (McConkey and Sheehan, 1981).

Sheehan and McConkey (1982; McConkey, 1991; Sheehan, 1991) argued that the hypnotized individual is a cognitively active participant who employs appropriate strategies to resolve the multiple problems that are posed by the hypnotic setting. In doing so, the hypnotized person develops a strong commitment to the phenomenal reality of their suggested experience. Sheehan and McConkey (1982; McConkey, 1991; Sheehan, 1991) also emphasized the relevance of the cognitions and attributions that hypnotized individuals make about their experiences during hypnosis, and especially the way in which they use these attributions to protect the integrity of their hypnotic responses. Sheehan and McConkey (1982) reported that relatively distinct styles of cognition (concentrative, independent, and constructive) emerged among high hypnotizable individuals, and that these styles also varied within individuals depending on the degree of complexity involved in the suggested hypnotic experience.

Recently and influentially, after 40 years of work in the field, Barber (1999a, 1999b, 1999c; see also Chapters 4 and 8) synthesized his view of high hypnotizability and hypnosis when he said:

> I understood the essence of hypnosis when I realized that there are really three dimensions or kinds of hypnosis, each associated with one of the three types of very good hypnotic subjects. One dimension or type of hypnosis is associated with very good

hypnotic subjects who have a secret life-long history of fantasizing 'as real as real'. A second type of hypnosis is associated with another group of very good subjects who have a surprising tendency to forget events in their life and also have amnesia for hypnosis. A third type of hypnosis is associated with very good subjects who are neither fantasy-prone nor amnesia-prone but, instead, have positive attitudes, motivations and expectancies towards the hypnotic situation and are thus 'positively set' to think with and flow with the suggestions.

(Barber, 1999b, p. 123)

Barber (1999a, 1999b, 1999c) supported this view through a consideration of empirical work on fantasy-prone persons (Barrett, 1990, 1996; Lynn and Rhue, 1986, 1988; Wilson and Barber, 1981, 1983), amnesia-prone individuals (Barrett, 1990, 1996), and positively set people (Barber 1969; Spanos and Chaves, 1989), as well as through a consideration of cluster analyses of the reports of hypnotic experiences (Pekala, 1991b; Pekala et al., 1995). Commentators have highlighted particular aspects of Barber's (1999a, 1999b, 1999c) three-dimensional theory of hypnosis. For instance, Chaves (1999) pointed to ambiguities and limitations in the empirical support for these three types of hypnotic responders, Gauld (1999) wondered whether researchers are dealing with a difference of degree rather than kind of hypnotic responder, and Heap (1999) considered that investigators are talking more about dimensions of response rather than types of responders. Barber (1999c) responded to the points made by these, and other, commentators, and underscored the need for a programme of research to be undertaken that investigates not only the dimensions of fantasy-prone, amnesia-prone, and positively set individuals, but also the dimensions of the social psychology of the experiment, the characteristics of the hypnotist, and the instructions and suggestions.

Apart from the views of Hilgard (1965), Sheehan and McConkey (1982; see also McConkey, 1991, Sheehan, 1991), and Barber (1999a, 1999b, 1999c), few theoretical accounts have come fully to grips with the ways in which high hypnotizables may differ from each other as well as their low and medium hypnotizable counterparts. This is particularly interesting given psychometric data that suggest that hypnotizability may be typological, rather than dimensional, in nature (or even typological above a certain dimensional level; Oakman and Woody, 1996), and that difficult hypnotic performances (usually limited to the most talented hypnotic individuals) may draw on different underlying factors from easy hypnotic performances (Register and Kihlstrom, 1986). We return to the issue of dimensions versus type later in this chapter, but we move now to consider a selection of the, often difficult, hypnotic behaviours and experiences that high hypnotizables can achieve.

Performance patterns of highly hypnotizable individuals

Selected hypnotic phenomena

Hilgard (1965) argued that high hypnotizables differ in the degree to which they can successfully experience cognitive distortions, positive and negative hallucinations, dreams and regressions, amnesia and posthypnotic compulsions, and loss of motor control. We review selected research from some of these areas.

Hypnotic sex change

One way to assess the performance patterns of high hypnotizable individuals is to test the limits of their hypnotic experience. Following Sutcliffe (1961), Noble and McConkey (1995) suggested a change of sex to hypnotized individuals. The experiment used Orne's (1959) real-simulating paradigm, which involves high hypnotizable subjects who are tested normally and low hypnotizable subjects who are instructed to fake hypnosis; the hypnotist is unaware who is and is not faking. The simulation condition is a quasi-control one that allows inferences to be drawn about the extent to which the responses of the hypnotized participants may be based on the cues operating in the experimental setting rather than in the subjective experience of hypnosis. Noble and McConkey (1995) used 'virtuoso' (see Register and Kihlstrom, 1986) hypnotic subjects and high hypnotizable participants as reals, and low hypnotizable participants as simulators. They reported that most, but not all, virtuoso participants and some, but not all, high hypnotizable participants showed a compelling hypnotic experience of sex change. In addition, Noble and McConkey (1995) reported that virtuosos were more likely than highs or simulators to maintain their response when challenged by contradiction (in which a hypothetical authority figure questioned their experience) and confrontation (in which they looked at an image of themselves on a video monitor). In response to the confrontation, virtuosos were especially likely to either reinterpret the image in line with the suggestion (e.g. one male subject commented 'Well, I'm not as pretty as I thought, but I have long, blond hair') or deny that the image was them (e.g. 'That's not me, I don't look like that'). In particular, some of these excellent hypnotic participants appeared willing and able to reinterpret the conflicting information in a way that confirmed their suggested experience.

Burn et al. (2001) extended this work to explore how subjects process information during a hypnotic sex change. They were interested in the degree to which participants selectively interpret information as consistent with their hypnotic experience. Participants received a suggestion for sex change and listened to a structured story that involved a male and a female character; following hypnosis, participants recalled the story. Burn et al. (2001) reported that virtuosos were less likely to identify with the character that was consistent with their suggested sex, but, when asked to recall the story after hypnosis, virtuosos recalled more information about the character that was consistent with their suggested sex than did highs or simulators. In other words, virtuosos were less likely to identify with the character consistent with their suggested sex, but they recalled significantly more information relevant to that character. Thus, virtuosos appeared to process information selectivity during encoding (i.e. during the sex change suggestion); character identification alone was not the major factor that influenced their enhanced recall. Comments by some virtuosos and high hypnotizables indicated that they perceived certain information as self-referential and very significant in the context of their sex change experience and selected it for more elaborate processing. These findings suggest that the virtuosos interpreted different aspects of the information as more significant to their internal belief, which implies the operation of different cognitive processes in the development and maintenance of the delusory experience in some, but not other, excellent hypnotic participants.

Hypnotic blindness

Hypnotic blindness involves a suggestion for total or partial loss of vision. Bryant and McConkey (1989a) used a task that involved participants looking at a small machine and turning off a tone that it emitted by pressing one of three switches on the frontplate of the machine. A light on a visual display above the frontplate indicated the correct switch, and the switch and the corresponding light varied across trials. Whereas hypnotized participants reported phenomenal blindness following a suggestion for blindness, most of them responded on the task as if they were processing the available visual information. In a second study, Bryant and McConkey (1989b) visually presented participants with uncommon spellings of homophones during hypnotic blindness, and subsequently asked them to spell a series of words that included the homophones that were presented previously. Post-experimentally the investigators presented participants with evidence that they had spelt the homophones in ways that were influenced by the uncommon spellings presented during their reported blindness. Bryant and McConkey (1989b) reported that the participants vehemently defended their experience of blindness by attributing their visual processing to a range of factors that did not involve a contradiction of their phenomenal blindness. For example, one participant insisted that he spelt the homophone 'stake' the uncommon way because as a child he had never been fed 'steak'. Another participant claimed that she did not spell the homophone 'break' the common way because her father was a mechanic and he often worked with 'brakes'.

Despite claims to the contrary, hypnotically blind individuals do process the visually presented information. For instance, Bryant and McConkey (1995) presented words to hypnotically blind participants and subsequently required them to complete a word-fragment task. Most hypnotized participants correctly completed more word-fragments of words that had been presented during hypnotic blindness than words that had not been presented, although this response was not uniform and clearly created considerable conflict for some hypnotizable individuals. More recently, Mallard and Bryant (2001) asked high hypnotizable participants to learn associations between colour names and shapes, gave them a suggestion for colour blindness, and then asked them to name the shapes when they appeared in colours that were either congruent or incongruent with the learned association. About half the high hypnotizable participants reported that they experienced the suggested colour blindness, but they nevertheless showed an interference effect for shapes for which they were reportedly colour blind; in other words, they were slower to name those shapes that were presented in a colour that was incongruent rather than congruent with the previously learned association. These findings indicate that some, but not all, high hypnotizable, hypnotized participants report phenomenal blindness, but that they show implicit perception by using visual information to complete various tasks. Importantly, many of them work hard to protect the integrity of their engagement in the suggested experience; the patterns of response here are similar to the 50 per cent phenomenon that is seen across other demanding hypnotic items, such as trance logic, hidden observer, amnesia, and sex change.

Hypnotic anaesthesia

Wilton and McConkey (1994) placed ordinary objects into the hypnotically anaesthetized and non-anaesthetized hands of high hypnotizable participants and asked them to identify those objects. The participants who reported experiencing complete anaesthesia identified fewer objects in the anaesthetized than in the non-anaesthetized hand. Notably, although some participants who experienced complete anaesthesia identified none of the objects, other participants identified some or all of the objects in the anaesthetized hand; that is, there was diversity in responding among this group of similarly high hypnotizable participants. Those participants who did not identify any objects reported greater success in experiencing anaesthesia than did those participants who identified at least one object in the anaesthetized hand. Also, those participants who did not identify any objects reported greater belief in the reality of their anaesthesia than did those who identified at least one object in their anaesthetized hand. The external reality of the task of identifying objects did not decrease the reported success or belief for participants who did not identify any of the objects; in fact, their ratings of success in experiencing anaesthesia increased from before hypnosis to after the object task. These findings underscore the complexities involved when an internal, subjective experience is challenged through the presentation of an external, objective stimulus. More importantly, it is unclear why individuals of equal (high) hypnotizability respond differently. It may be that this difference reflects the cognitive styles that they use to engage in the experience or their understanding of the meaning of the message coming from the hypnotist. Alternatively, some individuals may reach a point in the balance of internal and external influence where they cannot sustain their commitment to the suggested experiences. More precise specification and evaluation of these options is needed in future research.

Wilton et al. (1997; see also Barnier et al., 1997; McConkey et al., 1990) used the circle-touch test to further explore hypnotic anaesthesia. This test involves suggesting to participants that a circular area marked on their hand is anaesthetized and then testing their responses to touches inside and outside that defined area. Wilton et al. (1997) reported that some, but not other, high hypnotizable, hypnotized individuals could experience suggested anaesthesia in a compelling way and could sustain that experience when tested by aesthesiometers, even when the external stimulus was relatively strong. In this case, Wilton et al. (1997) reported that participants' success in achieving anaesthesia and their belief in the genuineness of the experience were associated with hypnotizability. This indicates that hypnotizability, even among a group of carefully selected individuals, might play a role in helping to understand the 50 per cent phenomenon that is sometimes observed, and it underscores the need for the specific, rather than the general, assessment of hypnotizability.

Types and phases of hypnotic suggestion

The findings across a range of hypnotic phenomena indicate that high hypnotizables respond differently, both from mediums and lows and also amongst themselves. These differences are apparent when analysis focuses on their response to the specific test of the suggestions. The nature of these differences becomes even clearer when we consider closely responding across types of items (i.e. ideomotor, challenge, cognitive; for descriptions see Chapter 2) and the time course of items (i.e. suggestion or onset, test, and cancellation or offset). To index and track ongoing hypnotic experience across item types, McConkey et al. (1999) developed and used a 'dial' method, which involved asking participants to turn a dial to indicate changes in the strength of their experience of the hypnotically suggested item. The dial was connected to a computer that recorded the position of the pointer (i.e. rating of experience) every second across the three phases of each item. These three phases can be illustrated in terms of the standard suggestion of hand lowering: the suggestion or onset involves asking the participant to hold his or her hand out and the hypnotist saying that the hand is becoming too heavy to hold out there; the test involves the hypnotist telling the participant to see how heavy it is, and then observing quietly for say 10 seconds; the cancellation or offset involves the hypnotist telling the participant to put his or her hand back into a resting position and saying that the hand is now back to normal and is no longer heavy. As indicated, most research in the field of hypnosis has focused on the test phase, and there is a need to explore the experience of participants during the onset and offset of selected hypnotic items.

McConkey et al. (1999) asked high, medium, and low hypnotizable participants to use the dial across three different hypnotic items: arm levitation (ideomotor item), arm rigidity (challenge item), and anosmia (cognitive item). They reported that participants showed different patterns of experience across these hypnotic items. In particular, participants overall showed greater experiential involvement in arm rigidity than arm levitation and anosmia; in other words, they showed greater involvement in the challenge item than in the ideomotor or cognitive items. Participants who passed an item in terms of the behavioural criterion reported a greater strength of experience for that item than did those who did not meet the behavioural criterion. In other words, there was a substantial match between behaviour as assessed by the specific criterion and experience as assessed by the dial. Although highs responded behaviourally more so than medium or low hypnotizable, the dial pattern of high and medium hypnotizable was essentially similar for each of the items and was different from that of lows. The different patterns of dial ratings across the items underscored that hypnotic items tap particular dimensions of hypnotic responding, and that these dimensions involve different aspects of experiential involvement as well as different behavioural responses. In particular, the findings suggested that these items do not differ simply in terms of difficulty, but rather that they differ in a more complex amalgam of demands that are placed on and experienced by the hypnotized person. Moreover, there was variability within high hypnotizables in terms of the match between their behaviour and their dial ratings.

In terms of the pattern of ratings across the phases of the hypnotic items, the findings indicated that the experience of participants changed across the phases and that these changes were different for different types of participants and for different types of items. For instance, whereas during cancellation of arm rigidity, both high and medium hypnotizable participants showed a decreasing strength of experience, during cancellation of anosmia, highs showed an increasing strength and mediums showed a decreasing strength of experience. It seems that for most of the high hypnotizable participants, their positive experience during the test of anosmia enhanced and encouraged the intensity of their experiential involvement and this intensity was not diminished by the explicit instruction from the hypnotist that was intended to cancel their experience. In this respect, it was striking that the pattern of dial ratings indicated that across the items the offset of the experience progressed relatively slowly and in a way that was very different from the pattern that characterized the onset of the experience; in particular, whereas some high hypnotizables could 'turn off' the hypnotic experience relatively quickly, other high hypnotizables took a considerable time. The cancellation, or offset, of hypnotic suggestions has not been the focus of investigation in the field (except in isolated studies; Perry, 1977), and we believe that substantial, theoretically interesting diversity exists within high hypnotizables in terms of how they experience the cancellation of hypnotic suggestions.

More recently, McConkey et al. (2001) suggested a change of sex to high hypnotizable participants in hypnosis and imagination conditions, and then indexed that experience with the dial method; also, they indexed participants' experience through retrospective ratings of realness, involuntariness, and active thinking. Notably, there were differences in the pattern of dial ratings across the hypnotic and imagination conditions. In particular, the dial ratings differed for the suggestion phase, but not the test or cancellation phases. This pattern indicated that the experience of sex change came about more quickly for hypnotic than for imagination participants. This implies that the presence of a hypnotic induction may influence the rate of onset of a suggested experience for high hypnotizable individuals. Thus, hypnotic induction may facilitate, rather than create, particular experiences. The finding that most hypnotized participants achieved their experience more quickly than did the high hypnotizable imagination participants was apparent because of the use of the dial method in this experiment; it was not revealed by the retrospective ratings or reports. Future research needs to investigate in more detail the nature of both the onset and offset of the experience. In this respect, McConkey et al. (1999) reported that although the strength of the suggested experience typically decreased during the cancellation phase of the ideomotor, challenge, and cognitive items they used, it did not do so for all individuals and it did not do so as rapidly as might be expected.

A perspective on unity and diversity

Although Kirsch and Lynn (1995), somewhat like Spanos and Barber (1974) before them, argued that broad areas of agreement exist among hypnosis researchers, Kihlstrom (1997) warned about the dangers of reaching a 'false consensus that obscures differences in approach and sweeps areas of conflict under the rug' (p. 329). From our perspective, as we have earlier stated, the hypnotized individual is an active participant who employs appropriate cognitive strategies (e.g. concentrative, independent, constructive; Sheehan and McConkey, 1982) to resolve the multiple problems posed by the hypnotic setting. This provides many opportunities for different patterns of responding to emerge among high hypnotizable individuals. Many such people develop strong belief in and commitment to the phenomenal reality of their subjective experience during hypnosis (but others of similar high hypnotizability do not), and this can be manifested in the attributions that they make about their experiences during hypnosis. The way in which these attributions appear to be used to protect the integrity of hypnotic responses also provides substantial opportunity for diversity in experience and response among high hypnotizable individuals. Both cognitive and social processes in the hypnotic setting contribute to the beliefs and attributions of hypnotized participants, and further systematic research is needed to explore these processes in detail.

Moreover, it may be that hypnotizability and hypnotic responding is dimensional in part and typological in part, and this needs to be examined both conceptually and empirically. Oakman and Woody (1996) provided evidence of a latent typology in hypnotizability scores, and it may be that there is not only something distinctively different between high and not-high hypnotizable persons, but also something distinctively different among certain types of high hypnotizable persons. This distinction between dimensional and typological accounts of hypnotic responding has not received enough consideration in the field, and it could have important implications for both theory and measurement of hypnotic experience and behaviour, particularly since most theories and measures assume dimensionality. The possibility of distinct types is relevant also as the field seeks a neural basis for hypnotic behaviour and experience; the successful application of neuroimaging techniques assumes and demands singular pathways to the phenomena of interest (Barnier and McConkey, 2003).

The different patterns of dial ratings reported by McConkey et al. (1999, 2001) underscore that hypnotic items tap different aspects of experiential involvement as well as different behavioural responses. Hypnotic items do not differ simply in terms of difficulty, but they differ in a more complex amalgam of demands that are placed on and experienced by the hypnotized individual. That amalgam of demands needs to be better distinguished, to better understand both the unity and the diversity of responding by high hypnotizable individuals. For instance, to respond to a hypnotic or posthypnotic suggestion, participants must develop an appropriate motivated set or preparedness to respond in a hypnotic fashion. It is not sufficient for participants to have received the suggestion and for the test simply to be presented; rather, they must actively process the information in a way that helps them to display the hypnotic behaviour. The processing of information by high hypnotizables to achieve a positive experience (and high hypnotizables differ in how they go about achieving this) is influenced by the extent to which the suggestion meets their expectations, the availability of cues in the setting that reinforces particular responses, and the degree to which they are able to tolerate and manage ambiguity in the totality of messages and cues that are available to them. The fact that many hypnotized participants work in different ways to give priority to particular features of the messages they receive underscores the potency of the hypnotist's message, the relevance of the relationship between themselves and the hypnotist, and their own cognitive predisposition and ability to assimilate conflicting and ambiguous information in a way that defines and promotes their experiences as special in the hypnotic setting.

The issues that we have discussed do not exhaust those that are relevant to the diversity of response of hypnotized participants. For example, the importance of the interpersonal relationship between the participant and hypnotist and the affective qualities of their dyadic interaction may be central to the responses of hypnotized individuals (Orne and Hammer, 1974; Sheehan, 1971, 1991). The relevance of emotional processes clearly needs to be explored and incorporated into the perspective that we have presented. Nevertheless, we have pointed to selected variables that influence the construction of information by hypnotized participants (high hypnotizables in particular) in a way that allows them both to experience the effects suggested by the hypnotist and to develop a belief in the reality of those experiences even in the face of challenging information from reality. To comprehend hypnotic experiences one must view hypnotized participants as sentient individuals who actively process the information they receive from both cognitive (internal) and social (external) sources. In a detailed analysis of the experience of two very highly hypnotizable individuals, McConkey et al. (1989) reported how differently these two participants responded to hypnotic suggestions in both experiential and behavioural terms. Whereas one participant reported using a range of particular cognitive strategies to respond to the suggestions, the other reported that the effects suggested by the hypnotist simply occurred.

Capturing these differences is crucial to both theory and method. Some understanding will be driven by new theoretical approaches and some will be driven by novel methodologies. Based on their use of the Experiential Analysis Technique, Sheehan and McConkey (1982) argued that there is an 'essential diversity of hypnotic reaction' and researchers need to explore 'the different patterns of cognitive processing that appear necessary to explain the variable ways in which participants may respond hypnotically' (p. 250). Given that the experience of the hypnotized participant is shaped by both cognitive and social processes, a change in such processes or an alteration in the hypnotic interaction can change the nature of the hypnotized person's experience and the ways in which they behaviourally express that experience. Our emphasis on the interaction between social and cognitive processes underscores the view that the behavioural response of the hypnotized participant is the result of a bi-directional interaction between internal personal factors and external environmental factors. Important theoretical gains can be obtained by focusing on the individual differences that exist among high hypnotizable individuals, to determine the particular patterns of abilities that exist among them, and to understand the differences that exist in the social cognitions they use to process the communications of the hypnotist.

References

Balthazard, C.G. and Woody, E.Z. (1985) 'The "stuff" of hypnotic performance: A review of psychometric approaches', *Psychological Bulletin*, 98:283–96.

—— and Woody, E.Z. (1989) 'Bimodality, dimensionality, and the notion of hypnotic types', *International Journal of Clinical and Experimental Hypnosis*, 37:70–89.

Bányai, E.A. (1991) 'Toward a social-psychobiological model of hypnosis', in S.J. Lynn and J.W. Rhue (eds), *Theories of Hypnosis: Current Models and Perspectives* (pp. 564–98), New York: Guilford Press.

Barber, T.X. (1969) *Hypnosis: A Scientific Approach*, New York: Van Nostrand Reinhold.

Barber, T.X. (1999a) 'A comprehensive three-dimensional theory of hypnosis', in I. Kirsch, A. Capafons, E. Cardeña-Buelna and S. Amigó (eds), *Clinical Hypnosis and Self-regulation: Cognitive-behavioral Perspectives* (pp. 21–48), Washington, DC: American Psychological Association.

—— (1999b) 'Hypnosis: A mature view', *Contemporary Hypnosis*, 16:123–7.

—— (1999c) 'The essence and mechanism of superb hypnotic performance', *Contemporary Hypnosis*, 16:192–208.

Barnier, A.J. and McConkey, K.M. (1999) 'Hypnotic and posthypnotic suggestion: Finding meaning in the message of the hypnotist', *International Journal of Clinical and Experimental Hypnosis*, 47:192–208.

—— and McConkey, K.M. (2003) 'Hypnosis, human nature, and complexity: Integrating neuroscience approaches into hypnosis research', *International Journal of Clinical and Experimental Hypnosis*, 51:282–308.

—— Wilton, H.J. and McConkey, K.M. (1997) 'Hypnotic anaesthesia and the circle-touch test: Exploring phenomena and method in hypnosis', *Contemporary Hypnosis*, 14:22–5.

Barrett, D. (1990) 'Deep trance subjects: A schema of two distinct subgroups', in R.G. Kunzendorf (ed.), *Mental Imagery* (pp. 101–12), New York: Plenum Press.

—— (1996) 'Fantasizers and dissociaters: Two types of high hypnotizables, two different imagery styles', in R.G. Kunsendorf, N.P. Spanos, and B. Wallace (eds), *Hypnosis and Imagination* (pp. 123–35), Amityville, NY: Baywood.

Bryant, R.A. and Mallard, D. (2002) 'Hypnotically induced emotional numbing: A real–simulating analysis', *Journal of Abnormal Psychology*, 111:203–7.

—— and McConkey, K.M. (1989a) 'Hypnotic blindness: A behavioural and experiential analysis', *Journal of Abnormal Psychology*, 98:71–7.

—— and McConkey, K.M. (1989b) 'Hypnotic blindness, awareness and attribution', *Journal of Abnormal Psychology*, 98:443–7.

—— and McConkey, K.M. (1995) 'Hypnotic blindness and the priming effect of visual material. *Contemporary Hypnosis*, 12:157–64.

Burn, C., Barnier, A.J. and McConkey, K.M. (2001) 'Information processing during hypnotically suggested sex change', *International Journal of Clinical and Experimental Hypnosis*, 49:231–42.

Chaves, J.F. (1999) 'Deconstructing hypnosis: A generative approach to theory and research', *Contemporary Hypnosis*, 16:139–43.

Davis, L.W. and Husband, R.W. (1931) 'A study of hypnotic susceptibility in relation to personality traits', *Journal of Abnormal and Social Psychology*, 26:175–82.

Gauld, A. (1999) 'Clearing the decks again?', *Contemporary Hypnosis*, 16:146–9.

Heap, M. (1999) 'High hypnotizability: Types and dimensions', *Contemporary Hypnosis*, 16:153–6.

Hilgard, E.R. (1965) *Hypnotic Susceptibility*, New York: Harcourt, Brace and World.

—— (1973) 'A neodissociation interpretation of pain reduction in hypnosis', *Psychological Review*, 80:396–411.

—— (1977) *Divided Consciousness: Multiple Controls in Human Thought and Action*, New York: Wiley.

—— (1978–9) 'The Stanford Hypnotic Susceptibility Scales as related to other measures of hypnotic responsiveness', *American Journal of Clinical Hypnosis*, 21:68–83.

—— Hilgard, J.R., Macdonald, H., Morgan, A.H. and Johnson, L.S. (1978) 'Covert pain in hypnotic analgesia: Its reality as tested by the real-simulator design', *Journal of Abnormal Psychology*, 87:655–63.

Kihlstrom, J.F. (1997) 'Convergence in understanding hypnosis?: Perhaps, but perhaps not quite so fast', *International Journal of Clinical and Experimental Hypnosis*, 45:324–32.

Kirsch, I. and Lynn, S.J. (1995) 'The altered state of hypnosis: Changes in the theoretical landscape', *American Psychologist*, 50:846–58.

Knox, V.J., Morgan, A.H. and Hilgard, E.R. (1974) 'Pain and suffering in ischemia: The paradox of hypnotically suggested anesthesia as contradicted by reports from the "hidden observer" ', *Archives of General Psychiatry*, 30:301–16.

Kumar, V.K., Marcano, G. and Pekala, R.J. (1996) 'Behavioral and subjective scoring of the Harvard Group Scale of Hypnotic Susceptibility: Further data and extension', *American Journal of Clinical Hypnosis*, 38:191–209.

Laurence, J.-R. and Perry, C. (1981) 'The "hidden observer" phenomenon in hypnosis: Some additional findings', *Journal of Abnormal Psychology*, 90:334–44.

Lynn, S.J. and Rhue, J.W. (1986) 'The fantasy-prone person: Hypnosis, imagination, and creativity', *Journal of Personality and Social Psychology*, 51:404–8.

—— and Rhue, J.W. (1988) 'Fantasy-proneness: Hypnosis, developmental antecedents, and psychopathology', *American Psychologist*, 43:35–44.

Mallard, D. and Bryant, R.A. (2001) 'Hypnotic color blindness and performance on the Stroop test', *International Journal of Clinical and Experimental Hypnosis*, 49:330–8.

McConkey, K.M. (1991) 'The construction and resolution of experience and behavior in hypnosis', in S.J. Lynn and J.W. Rhue (eds), *Theories of Hypnosis: Current Models and Perspectives* (pp. 542–63), New York: Guilford Press.

—— and Sheehan, P.W. (1981) 'The impact of videotape playback of hypnotic events on posthypnotic amnesia', *Journal of Abnormal Psychology*, 90:46–54.

—— Glisky, M.L. and Kihlstrom, J.F. (1989) 'Individual differences among hypnotic virtuosos: A case comparison', *Australian Journal of Clinical and Experimental Hypnosis*, 17:131–40.

McConkey, K.M., Bryant, R.A., Bibb, B.C., Kihlstrom, J.F. and Tataryn, D.J. (1990) 'Hypnotically suggested anaesthesia and the circle-touch test: A real–simulating comparison', *British Journal of Experimental and Clinical Hypnosis*, 7:153–7.

—— Bryant, R.A., Bibb, B.C. and Kihlstrom, J.F. (1991) 'Trance logic in hypnosis and imagination', *Journal of Abnormal Psychology*, 100:464–72.

—— Wende, V. and Barnier, A.J. (1999) 'Measuring change in the subjective experience of hypnosis', *International Journal of Clinical and Experimental Hypnosis*, 47:23–39.

—— Szeps, A. and Barnier, A.J. (2001) 'Indexing the experience of sex change in hypnosis and imagination', *International Journal of Clinical and Experimental Hypnosis*, 49:123–38.

Noble, J. and McConkey, K.M. (1995) 'Hypnotic sex change: Creating and challenging a delusion in the laboratory', *Journal of Abnormal Psychology*, 104:69–74.

Nogrady, H., McConkey, K.M., Laurence, J.-R. and Perry, C. (1983) 'Dissociation, duality, and demand characteristics in hypnosis', *Journal of Abnormal Psychology*, 92:223–35.

Oakman, J.M., and Woody, E.Z. (1996) 'A taxometric analysis of hypnotic susceptibility', *Journal of Personality and Social Psychology*, 72:981–91.

Orne, M.T. (1959) 'The nature of hypnosis: Artifact and essence', *Journal of Abnormal and Social Psychology*, 58:277–99.

—— (1972) 'On the simulating subject as a quasi-control group in hypnosis research: What, why, and how', in E. Fromm and R.E. Shor (eds), *Hypnosis: Research Developments and Perspectives* (pp. 519–65), Chicago: Aldine-Atherton.

—— and Hammer, A.G. (1974) 'Hypnosis', *Encyclopaedia Britannica* (vol. 15), Chicago: Benton.

—— and O'Connell, D.N. (1967) 'Diagnostic ratings of hypnotizability', *International Journal of Clinical and Experimental Hypnosis*, 15:125–33.

Pekala, R.J. (1991a) *The Phenomenology of Consciousness Inventory* (PCI) West Chester, PA: Mid-Atlantic Educational Institute. (Original work published 1982).

—— (1991b) 'Hypnotic types: Evidence from a cluster analysis of phenomenal experience', *Contemporary Hypnosis*, 8:95–104.

—— Kumar, V.J. and Marcano, G. (1995) 'Hypnotic types: A particular replication concerning phenomenal experience', *Contemporary Hypnosis*, 12:194–200.

Perry, C. (1977) 'Variables influencing the posthypnotic persistence of an uncancelled hypnotic suggestion', *Annals of the New York Academy of Sciences*, 296:264–73.

Register, P.A. and Kihlstrom, J.F. (1986) 'Finding the hypnotic virtuoso', *International Journal of Clinical and Experimental Hypnosis*, 34:84–97.

Sheehan, P.W. (1971) 'Countering preconceptions about hypnosis: An objective index of involvement with the hypnotist' [Monograph], *Journal of Abnormal Psychology*, 78:299–322.

—— (1980) 'Factors influencing rapport in hypnosis', *Journal of Abnormal Psychology*, 89:263–81.

—— (1991) 'Hypnosis, context, and commitment', in S.J. Lynn and J.W. Rhue (eds), *Theories of Hypnosis: Current Models and Perspectives* (pp. 520–41), New York: Guilford Press.

—— and McConkey, K.M. (1982) *Hypnosis and Experience: The Exploration of Phenomena and Process*, Hillsdale, NJ: Erlbaum.

—— McConkey, K.M. and Cross, D. (1978) 'Experimental analysis of hypnosis: Some new observations on hypnotic phenomena', *Journal of Abnormal Psychology*, 87:570–3.

Shor, R.E. (1962) 'Three dimensions of hypnotic depth', *International Journal of Clinical and Experimental Hypnosis*, 10:23–8.

—— (1979) 'A phenomenological method for the measurement of variables important to an understanding of the nature of hypnosis', in E. Fromm and R.E. Shor (eds), *Hypnosis: Developments in Research and New Perspectives*, 2nd edn (pp. 105–35), Hawthorne, NY: Aldine.

—— Orne, M.T, and O'Connell, D.N. (1966) 'Psychological correlates of plateau hypnotizability in a special volunteer sample', *Journal of Personality and Social Psychology*, 3:80–95.

Spanos, N.P. (1981) 'Hypnotic responding: Automatic dissociation or situation relevant cognizing?', in E. Kinger (ed.), *Imagery: Concepts, Results and Applications* (pp. 105–32), New York: Plenum Press.

—— and Barber, T.X. (1974) 'Toward a convergence in hypnosis research', *American Psychologist*, 29:500–11.

—— and Chaves, J.F. (eds) (1989) *Hypnosis: The Cognitive-behavioral Perspective*, Buffalo, NY: Prometheus Books.

Sutcliffe, J.P. (1961) ' "Credulous" and "skeptical" views of hypnotic phenomena: Experiments on esthesia, hallucination, and delusion', *Journal of Abnormal and Social Psychology*, 62:189–200.

Tellegen, A. (1978–9) 'On measures and conceptions of hypnosis', *American Journal of Clinical Hypnosis*, 21:219–37.

Varga, K., Jozsa, E., Bányai, E.I., Gosi-Greguss, A.C. and Kumar, V.K. (2001) 'Phenomenological experiences associated with hypnotic susceptibility', *International Journal of Clinical and Experimental Hypnosis*, 49:19–29.

Weitzenhoffer, A.M. and Hilgard, E.R. (1959) *Stanford Hypnotic Susceptibility Scales, Forms A and B*, Palo Alto, CA: Consulting Psychologists Press.

—— and Hilgard, E.R. (1962) *Stanford Hypnotic Susceptibility Scales, Form C*, Palo Alto, CA: Consulting Psychologists Press.

Weitzenhoffer, A.M. and Hilgard, E.R. (1963) *Stanford Profile Scales Hypnotic Susceptibility Scales: Forms I and II*, Palo Alto, CA: Consulting Psychologists Press.

—— and Hilgard, E.R. (1967) *Revised Stanford Profile Scales Hypnotic Susceptibility Scales: Forms I and II*, Palo Alto, CA: Consulting Psychologists Press.

West, V. and Fellows, B. (1996) 'How to be a "good" hypnotic subject', *Contemporary Hypnosis*, 13:143–9.

Wilson, S.C. and Barber, T.X. (1981) 'Vivid fantasy and hallucinatory abilities in the life histories of excellent hypnotic subjects ("somnambules"): Preliminary report with female subjects', in E. Klinger (ed.) *Imagery: Concepts, Results, and Applications* (pp. 133–49), New York: Plenum Press.

—— and Barber, T.X. (1983) 'The fantasy-prone personality: Implications for understanding imagery, hypnosis, and parapsychological phenomena', in A.A. Sheikh (ed.), *Imagery: Current Theory, Research, and Application* (pp. 340–87), New York: Wiley.

Wilton, H.J. and McConkey, K.M. (1994) 'Hypnotic anaesthesia and the resolution of conflict', *Contemporary Hypnosis*, 11:1–8.

—— Barnier, A.J. and McConkey, K.M. (1997) 'Hypnotic anaesthesia and the circle-touch test: Investigating the components of the instructions', *Contemporary Hypnosis*, 14:9–15.

Woody, E.Z., Bowers, K.S. and Oakman, J.M. (1992) 'A conceptual analysis of hypnotic responsiveness: Experience, individual differences, and context', in E. Fromm and M.R. Nash (eds), *Contemporary Perspectives in Hypnosis Research* (pp. 3–33), New York: Guilford Press.

Chapter 4

High hypnotizability in a sociocognitive framework

Graham F. Wagstaff

Introduction: the traditional view of hypnosis

The traditional view of hypnosis as described by its proponents in the 19th century is that of a special sleep-like brain state or trance, and up until at least the mid-1980s it was quite common for theorists and researchers to talk about hypnosis using the terminology of this tradition. For example, many emphasized a differentiation between the 'hypnotic' and 'waking' states (see, for example, Bowers, 1976; Gibson, 1977; Hilgard and Hilgard, 1983; Sheehan and Perry, 1976). The unusual nature of the hypnotic trance or state condition was reinforced by the view that the phenomena associated with it were not explicable in terms of processes familiar to most psychologists, such as suggestibility, placebo effects, motivation, imagination, absorption, shifts in attention, and compliance with instructions (see, for example, Bowers, 1976; Hilgard, 1986; Hilgard and Hilgard, 1983; Kihlstrom, 1978; Kihlstrom et al., 1980; Orne, 1959, 1970; Zamansky, 1977).

Another significant feature of state accounts of hypnosis was the idea that susceptibility to this state is a relatively fixed and unmodifiable trait (e.g. Bowers, 1976). From this point of view, therefore, the core feature of the highly hypnotizable subject is an aptitude and ability to enter this special altered state of consciousness, the hypnotic trance. Moreover, it is the production and experience of this trance that enables the very highly hypnotizable subject to experience a range of quite extraordinary phenomena in a unique and compelling way.

Throughout its history, the state approach to hypnosis has been through various incarnations (see Chapter 1), and degrees of popularity (Kirsch and Lynn, 1995). Recently, however, with increasing application of the technologies of cognitive neuroscience, the notion that hypnosis involves a special psychological and physiological condition or altered state has experienced something of a revival (Gruzelier, 2000; see also Chapter 1).

The development of the sociocognitive view

It was very much as a response to the traditional portrayal of hypnosis that the 'sociocognitive' view of hypnosis evolved. The term 'sociocognitive' in relation to hypnosis was first used by the present author in a book chapter published in 1986, to denote an already established approach to hypnosis that employed a range of 'ordinary' concepts derived from social and cognitive psychology. According to Spanos (1991), the modern precursor to the sociocognitive tradition was, in fact, Robert White (1941) who conceptualized hypnotic behaviour in terms of an interaction between subjects' implicit expectations about what was to happen, and their attempts to present themselves in a manner appropriate to what they believed the hypnotist was looking for. It was, however, T.R. Sarbin who really pioneered the idea of hypnosis as a social phenomenon (see, for example, Sarbin, 1950; Sarbin and Coe, 1972). Sarbin construed hypnosis primarily in terms of a role-enactment in which the subject and the hypnotist can be seen as enacting roles appropriate to their conceptions of a developing script.

At the time, however, Sarbin's role-theory approach met with considerable resistance from those who continued to maintain that there was something special about hypnosis that enabled 'hypnotized subjects' to transcend their 'waking capacities'. It was this belief in the special status of hypnosis that very much motivated the research programme of T.X. Barber (1969). Barber set out to demonstrate that all hypnotic phenomena could be explained in other ways using terms of social and cognitive processes drawn from general psychology. Those working with Sarbin and with Barber, in particular N.P. Spanos, J.F. Chaves, and W.C. Coe, and others influenced by them, then took up the mantle, stressing the social-psychological nature of hypnotic responding, and the importance of context in guiding the behaviour of the hypnotic subject (Coe and Sarbin, 1991; Kirsch, 1991, Lynn and Rhue, 1991; Spanos, 1986, 1991; Spanos and Chaves, 1989; Wagstaff, 1977, 1981, 1991). In relation to this view, they also noted that most hypnotic behaviour is relatively easy to simulate, and suitably motivated 'non-hypnotized' groups can equal hypnotic groups on a variety of performance measures, including feats of strength and endurance, pain tolerance, and age regression (for examples of this kind of research, see Barber, 1969; Spanos, 1982, 1986; Spanos and Chaves, 1989; Wagstaff, 1981). Significantly, they also found that subjects' descriptions of the experience of being 'hypnotized' do not indicate the operation of some unique process; indeed, they are indistinguishable from those who have undergone, for example, relaxation training, or instructions in the use of imagery (Barber et al., 1974, and more recently, Kirsch et al., 1992; Lynn et al., 2000).

Certainly, sociocognitive theorists differ in the extent to which they emphasize the various elements that they believe account for hypnotic experience and performance; they have in common, however, a commitment to the following three fundamental ideas.

1 Hypnosis is best construed as a culturally devised role; thus although subjects may experience changes in consciousness as they play this role (as most people do when they close their eyes, relax, focus attention, etc.), it is actually misleading and unhelpful to conceptualize hypnosis in terms of some special biologically based state or trance condition.

2 Hypnotizable subjects are actively cognizing agents who adapt their behaviour to the demands of the situation; they are not passive respondents automatically displaying the phenomena associated with a special hypnotic state.

3 Hypnotic behaviour and experience are best explained in terms of concepts and processes drawn from everyday psychology without the postulation of special hypnotic processes.

According to a sociocognitive perspective, therefore, 'hypnosis' and related terms can be defined operationally in a way that does not imply the existence of a unitary altered state of consciousness. In fact, operationally, hypnosis has two meanings, referring to (i) the *belief* or *suggestion* that there exists an altered state of consciousness with definable characteristics (such as a loss of control and volition, and increased suggestibility); and (ii) any *procedure* or ritual in which the participants are invited to take the roles of hypnotist and hypnotic subject as they understand these roles.

How subjects enact these 'hypnotic' roles will vary according to their role attitudes and expectations (that is, their beliefs about, and attitudes towards, hypnosis and how well they will respond), their role skills (their abilities to enact the hypnotic role convincingly), and how they interpret and respond to the cues provided by the situation, particularly the nature of the hypnotic induction ritual (i.e. their interpretational 'sets'; e.g. whether they are prepared to accept that simply being relaxed justifies the label of being 'hypnotized'). Accordingly, 'hypnotic' subjects are those who have received the hypnosis role ritual, and 'hypnotizable' subjects are those who respond in some way to the instructions and suggestions given in the context of this ritual.

From a sociocognitive perspective, the highly hypnotizable hypnotic subject is simply someone *who is willing and able to enact the hypnotic role, as he or she defines it, to its fullest extent.* So, how is the role enacted?

Enacting the hypnotic role

According to the author's sociocognitive view (Wagstaff, 1986, 1991), when highly hypnotizable subjects enter a situation defined as hypnosis, they will involve themselves in a three-stage 'ESC' process (expectation, strategy, compliance), which involves the following.

1   They will work out what is appropriate to the role.
2   They will apply 'normal' cognitive strategies to make the experiences veridical or believable, in line with existing expectations and what is explicitly or implicitly demanded in the suggestions.
3   If the application of normal strategies fails, is not possible, or is deemed inappropriate in the context, they will behaviourally comply or 'sham'.

The kinds of strategies employed in stage 2 of the ESC process have been detailed extensively by sociocognitive theorists (see, for example, Barber et al., 1974; Gorassini and Spanos, 1999; Lynn et al., 1990; Spanos et al., 1977; Spanos and Chaves, 1989; Wagstaff, 1981). Hence, in response to the induction procedure, highly hypnotizable subjects will listen carefully to the hypnotist's voice, and quite literally follow the instructions, relaxing if appropriate, closing their eyes, imagining they are going to sleep, and so on, as the particular induction demands. Then, in response to an ideomotor suggestion such as arm lowering, they will try hard to imagine their arms are heavy, or they will move their arms whilst distracting themselves (focusing attention away from thoughts such as 'I am moving my arm'), so that the movement is experienced as involuntary. In non-hypnotic situations, many people seem to have little difficulty passing this suggestion so long as they 'think along with the suggestion' and do not just 'wait for something to happen'. To respond to a challenge suggestion, all that is necessary is simply to obey the instructions. For example, if it is suggested to subjects that they cannot unclasp their hands because they are 'glued together' then as long as they concentrate on the instruction that their hands are glued together, they will not be able to separate them (this is akin to trying to stand up and sit down at the same time). To respond to an analgesia suggestion, subjects may try hard to distract themselves (one way is to concentrate on elements of 'being hypnotized', such as deep breathing, or thinking about sleep), or simply keep calm and tolerate the pain, or even concentrate on the pain and attempt to reinterpret it as pleasant. To respond to a positive hallucination suggestion, subjects may try to imagine the suggested object in their 'mind's eye', and in response to an amnesia suggestion they may, again, distract themselves by thinking about something else other than the material to be remembered, or simply fail to apply the effort to think back.

Importantly, as previously noted, one of the key features of the hypnotic role is that subjects should experience the effects as involuntary or 'happening to them'; hence good hypnotic subjects will also attempt, with every means at their disposal, to interpret their responses as involuntary and veridical happenings (Kirsch and Lynn, 1999; Gorassini, 1996, 1997, 1999; Gorassini and Spanos, 1999). The issue of how a good hypnotic subject may come to report his or her responses as involuntary (which good hypnotic subjects do) has been a source of considerable speculation amongst socio-cognitive theorists. One possible explanation can be derived from current cognitive psychological models of memory and attention.

Cognitive aspects of hypnotic responding

The last two decades have seen an increase in interest amongst hypnosis researchers of all persuasions in models of cognitive performance drawn from mainstream psychology, particularly those involving working memory and attention.

Many cognitive psychological models propose that working memory should be viewed in terms of a number of subcomponents that can operate relatively autonomously and automatically (Baddeley and Hitch, 1974; Gathercole and Baddeley, 1994; Logie, 1995; Posner,

1978; Shallice, 1988). This, in turn, has led to speculation about a supervisory mechanism or executive system involved in controlling the on-line operation of specific information-processing subsystems. Although this hypothesized executive mechanism has been labelled in various ways, such as the Central Executive (Baddeley, 1996), and the Supervisory Attentional System (Norman and Shallice, 1986), its existence and function are widely endorsed within models of memory and attention. Moreover, the types of operation which would require a central processor are now broadly agreed upon; these include situations that involve planning, decision making and error correction, particularly where the responses are not well learned or contain novel sequences of action, situations that are dangerous or technically difficult, and situations that require over-coming a strong habitual response or resisting temptation (see, for example, Norman and Shallice 1986; Shallice and Burgess, 1993).

Because it has been assumed that the central executive is a limited-capacity system, one approach to testing these ideas has been to assess the effects on performance of overloading the executive sys-tem by running two or more tasks assumed to tap executive function concurrently, the prediction being that a decline in performance would be expected on such tasks, while tasks that require processing by the slave systems alone should not have a deleterious effect on performance. For instance, Baddeley (1993) found that random number generation, which allegedly requires executive processing, was substantially disrupted when it was performed concurrently with other 'executive tasks' such as card sorting or sorting by category. In contrast, a task that could be handled without executive intervention (such as counting repeatedly from 1 to 6) did not affect performance on random number generation when used as a secondary task (see also e.g. Baddeley et al., 1998).

The appeal of such an approach is that it appears to provide an explanation of some of the effects attributed to hypnosis. If the operation of the central executive is deemed to be equivalent to the operation of a voluntary monitoring component in hypnotic responding, then by 'loading up' the processor by focusing attention, (for example), or by suppressing the operation of this processor (by adopting a passive responsive mode), fairly simple actions, such as arm movements, may be experienced as relatively automatic; for instance, the act of imagining one's arm being heavy, or simply focusing attention on the hypnotist's instructions, might 'load up' the central executive, such that the relatively simple act of arm lowering, though initiated voluntarily, is subsequently experienced as automatic.

Kirsch and Lynn (1999) have extended such ideas to explain why highly hypnotizable subjects may come to experience whole sequences of actions as involuntary. They start from the premise that automatic or involuntary behaviour is, in fact, a feature of everyday life. Indeed, evidence suggests that much everyday behaviour is routinized and scripted to be carried out fairly automatically without continual monitoring from a central executive; a good example would be driving a car on a familiar route to work (Norman and Shallice, 1986). All that is needed, therefore, for a highly hypnotizable subject to respond to suggestions is to *intend* to enact the hypnotic role. Although the central executive is likely to be involved in planning this initial stage, having established this intention, the subject is then in a position to essentially 'hand over' the executive control of his or her actions to the hypnotist, in the same way that a driver might hand over control of directing the car he or she is driving to a navigator. According to this analysis, therefore, one characteristic of the highly hypnotizable hypnotic subject is a willingness to let the 'hypnotic script' unfold without constant monitoring or interruption from some high-level executive process; if he or she does this, then there is no contradiction between the idea that, overall, the hypnotic role is controlled and intentional (as driving a car to work is intentional) yet the elements of the role can be experienced as automatic (like following certain directions with little thought or deliberation).

Kirsch and Lynn (1998) have noted a certain correspondence between their own viewpoint and the 'state' theory of dissociated control put forward by Woody and Bowers (1994), which also invokes the ideas of Norman and Shallice (1986). According to Woody and Bowers, hypnosis is essentially an altered state of consciousness in which the frontal lobes are inhibited; as a result, the hypnotic subject loses executive control over his or her behaviour and exhibits behaviours in a way similar to patients with frontal lobe pathology. Kirsch and Lynn (1998), however, criticize Woody and Bowers for putting too much emphasis on loss of control during hypnosis; for example, they argue that Woody and Bowers cannot account for self-hypnosis. In Kirsch and Lynn's model, however, the good hypnotic subject does not lose the capacity to employ executive control any more than a car driver following the instructions of a navigator. Hence, the hypnotic subject can himself or herself dictate the degree of absorption in suggestions, as in self-hypnosis. Kirsch and Lynn (1998) also suggest that the theory of dissociated control cannot readily account for novel and complex hypnotic behaviours that would seem to require executive processing. Arguably, however, in this latter respect, their theory may have similar difficulties.

Compliance and the highly hypnotizable subject

Many of the behaviours shown by high hypnotizables typically look very different from the mundane actions and experiences involved in driving a car, taking the bus to work, or making the dinner. For example, the negative hallucination is one of the most dramatic of all hypnotic effects, and one of the hallmarks of the highly hypnotizable subject. That is, in response to suggestion, some hypnotic subjects will claim that they cannot see someone or have not seen something, such as a person, part of a person, or one of a number of objects, set before their eyes. A possible explanation is that subjects may be using strategies to bring the suggested effect about, such as looking away, or closing or defocusing their eyes. It is also possible that subjects may try to visualize an image that will 'blot out' the material that is not supposed to be seen. However, even though all of these strategies may to some extent be successful, it is still debatable whether any would enable a subject to selectively yet fully obliterate a small part of the visual field, and be unaware that they have done so. Indeed, two studies have shown that virtually all subjects who claim to have seen nothing in response to a negative hallucination suggestion are subsequently able to report what was presented to them if they are told that there is another 'hidden part' of the mind that actually saw what was presented (Spanos et al., 1988; Zamansky and Bartis, 1985). So how do we explain these reports? Of course, it could be argued that there really is another dissociated 'part of the mind' that saw what happened. This seems a rather unlikely explanation, however, given that highly hypnotizable subjects will even report a *reversal* of a previously 'unseen' number (such as 81 instead of 18) if they are led to believe that the 'hidden part of the mind' sees a reversed version of the stimulus (Spanos et al., 1988).

It is also unlikely that hypnotic negative hallucinations can be interpreted purely in terms of expectancy effects (Kirsch, 1991), that is, the proposal that subjects genuinely experience negative hallucinations simply because they 'expect' to experience them. In a recent study at the University of Liverpool we led subjects to believe that a piece of paper to be presented to them would be blank; in fact it had a large number written on it. The results showed that not one person who was 100 per cent certain that he or she would see a piece of paper as blank, subsequently reported the paper as blank; moreover expectancy did not relate to the perceived clarity of the image (Wagstaff et al., 2002).

As Kirsch and Lynn (1998) have noted, suggested negative hallucinations are novel events, and may be construed as cognitively complex to execute; consequently, an analysis of profound negative hallucination effects purely in terms of non-executive automatic processes is difficult to entertain. Although Kirsch and Lynn have argued that their analysis may be extended to encompass more novel events, a further, and perhaps more parsimonious, explanation of negative hallucination effects, is that they are primarily manifestations of behavioural compliance; that is, subjects move to stage 3 of the ESC process outlined earlier, and simply pretend that they cannot see something (Spanos, 1992; Perlini et al., 1996; Wagstaff, 1981, 1991).

The issue of the extent to which hypnotic subjects may be exaggerating or lying has been contentious even amongst sociocognitive theorists (see, for example, Council et al., 1996; Kinnunen et al., 1994, 2001; Kirsch et al., 1989; Perlini et al., 1996; Spanos, 1991; Wagstaff, 1981, 1999). However, supporters of the compliance viewpoint can point to a number of classic examples in the hypnosis literature (Wagstaff, 1996). For example, Pattie (1935) reports the case of a woman who claimed that, under hypnosis, she was blind in one eye, and she passed a number of tests that seemed to indicate her blindness was genuine. However, she subsequently failed a more complex test. It was then discovered that she had managed to achieve the appearance of blindness in one eye on the earlier tests by practising at home with a friend.

Particularly notable here is some work using an experimental design developed by Spanos and his associates to assess the influence of compliance (Perlini et al., 1996; Spanos, 1992). For example, Spanos and his colleagues have demonstrated that highly hypnotizable subjects will tend to report that various suggestions were effective, or not effective, depending on whether *afterwards* the experimenter conveys to them that they had 'drifted into hypnosis' when the suggestions were presented. Although this might suggest that 'highs' deliberately bias their reports to comply with experimental demands (i.e. lie about their experiences), it has been argued that the suggestion to 'highs' that they had 'drifted into hypnosis' might have led them to reinterpret what they experienced to fit in with experimental demands or expectancies (Council et al., 1996).

In another more definitive study, Spanos et al. (1989) gave subjects a negative hallucination suggestion that they would not see a number '8' that was presented clearly in front of them. Some subjects subsequently claimed they had seen nothing. These same subjects were then told that 'reals', unlike 'fakers', *do* see the number for a short period, but then it fades. Having been given this information, virtually all of these subjects confirmed they *had* seen the number. These results seem to indicate strongly that the subjects were not entirely truthful when they originally claimed they could not see the number. Significantly, Spanos and his associates also found that those who complied on this task tended to be the sort of highly hypnotizable subjects who perform well on other 'difficult' hypnotic tasks, such as seeing a stimulus in a different colour (see Perlini et al., 1996; Spanos, 1992). Hence Perlini et al.'s (1996) conclusion that 'compliance is a central component of hypnotic responding' (p. 206).

The issue of compliance figures again in discussions of another phenomenon usually manifested by highly hypnotizable subjects, hypnotic amnesia. Compliance is undeniably present in reports of hypnotic amnesia; indeed, a large proportion of subjects (as many as 60 per cent) will subsequently confess on questioning that they deliberately suppressed their reports so that they might appear 'amnesic' (Coe, 1989). As Coe asks, 'Perhaps we should wonder how many did not confess?' (p. 118).

From a sociocognitive perspective, hypnotic amnesia is primarily a consequence of strategies in response to task demands; that is, because hypnotic subjects have a strong investment in presenting themselves as 'hypnotized', when given an amnesia suggestion they engage in strategies such as distraction, inattention, and voluntarily withholding responses (compliance), to give the appearance of amnesia until the experimental demands (the reversal cue) indicate otherwise (Coe, 1989; Coe and Sarbin, 1991; Spanos, 1986, 1991; Wagstaff, 1977, 1981, 1986, 1991; Wagstaff and Frost, 1996).

A number of studies support this interpretation. For instance, posthypnotic amnesia in high hypnotizables can be eliminated almost entirely using a package that involves exhorting subjects to be honest and not to lie, presenting them with a videotape of their actions, and rigging them up to a lie detector (Coe, 1989). Other successful 'face saving' breaching techniques include requesting subjects to 'trust their imaginary memories' (Kunzendorf, 1990), and suggesting to them that memory can be recovered in 'deep hypnosis' (Silva and Kirsch, 1987). Hypnotic amnesia can also be eliminated entirely if subjects are given an opportunity to say they were 'role-playing' rather than in a 'trance' before being tested for amnesia, that is, before committing themselves to appearing amnesic (Wagstaff, 1977; Wagstaff and Frost, 1996). Arguably again, however, whilst such studies indicate that hypnotic amnesia is very much under the control of the hypnotic subject, they do not necessarily indicate that reports of amnesia are exaggerated; these manipulations might simply serve to stop subjects applying the attentional strategies necessary to suppress their memories. Nevertheless, other studies of amnesia suggest a more crucial role for compliance.

For example, Spanos et al. (1984) found that hypnotic amnesia was eliminated in highly hypnotizable subjects when they were told (incorrectly) that different classes of items (concrete and abstract) can be made available by contacting different hemispheres of the brain. This task required hypnotic subjects to selectively reverse 'amnesia' for either concrete or abstract items depending on what hemisphere was 'contacted'; as the items were not originally encoded in this way, the task would necessitate bringing all items to mind and then deliberately selecting those in the right category and eliminating those in the wrong category. In a further study, hypnotically amnesic subjects, like simulators, tended to score significantly lower (i.e. show more memory loss) than patients who suffer profound amnesia due to brain damage (Wagstaff et al., 2001).

Another technique for assessing the operation of compliance is the surreptitious observation paradigm, which compares the behaviours of 'real' hypnotic subjects and simulators when the experimenter leaves the room. Sometimes, although not always, the results show that reals continue to respond in the absence of the experimenter, whilst simulators do not. The problem with this paradigm, however, is that reals and simulators operate under different role demands. Thus, for reals, continuing the compliant role in the absence of the hypnotist may feel more natural; moreover, whilst it is legitimate for simulators to be 'found out' during suspected surreptitious observation (because simulation is their prescribed role), the same is not true for 'real' hypnotic subjects, who may be considerably more cautious about revealing themselves (Sarbin and Coe, 1972;

Spanos, 1991; Wagstaff, 1981). As a more definitive test, therefore, Spanos et al. (1987) set up a situation in which highly hypnotizable subjects were given a posthypnotic suggestion that, for a week, they would cough whenever they heard the word 'psychology'. They were then tested in the laboratory and then outside by two confederates who ostensibly had no connection whatsoever with the experimenters. Whilst all high hypnotizables responded to the suggestion in the laboratory (like the simulators), none responded when the word 'psychology' was voiced by the confederates. The posthypnotic response returned for about half of the subjects (both reals and simulators), however, when they were retested in the laboratory a week later (see also, Fisher, 1954). These results again strongly attest to the role of compliance in the behaviour of highly hypnotizable subjects.

The hypnotic virtuoso past and present

Recently, however, a challenge to the sociocognitive view of hypnotic responding has come from the claim by T.X. Barber (1999) that, in their samples, the vast majority of modern scientific studies on hypnosis have ignored the true hypnotic virtuosos described in historical accounts. In support of this view, Barber cites a study by Barrett (1996) on 1200 students, which found that only 34 subjects could be classed as really excellent subjects (see also Chapter 8). Of these, 19 could be classed as 'fantasy-prone'; these subjects reported that they had a vivid fantasy life, which they brought to the hypnosis situation. Perhaps more interesting were the 15 excellent subjects whom Barber classes as 'amnesia-prone', and Barrett as 'dissociators'. In hypnosis situations, these subjects typically displayed behaviours including the following: looking disoriented when 'awakened' from hypnosis and asking 'what happened'; showing unsuggested (spontaneous) amnesia; experiencing profound hallucinatory experiences that they believed were real events; being surprised at these responses; expressing little use of imagination and fantasy involvement; and requiring a lengthy hypnotic induction procedure during which they show a subdued voice and loss of muscle tone. In other words, these subjects look like the truly 'hypnotizable' individuals who fall into the classic 'hypnotic trance'. Added to this, most of them displayed dissociated 'hidden observers' who could be contacted in different parts of their mind; moreover, these hidden parts would often speak in strange voices. But how valid is this interpretation?

Investigators studying hypnosis and criminal behaviour have come up with a number of phenomena which, they claim, can be used to detect whether a person is 'faking hypnosis' (see for example, Aldridge-Morris, 1989; McConkey and Sheehan, 1995). These include a lack of imaginative involvement, overplaying and over-emphasis in the hypnotic role, and acting with surprise at responses. The overlap between these and some of the major defining character-istics of the 'amnesia-prone' individual hardly requires comment; perhaps, therefore, a more parsimonious explanation of the behaviour of the so-called amnesia-prone individual is that this per-son, more than any other, enacts the stereotypical, classic role of the hypnotic subject in a 'deep somnambulistic trance' (see Wagstaff, 1999). However, this invites the question as to why these particular subjects are motivated to enact the hypnotic role in this way. As we know very little about the origins of individual differences in com-pliant behaviour generally, any attempt to address this question must be speculative. Nevertheless, it may be of some interest that virtually all of the dissociaters reported by Barrett reported or showed signs that they had been physically abused and maltreated as children. Significantly, many of the important manifestations of maltreatment are to be found in social interaction; thus victims of neglect and physical abuse may learn to adapt to and overcome their feelings of isolation and powerlessness by engaging in attention- and approval-seeking behaviours. Arguably, such a factor might contribute to a predisposition to enact the hypnotic role in accordance with situational demands (Wagstaff, 1996).

The idea that most modern investigators are not and have not been investigating classic 'true hypnosis' as it was evidenced historically is, of course, impossible to deny or substantiate. Nevertheless, historical investigation can be revealing. For example, one of the first recorded cases of alleged hypnotic 'somnambulism' involved the French land-owner, the Marquis de Puységur, and, in fact, this is cited by Barber as an early example of the amnesia-prone individual. In 1784, Puységur 'magnetized' one of his peasants, a young man called Victor Race. Victor promptly adopted a sleep-like appearance. However, two features of Victor Race's behaviour intrigued Puységur. First, whilst in this state, Victor treated Puységur as an equal instead of adopting his usual humble and subordinate manner; and second, when Victor awoke, he was unable to remember having done this (Mackay, 1869). A motive for Victor's claim of amnesia is thus not difficult to establish; it gave him a chance to challenge his master whilst denying any responsibility. It can also be noted that further claims made by Puységur's 'somnambulistic' subjects included telepathy and being able to see into the interior of another's stomach.

Significantly, Martin and Lynn (1996) found that a standard hypnotic susceptibility test successfully classified 76 per cent of a sample as either 'real' or 'simulating'. This success is due to the fact that, typically, simulators pass more items than 'non-virtuoso' 'real' subjects. In other words, one of the main characteristics of 'virtuoso' performance on measures of hypnotizability is that it is similar to the behaviour of those faking hypnosis.

It must be emphasized that sociocognitive theorists who have argued for the role of compliance in hypnotic behaviours certainly do not argue that all of the behaviours of the highly hypnotizable subject are faked or sham (Coe, 1989; Spanos, 1991; Wagstaff, 1981, 1991). For example, Spanos (1991) reviews a large amount of evidence that he interprets as indicating the real effects of suggestions for analgesia. However, they do argue, in particular, that compliance may provide a very plausible and parsimonious explanation of behaviours that do not fit into current mainstream psychological theorizing on perception and cognition.

The sociocognitive neuropsychology of hypnosis

Another way that researchers have attempted to determine whether high hypnotizables have the capacity to enter a special altered state is to search for some unique physiological marker of being 'hypnotized'. Although a vast number of physiological effects have been attributed to hypnosis and the hypnotic 'state', attempts to develop an integrated meaningful physiological theory of hypnosis have so far failed, largely because the findings are often contradictory, or impossible to interpret at our present state of knowledge (Wagstaff, 1998, 2000). However, viewed in terms of role strategies that individuals might use to carry out instructions and suggestions, these findings make considerable sense.

As noted previously, sociocognitive theorists suggest that the role requirement of being a good hypnotic subject often involves employing strategies aimed at bringing about the suggested effects; that is, all good 'hypnotizable' subjects should at least *try* to experience what is suggested or expected of them (Spanos, 1991, 1992; Wagstaff,

1986, 1991, 1996; see also Chapter 9). In contrast, low hypnotizables ('lows') tend not to employ these strategies, and fail to carry out instructions in a situation defined as 'hypnosis'. Reasons for 'non-compliance' would include the following.

1   Negative attitudes and/or expectancies about hypnosis (for instance, they might fear going out of control, or want to show their 'iron willpower', or simply believe they will not be able to respond).
2   A failure to understand that responsiveness to suggestions involves active involvement not passive responsivity. (This would be manifested by an unwillingness to employ the strategies in a situation defined as hypnosis because this is 'not what is supposed to happen'.)
3   Difficulty in using the strategies (i.e. they might find it difficult, or not have the ability to imagine sounds and images). There seems to be some support for all of these characteristics in 'lows' (see, for example, Jan and Wagstaff, 1994; Lynn and Rhue, 1991; Spanos, 1986; Spanos and Chaves, 1989).

If we apply this analysis to psychophysiological work on correlates of hypnosis, then not only is much of it consistent with the sociocognitive view, it could actually be considered to lend considerable support for it. Consider, for example, modern physiological studies of hypnotic negative hallucinations (see, for example, Barabasz et al., 1999; Perlini et al., 1996; Spiegel and Barabasz, 1988; Spiegel et al., 1985, 1989). Some investigators have reported that when highly hypnotizable subjects are told during a hypnosis session to construct an obstructive image that will mask an incoming visual stimulus, the evidence from their brain-event-related potential recordings shows that the component known as P300 is suppressed. This is significant, because the P300 component occurs in response to an incoming stimulus when we are waiting for, or attending to, the occurrence of this stimulus. From a strategic enactment perspective, the suppression of P300 could occur as subjects divert their attention away from the incoming stimulus in an effort to construct the obstructive image. In contrast, some findings indicate that when hypnotic subjects are instructed, in a more straightforward way, to obliterate an incoming stimulus, their evoked potentials show, paradoxically, and contrary to their verbal reports, that P300 is enhanced. That is, though claiming they cannot see it, subjects are singularly unsuccessful in eliminating the stimulus. The latter finding makes sense if one assumes that subjects are now strategically concentrating on the incoming stimulus in an unsuccessful attempt to 'obliterate it' or 'make it go away'. Not surprisingly, from a sociocognitive perspective, low susceptibles do not generally show these results as they would not be applying, or would find it more difficult to apply, such strategies.

Interestingly also, in an investigation of negative auditory hallucinations, Kunzendorf and Boisvert (1996) gave subjects a music hallucination suggestion to 'mask' a simple auditory stimulus. In response, some highly susceptible subjects showed physiological responses consistent with the successful use of suggested auditory masking imagery (i.e. the music imagery suppressed the evoked potential responses to the auditory 'click' stimulus). However, these responses were not suppressed in high hypnotizables who claimed initially to be totally deaf to the click stimulus, but subsequently reported a 'hidden observer' in another part of the mind who could hear the stimulus. This result fits well with the sociocognitive perspective. Strategically, the tasks of attending away from the auditory stimulus and imaging an auditory masking sound could be seen as incompatible with the task of reporting a 'hidden observer' who can recall the allegedly 'unheard' stimulus. The fact that subjects with 'hidden observers' claimed deafness in the absence of any supporting physiological evidence again suggests a prime role for compliance in these subjects. It may not be coincidence, therefore, that Barber's (1999) hypnotic amnesia-prone 'virtuosos' described earlier tended to display 'hidden observers'.

If the strategic enactment view is correct, therefore, we should expect the physiological correlates of hypnotic responding to vary according to the particular task. In other words, there will be no fixed set of physiological indicators of a 'hypnotic state'; rather the physiological correlates of hypnotic responding should vary according to the nature of the task and the strategies involved. This view is consistent with many of the findings of Gruzelier and his co-workers.

In a series of studies, Gruzelier and his co-workers found that high and low hypnotizables tend to show a different pattern of responding during a standard hypnotic induction. 'Highs' start off showing left-hemisphere dominance, but as the induction continues, increased electrophysiological activity shifts to the right hemisphere, leaving the hypnotized subject in a state of right-hemisphere dominance (Gruzelier, 1988; McCormack and Gruzelier, 1993). In another

study by Jasiukaitis et al. (1996), however, neurophysiological correlates of a hypnotic hallucination suggestion were found to be
associated with left-hemisphere superiority. In other words, no one
working in this area has yet claimed to have found a laterality measure that can tell us whether or not someone is 'in' or 'out of' a
'hypnotic state'. Instead, as Crawford (1996) comments, 'There is
growing evidence that hypnotic phenomena selectively involve cortical and subcortical processes of either hemisphere, dependent upon
the nature of the task' (p. 272; see also Chapter 7).

From a sociocognitive perspective, however, the patterns of hemispheric activation shift are predictable in terms of the ways in which
high hypnotizables enact role requirements. That is, the results are
what might be predicted from two groups of individuals, some (the
'highs') 'thinking and imagining' along with the induction, others
(the 'lows') not, or less so. The standard hypnotic induction first
requires one to concentrate on the words of the hypnotist. This form
of analytical processing might be considered typical of left-
hemisphere function. After a while, however, the induction shifts
towards the idea of concentrating on one's feelings and internal
states, i.e. 'holistic' activity associated with the right hemisphere (see
Springer and Deutsch, 1981). In contrast, 'lows', who for the reasons
stated earlier fail to carry out the instructions, would not be expected
to show these laterality shifts. Also, predictably, Jutai et al. (1993)
have shown that when 'highs' and 'mediums' are given an induction
procedure that requires holistic processing, their responses differ not
only from those of 'lows', but also from those of controls who are
attending to verbal material (a more left-hemisphere task). In contrast, the task of trying to conjure up an image in response to a
hallucination suggestion requires considerable non-holistic attention
to detail. As Jasiukaitis et al. (1996) note, 'Such narrow attentional
focus would seem to be a function of the left hemisphere's detailed
analytical and sequential processing' (p. 667). Consequently, high
hypnotizables show a shift to right-hemisphere processing as they
concentrate on the induction, and left-hemisphere processing as they
shift to trying to conjure up an image.

In another study, Gruzelier and Warren (1993) found that highly
hypnotizable subjects show poorer performance on a left frontal
phonemic fluency task immediately following an initial hypnotic
induction procedure. This is significant, as it has been demonstrated
outside of hypnosis that motor acts generated by will are associated
with blood flow increases in the dorsolateral prefrontal cortex while

instruction guided acts are not (Frith, 1996; Jahanshahi and Frith, 1998). Moreover, some patients with damage to the prefrontal cortex appear to show specific disruptions of the executive processes assumed in cognitive models (Leclercq et al., 2000; Shallice and Burgess, 1993). From this viewpoint, therefore, it is tempting to believe that we have a model for explaining the behaviour of high hypnotizables; that is, their frontal function is impaired under hypnosis and they lose the capacity to control their own actions (Gruzelier, 2000; Woody and Bowers, 1994). However, Crawford (1996) concludes that, 'Rather consistently there is *increased* involvement of regions within the frontal cortex during hypnotic suggestion', and, as Crawford points out, and as noted above (Frith, 1996; Jahanshahi and Frith, 1998), 'PET studies show increased activity in the frontal cortex during the performance of *willed actions*' (pp. 269–71, my emphasis). Increased activity in the frontal cortex is also associated with better performance on tasks assumed to require executive processing (Elfgren and Risberg, 1998). If we accept an association between increased activity in the frontal cortex and willed, executive actions, then such results present problems for those attempting to identify hypnosis with a special brain state typified by inhibition of the frontal cortex. Viewed from a sociocognitive perspective, these apparently contradictory results are again very predictable.

A standard hypnotic induction procedure typically involves suggestions for concentration and passive acceptance of instructions. Compliance with either type of suggestion might initially result in a reduction in left frontal performance. For example, in a study that did not involve hypnosis, Troyer et al. (1997) found that requiring subjects to perform a finger-tapping task during a left frontal phonemic fluency test resulted in a reduction in performance on the latter. In other words, 'loading up the left frontal lobe' with a secondary task resulted in a reduction in residual left frontal capacity. In the same way, the simple act of concentrating hard on the induction instructions might reduce residual frontal capacity. Alternatively, consider another study on normal, psychologically healthy individuals that did not involve hypnosis. In this, Morris et al. (1993) looked at regional blood flow in the frontal cortex in two conditions. In one, subjects had to work out what moves to make to complete a task, and in the other the moves were guided by a computer (i.e. they simply followed the moves as dictated by the computer). The results showed that when subjects deliberately planned their moves, activity in the left frontal lobe was increased; conversely, when asked to simply follow the instructions of the computer, left frontal activity was depressed in comparison. One of the implications of this study is that when normal, fully conscious, individuals passively 'follow instructions', rather than plan their behaviours by themselves, they tend to show less left frontal activity than when they are planning their activities.

Which of these two explanations best accounts for physiological responses during hypnotic induction remains to be established (perhaps both operate). However, the main point is that changes in frontal activity and performance in normal subjects are not limited to situations involving hypnotic induction. To show a relative decline in the performance of activities related to the left frontal lobe, and perhaps other areas of the brain that have been associated with 'planning' or regulatory control, one does not need to be in some unique hypnotic brain state. Rather, all one needs is to be in a frame of mind to concentrate hard on a competing task or passively accept and act on the instructions of others (including a computer). Importantly, however, presumably no one would wish to argue that when Troyer et al.'s subjects performed a finger-tapping task, or Morris et al.'s subjects followed computer instructions, they had become ultra-suggestible automata, unable to control their behaviour. Moreover, as a sociocognitive theory would predict, when the hypnosis session switches from the induction to specific suggestions that may require a degree of strategic planning, such as working out a way to respond to an analgesia suggestion, the physiological evidence suggests an increase in frontal involvement, not a decrease; hence the results reported by Crawford (1996).

Another physiological phenomenon that has been linked to the notion of a hypnotic state is activation of the cingulate cortex. For example, Rainville et al. (1997) showed that when hypnotic subjects are given a pain stimulus and are asked to experience it as pleasant or unpleasant, the neurophysiological data from the cingulate cortex and other parts of the brain are consistent with the view that the pain can be experienced as pleasant and unpleasant, even though its perceived intensity remains the same; that is, even though the brain shows that it is clearly registering a pain stimulus, this stimulus can be experienced as pleasant or unpleasant depending on the suggestion given. However, as is typical in neurophysiological studies of hypnosis, Rainville et al., did not include an independent unhypnotized control group given the same analgesia suggestions. If they had, they would probably have found that 'hypnosis' was an irrelevant consideration. For example, a number of studies indicate that in both hypnotic and non-hypnotic situations, subjects report that suggestions for analgesia are effective even when there is no evidence that the pain stimulus is any less discriminable; in other words, although subjects, regardless of whether they have received hypnosis, often report that they feel less pain in response to an analgesia suggestion, there is no evidence that their brains are successfully 'blocking out' the pain stimulus (see, for example, Spanos, 1989, 1991).

The explanation put forward by Spanos is that many subjects who successfully experience suggested analgesia may do so, not through blocking out the painful stimulus, but by interpreting the stimulus in a more positive way. He concludes, 'These findings may indicate that suggestions for reduced sensitivity produce their effects by inducing subjects to reinterpret (rather than to "block out") sensory activity' (1991, p. 341). It seems, therefore, that Rainville et al., may have found neurophysiological support for Spanos's proposal that many individuals respond to suggestions for analgesia by trying to reinterpret the pain stimulus such that it is not perceived as unpleasant. However, it is worth noting that, at our present stage of knowledge, activation of the cingulate cortex could mean more or less anything. The cingulate cortex is thought to be the interface between subcortical and cortical regions and has a variety of functions including that of imparting emotional significance during attentional processing; the anterior part is also important in selecting responses from complex arrays in conflict situations (Banich, 1997). One can, therefore, imagine the cingulate 'lighting up' in a variety of, so far untested, social situations.

The study by Rainville et al., also draws attention to the importance of using appropriate control groups when attempting to assess the significance of the context of 'hypnosis' in accounting for physiological and other effects. As noted above, the appropriate experimental design for assessing the influence of the context of hypnosis is one in which an independent group of subjects receive exactly the same instructions or suggestions in a situation not defined as hypnosis. It is not, for example, one in which 'highs' are compared with 'lows' in the same context, or 'highs' act as their own 'waking imagination' controls. In the case of the latter, there is a variety of evidence to show that 'highs' strategically 'hold back' or fail to respond in the 'waking' situation so that their performance in the hypnosis condition will look 'special' (see, for example, Barber, 1969; Sheehan and Perry, 1976; Spanos and Chaves, 1989; Wagstaff, 1981).

Non-hypnotic correlates of high hypnotizability

Another advantage of viewing the highly hypnotizable subject from a sociocognitive perspective is that sense can also be made of various characteristics that have been associated with individual differences in hypnotizability in non-hypnotic situations. Hypnotizability correlates with positive expectancies about responding (Braffman and Kirsch, 1999), and strong and significant correlations have also been found between hypnotizability and the abilities to act out a drama, and convincingly fake items on a hypnosis scale (Sarbin and Coe, 1972). This fits with other evidence that, in non-hypnotic situations, high hypnotizables give a more convincing performance of childlike behaviour than low hypnotizables (Troffer, 1966). Given that the hypnotic role demands a generous amount of imaginative and fantasy involvement, it is also not surprising that hypnotizability also correlates, to some extent, with a tendency to report becoming absorbed in fantasy and imagination in everyday life (Tellegen and Atkinson, 1974; Wilson and Barber, 1982). However, these correlations are poorer than those between hypnotizability and positive expectancies (Braffman and Kirsch, 1999). At the same time, hypnotizability has also been shown to correlate with conformity in the Asch conformity paradigm (Shames, 1981), and even annual alumni giving (i.e. making donations to one's old college, Graham and Green, 1981). Particularly significant in terms of a propensity for compliance, Wilson and Barber (1982) observed that some of their high hypnotizables stated that they enjoyed deceiving others; for instance, while riding on a bus just one day before the interview, one of their high hypnotizable subjects who had lived in New York all of her life introduced herself as an 'Eskimo' to the person sitting next to her, and then proceeded to tell the stranger all about her (deliberately fantasized) life in Alaska. Thus, the picture that seems to emerge is that of a person who essentially has a set of role enactment skills (including the ability to deceive, if necessary) that he or she often applies in everyday situations, coupled with a willingness and positive attitude towards applying them in contexts defined as hypnosis.

From this perspective then, although a minority of high hypnotizables may exhibit signs of psychopathology (Lynn et al., 1996; see also Chapter 8), the majority do not have a frontal lobe or other kind of functional brain deficit; rather they are supremely astute social beings who are willing and able to adapt their behaviour in a convincing way to conform with social expectations. This capacity for social monitoring may be reflected in the superior frontal and attentional functioning that some display in non-hypnotic situations (for example, Braffman and Kirsch, 2001; Graham and Evans, 1977; Gruzelier and Warren, 1993; Sigman et al., 1985).

Conclusions

If the view expressed in this chapter is valid, then if we are to understand the behaviours of highly hypnotizable subjects we must avoid endowing them with magical or peculiar brain characteristics and concentrate on mainstream psychological processes. For example, from the perspective of contemporary models of working memory and attention, one can see how the use of ordinary attentional focus by high hypnotizables might lead to the production of certain hypnotic behaviours and experiences, including reports of involuntariness. Indeed, some state theorists have long embraced the notion of 'focused attention' in their definitions of hypnosis (see Wagstaff, 1998). A major difficulty, however, has been the tendency of others to write off this idea, and emphasize a special state that is more esoteric and ill-defined, because simple 'focused attention' cannot explain the range of hypnotic behaviours shown by high hypnotizables (e.g. Gruzelier, 2000). According to the present approach, however, this is a mistake. As sociocognitive theorists have long suggested, variations in attention may indeed be the basis of some important hypnotic responses and experiences. However, the reason why the concept of attentional focus is incapable of explaining the full range of hypnotic phenomena is not because there is another, unique, 'hypnotic' state, or brain condition shown only by high hypnotizables, but because the behaviours of high hypnotizables are best construed within the context of the enactment of a complex, socially constructed role in which 'focused attention' is only one component.

This message may be particularly pertinent for those who are attempting to apply the latest techniques in neuroscience to the study of hypnosis. Results so far have been very interesting, but it is difficult to see how the neurophysiological responses of high hypnotizables can be understood in the absence of a developed discipline of *socio*cognitive neuroscience that looks at the neurophysiological processes involved in a range of everyday social situations and experiences.

References

Aldridge-Morris, R. (1989) *Multiple Personality: An Exercise in Deception*, Hove, Sussex: Lawrence Erlbaum Associates.

Baddeley, A.D. (1993) 'Working memory or working attention', in A.D. Baddeley and L. Weiskrantz (eds), *Selection, Awareness and Control*, Oxford: Oxford University Press.

—— (1996) 'Exploring the Central Executive', *Quarterly Journal of Experimental Psychology: A*, 49:5–28.

—— and Hitch, G. (1974) 'Working Memory' in G.A. Bower (ed.), *Recent Advances in Learning and Motivation* (vol. 8, pp. 47–90), New York: Academic Press.

—— Emslie, H., Kolodny, J. and Duncan, J. (1998) 'Random generation and the executive control of working memory', *Quarterly Journal of Experimental Psychology: A*, 51:819–52.

Banich, M.T. (1997) *Neuropsychology: The Neural Bases of Mental Function*, New York: Houghton Mifflin.

Barabasz, A., Barabasz, M., Jensen, S., Calvin, S., Trevisan, M. and Warner, D. (1999) 'Cortical event-related potentials show the structure of hypnotic suggestions is crucial', *International Journal of Clinical and Experimental Hypnosis*, 47:5–22.

Barber, T.X. (1969) *Hypnosis: A Scientific Approach*, New York: Van Nostrand.

—— (1999) 'A comprehensive three-dimensional theory of hypnosis', in I. Kirsch, A. Capafons, E. Cardeña-Buelna and S. Amigó (eds), *Clinical Hypnosis and Self-regulation: Cognitive-behavioral Perspectives* (pp. 21–48), Washington, DC: American Psychological Association.

—— Spanos, N.P. and Chaves, J.F. (1974) *Hypnotism, Imagination and Human Potentialities*, New York: Pergamon.

Barrett, D. (1996) 'Fantasizers and dissociators. Two types of high hypnotizables, two different imagery styles', in R.G. Kunzendorf, N.P. Spanos and B. Wallace (eds), *Hypnosis and Imagination* (pp. 123–35), Amityville, NY: Baywood.

Bowers, K.S. (1976) *Hypnosis for the Seriously Curious*, Monteray, CA: Brooks/Cole.

Braffman, W. and Kirsch, I. (1999) 'Imaginative suggestibility and hypnotizability: An empirical analysis', *Journal of Personality and Social Psychology*, 77:578–87.

—— and Kirsch, I. (2001) 'Reaction time as a predictor of imaginative suggestibility and hypnotizability', *Contemporary Hypnosis*, 18:107–19.

Coe, W.C. (1989) 'Posthypnotic amnesia: Theory and research', in

108   Graham F. Wagstaff

N.P. Spanos and J.F. Chaves (eds), *Hypnosis: The Cognitive-behavioral Perspective* (pp. 110–48), Buffalo, NY: Prometheus.

Coe, W.C. and Sarbin, T.R. (1991) 'Role Theory: Hypnosis from a dramaturgical and narrational perspective', in S.J. Lynn and J.W. Rhue (eds), *Theories of Hypnosis: Current Models and Perspectives* (pp. 303–23), New York: Guilford Press.

Council, J.R., Kirsch, I. and Grant, D.L. (1996) 'Imagination, expectancy and hypnotic responding', in R.G. Kunzendorf, N.P. Spanos and B.J. Wallace (eds), *Hypnosis and Imagination* (pp. 41–66). New York: Baywood.

Crawford, H.J. (1996) 'Cerebral brain dynamics of mental imagery: Evidence and issues for hypnosis', in R.G. Kunzendorf, N.P. Spanos and B.J. Wallace (eds), *Hypnosis and Imagination* (pp. 253–82), New York: Baywood.

Elfgren, C.I. and Risberg, J. (1998) 'Lateralized frontal blood flow increases during fluency tasks: Influence of cognitive strategy', *Neuropsychologia*, 36:505–12.

Fisher, S. (1954) 'The role of expectancy in the performance of posthypnotic behavior', *Journal of Abnormal and Social Psychology*, 49:503–7.

Frith, C.D. (1996) 'The role of the prefrontal cortex in higher cognitive functions', *Cognitive Brain Research*, 5:175–81.

Gathercole, S.E. and Baddeley, A.D. (1994) *Working Memory and Language*, Hove: Lawrence Erlbaum Associates.

Gibson, H.B. (1977) *Hypnosis: Its Nature and Therapeutic Benefits*, London: Peter Owen.

Gorassini, D.R. (1996) 'Conviction management: Lessons from hypnosis research about how self-images of dubious validity can be wilfully sustained', in R.G. Kunzendorf, N.P. Spanos and B.J. Wallace (eds), *Hypnosis and Imagination* (pp. 177–98), New York: Baywood.

—— (1997) 'Strategy selection and hypnotic performance', *Contemporary Hypnosis*, 14:37–47.

—— (1999) 'Hypnotic responding: A cognitive-behavioral analysis of self-deception', in I. Kirsch, A. Capafons, E. Cardeña-Buelna and S. Amigó (eds), *Clinical Hypnosis and Self-regulation: Cognitive-behavioral Perspectives* (pp. 73–104), Washington, DC: American Psychological Association.

—— and Spanos, N.P. (1999) 'The Carleton Skill Training Program for modifying hypnotic suggestibility: Original version and variations', in I. Kirsch, A. Capafons, E. Cardeña-Buelna and S. Amigó (eds), *Clinical Hypnosis and Self-regulation: Cognitive-behavioral Perspectives* (pp. 141–80), Washington, DC: American Psychological Association.

Graham, C. and Evans, F.J. (1977) 'Hypnotizability and the deployment of waking attention', *Journal of Abnormal Psychology*, 86:631–8.

Graham, K.R. and Green, L.D. (1981) 'Hypnotic susceptibility related to an independent measure of compliance – alumni annual giving', *International Journal of Clinical and Experimental Hypnosis*, 29:351–4.

Gruzelier, J. (1988) 'The neuropsychology of hypnosis', in M. Heap (ed.), *Hypnosis: Current Clinical, Experimental and Forensic Practices* (pp. 68–76), London: Croom Helm.

—— (2000) 'Redefining hypnosis: Theory, methods and integration', *Contemporary Hypnosis*, 17:51–70.

—— and Warren, K. (1993) 'Neuropsychological evidence of reductions on left frontal tests with hypnosis', *Psychological Medicine*, 23:93–101.

Hilgard, E.R. (1986) *Divided Consciousness: Multiple Controls in Human Thought and Action*, New York: Wiley.

—— and Hilgard, J.R. (1983) *Hypnosis in the Relief of Pain*, Los Altos, CA: William Kaufmann.

Jahanshahi, M. and Frith, C.D. (1998) 'Willed action and its impairments', *Cognitive Neuropsychology*, 15:483–533.

Jan, N. and Wagstaff, G.F. (1994) 'Attitudes towards state and cognitive-behavioural approaches to hypnotherapy before and after hypnotic induction', *Contemporary Hypnosis*, 11:66–70.

Jasiukaitis, P., Nouriani, B. and Spiegel, D. (1996) 'Left hemisphere superiority for event related potential effects of hypnotic obstruction', *Neuropsychologia*, 34:661–8.

Jutai, J., Gruzelier, J., Golds, J. and Thomas, M. (1993) 'Bilateral auditory evoked potentials in conditions of hypnosis and focused attention', *International Journal of Psychophysiology*, 15:167–76.

Kihlstrom, J.F. (1978) 'Context and cognition in posthypnotic amnesia', *International Journal of Clinical and Experimental Hypnosis*, 26:246–67.

—— Evans, F.J., Orne, E.C. and Orne, M.T. (1980) 'Attempting to breach posthypnotic amnesia', *Journal of Abnormal Psychology*, 89:603–16.

Kinnunen, T., Zamansky, H.S. and Block, M. (1994) 'Is the hypnotized subject lying?', *Journal of Abnormal Psychology*, 2:184–91.

—— Zamansky, H.S. and Nordstrom, B.L. (2001) 'Is the hypnotized subject complying?', *International Journal of Clinical and Experimental Hypnosis*, 49:83–94.

Kirsch, I. (1991) 'The social learning theory of hypnosis', in S.J. Lynn and J.W. Rhue (eds), *Theories of Hypnosis: Current Models and Perspectives* (pp. 439–66), New York: Guilford Press.

—— and Lynn, S.J. (1995) 'Altered state of hypnosis: Changes in the theoretical landscape', *American Psychologist*, 50:846–58.

—— and Lynn, S.J. (1998) 'Dissociation theories of hypnosis', *Psychological Bulletin*, 123:100–15.

—— and Lynn, S.J. (1999) 'Hypnotic involuntariness and the automaticity of everyday life', in I. Kirsch, A. Capafons, E. Cardeña-Buelna and S. Amigó (eds), *Clinical Hypnosis and Self-regulation: Cognitive-behavioral Perspectives* (pp. 49–72), Washington: American Psychological Association.

Kirsch, I., Silva, C.E., Carone, J.E., Johnstone, J.D. and Simon, B. (1989) 'The surreptitious observer design: An experimental paradigm for distinguishing artifact from essence in hypnosis', *Journal of Abnormal Psychology*, 98:132–6.

—— Mobayed, C.P., Council, J.R. and Kenny, D.A. (1992) 'Expert judgments of hypnosis from subjective state reports', *Journal of Abnormal Psychology*, 101:657–62.

Kunzendorf, R.G. (1990) 'Post-hypnotic amnesia: Dissociation of self concept or self-consciousness?', *Imagination, Cognition and Personality*, 9:321–34.

—— and Boisvert, P. (1996) 'Presence vs. absence of a "hidden observer" during total deafness: The hypnotic illusion of subconsciousness vs. imaginal attenuation of brainstem evoked potentials', in R.G. Kunzendorf, N.P. Spanos and B.J. Wallace (eds), *Hypnosis and Imagination* (pp. 223–34), New York: Baywood.

Leclercq, M., Couillet, J., Azouvi, P., Marlier, N., Martin, Y., Strypstein, E. and Rousseaux, M. (2000) 'Dual task performance after severe diffuse traumatic brain injury or vascular prefrontal damage', *Journal of Clinical and Experimental Neuropsychology*, 22:339–50.

Logie, R.H. (1995) *Visuo-spatial Working Memory*, Hove: Lawrence Erlbaum Associates.

Lynn, S.J. and Rhue, J.W. (1991) 'An integrative model of hypnosis', in S.J. Lynn and J.W. Rhue (eds), *Theories of Hypnosis: Current Models and Perspectives* (pp. 397–438), New York: Guilford Press.

—— Rhue, J.W. and Weekes, J.R. (1990) 'Hypnotic involuntariness: A social cognitive analysis', *Psychological Review*, 97:169–84.

—— Neufield, V., Green, J.P., Sandberg, D. and Rhue, J. (1996) 'Daydreaming, fantasy and psychopathology', in R.G. Kunzendorf, N.P. Spanos and B.J. Wallace (eds), *Hypnosis and Imagination* (pp. 67–98), New York: Baywood.

—— Myer, E. and Mackillop, J. (2000) 'The systematic study of negative post-hypnotic effects: Research hypnosis, clinical hypnosis and stage hypnosis', *Contemporary Hypnosis*, 17:127–31.

Mackay, C. (1869) *Memoirs of Extraordinary Popular Delusions and the Madness of Crowds*, London: Routledge.

Martin, D.J. and Lynn, S.J. (1996) 'The hypnotic simulation index: Successful discrimination of real versus simulating participants', *International Journal of Clinical and Experimental Hypnosis*, 154:338–53.

McConkey, K.M. and Sheehan, P.W. (1995) *Hypnosis, Memory, and Behavior in Criminal Investigation*, New York: Guilford Press.

McCormack, K. and Gruzelier, J. (1993) 'Cerebral asymmetry and hypnosis: A signal detection analysis of divided field stimulation', *Journal of Abnormal Psychology*, 102:352–7.

Morris, R.G., Ahmed, S., Syed, G.M. and Toone, B.K. (1993) 'Neural correlates of planning ability: Frontal lobe activation during the Tower of London test', *Neuropsychologia*, 31:1367–78.

Norman, D.A and Shallice, T. (1986) 'Attention to action: Willed control of behavior', in R.J. Davidson, G.E. Schwartz and D. Shapiro (eds), *Consciousness and Self-regulation* (vol. 4, pp. 1–18), New York: Plenum.

Orne, M.T. (1959) 'The nature of hypnosis: Artifact and essence', *Journal of Abnormal Psychology*, 58:277–99.

—— (1970) 'Hypnosis, motivation and the ecological validity of the psychological experiment', in W.J. Arnold and M.M. Page (eds), *Nebraska Symposium on Motivation* (pp. 187–265), Lincoln, NE: Nebraska Press.

Pattie, F.A. (1935) 'A report of attempts to produce uniocular blindness by hypnotic suggestion', *British Journal of Medical Psychology*, 15:230–41.

Perlini, A.H., Spanos, N.P. and Jones, W. (1996) 'Hypnotic negative hallucinations: A review of subjective, behavioral and physiological methods', in R.G. Kunzendorf, N.P. Spanos and B.J. Wallace (eds), *Hypnosis and Imagination* (pp. 199–222), New York: Baywood.

Posner, M.I. (1978) *Chronometric Explorations of Mind*, Hillsdale, NJ: Erlbaum Associates.

Rainville, P., Duncan, G.H., Price, D.D., Carrier, B. and Bushnell, M.C. (1997) 'Pain affect encoded in human anterior cingulate but not somatosensory cortex', *Science*, 277: 986–71.

—— (1999) 'Whither hypnosis? A rhetorical analysis', in I. Kirsch, A. Capafons, E. Cardeña-Buelna and S. Amigó (eds), *Clinical Hypnosis and Self-regulation: Cognitive-behavioral Perspectives* (pp. 105–18), Washington, DC: American Psychological Association.

—— and Coe, W.C. (1972) *Hypnosis: A Social Psychological Analysis of Influence Communication*, New York: Holt, Rinehart and Winston.

Shallice, T. (1988) *From Neuropsychology to Mental Structure*, Cambridge: Cambridge University Press.

—— and Burgess, P. (1993) 'Supervisory control of action and thought selection', in A. Baddeley and L. Weiskrantz (eds), *Attention: Selection, Awareness and Control* (pp. 171–87), Oxford: Oxford University Press.

Shames, M.L. (1981) 'Hypnotic susceptibility and conformity: On the mediational mechanism of suggestibility', *Psychological Reports*, 49:563–5.

Sheehan, P.W. and Perry, C. (1976) *Methodologies of Hypnosis: A Critical Appraisal of Contemporary Paradigms of Hypnosis*, Hillsdale, NJ: Erlbaum.

Sigman, A., Phillips, K. and Clifford, B. (1985) 'Attentional concomitants of hypnotic susceptibility', *British Society of Experimental and Clinical Hypnosis*, 2:69–75.

Silva, C.E. and Kirsch, I. (1987) 'Breaching hypnotic amnesia by manipulating expectancy', *Journal of Abnormal Psychology*, 96:325–9.

Spanos, N.P. (1982) 'A social psychological approach to hypnotic behavior', in G. Weary and H.L. Mirels (eds), *Integrations of Clinical and Social Psychology* (pp. 231–71), New York: Oxford University Press.

Spanos, N.P. (1986) 'Hypnotic behavior: A social psychological interpretation of amnesia, analgesia, and "trance logic" ', *The Behavioral and Brain Sciences*, 9:449–502.

—— (1989) 'Experimental research on hypnotic amnesia', in N.P. Spanos and J.F. Chaves (eds), *Hypnosis: The Cognitive-Behavioral Perspective* (pp. 206–40), Buffalo, NY: Prometheus.

—— (1991) 'A sociocognitive approach to hypnosis', in S.J. Lynn and J.W. Rhue (eds), *Theories of Hypnosis: Current Models and Perspectives* (pp. 324–63), New York: Guilford Press.

—— (1992) 'Compliance and reinterpretation in hypnotic responding', *Contemporary Hypnosis*, 9:7–14.

—— and Chaves, J.F. (eds) (1989) *Hypnosis: The Cognitive-Behavioral Perspective*, Buffalo, NY: Prometheus.

—— Rivers, S.M. and Ross, S. (1977) 'Experienced involuntariness and response to hypnotic suggestions', *Annals of the New York Academy of Sciences*, 296:208–21.

—— Cobb, P.C. and Gorassini, D.R. (1984) 'Failing to resist test suggestions: A strategy for self-presenting as deeply hypnotized', *Psychiatry*, 48:282–92.

—— Menary, E., Brett, P.J., Cross, W. and Ahmed, Q. (1987) 'Failure of the posthypnotic responding to occur outside the experimental setting', *Journal of Abnormal Psychology*, 96:63–7.

—— Flynn, D.M. and Gwynn, M.I. (1988) 'Contextual demands, negative hallucinations, and hidden observer responding: Three hidden observers observed', *British Journal of Experimental and Clinical Hypnosis*, 5:5–10.

—— Flynn, D.M. and Gabora, N.J. (1989) 'Suggested negative visual hallucinations: When no means yes', *British Journal of Experimental and Clinical Hypnosis*, 4:15–23.

Spiegel, D. and Barabasz, A.E. (1988) 'Effects of hypnotic instructions on P300 event related potential amplitudes: Research and clinical implications', *American Journal of Clinical Hypnosis*, 31:11–7.

—— Cutcomb, C., Ren, C. and Pribram, K. (1985) 'Hypnotic hallucination alters evoked potentials', *Journal of Abnormal Psychology*, 94:140–3.

—— Bierre, P. and Rootenberg, J. (1989) 'Hypnotic alteration of somatosensory perception', *American Journal of Psychiatry*, 146:749–54.

Springer, S.P. and Deutsch, G. (1981) *Left Brain, Right Brain*, San Francisco: Freeman.

Tellegen, A. and Atkinson, G. (1974) 'Openness to absorbing and self-altering experiences ("absorption"): a trait related to hypnotic susceptibility', *Journal of Abnormal Psychology*, 83:268–77.

Troffer, S.A.H. (1966) 'Hypnotic age regression and cognitive functioning', unpublished doctoral dissertation, University of Stanford. (Cited by Barber, 1969.)

Troyer, A.K., Moscovitch, M. and Winocur, G. (1997) 'Clustering and switching as two components of verbal fluency: Evidence from younger and older healthy adults', *Neuropsychology*, 11:138–46.

Wagstaff, G.F. (1977) 'An experimental study of compliance and post-hypnotic amnesia', *British Journal of Social and Clinical Psychology*, 16:225–8.

—— (1981) *Hypnosis, Compliance and Belief*, Brighton: Harvester/New York: St Martin's Press.

—— (1986) 'Hypnosis as compliance and belief: A sociocognitive view', in P.L.N. Naish (ed.), *What Is Hypnosis?*, Philadelphia: Open University Press.

—— (1991) 'Compliance, belief and semantics in hypnosis: A non-state, sociocognitive perspective', in S.J. Lynn and J.W. Rhue (eds), *Theories of Hypnosis: Current Models and Perspectives* (pp. 362–96), New York: Guilford Press.

—— (1996) 'Compliance and imagination in hypnosis', in R.G. Kunzendorf, N.P. Spanos and B.Wallace (eds), *Hypnosis and Imagination* (pp. 19–40), Amityville NY: Baywood.

—— (1998) 'The semantics and physiology of hypnosis as an altered state', *Contemporary Hypnosis*, 15:149–64.

—— (1999) 'The amnesia-prone syndrome: Brain state or cultural role?' *Contemporary Hypnosis*, 16:176–81.

—— (2000) 'On the physiological redefinition of hypnosis: A reply to Gruzelier', *Contemporary Hypnosis*, 17:154–62.

—— and Frost, R. (1996) 'Reversing and breaching posthypnotic amnesia and hypnotically created pseudomemories', *Contemporary Hypnosis*, 13:191–7.

—— Toner, S. and Cole, J. (2002) 'Is response expectancy sufficient to account for hypnotic negative hallucinations?', *Contemporary Hypnosis*, 19:133–8.

—— Parkes, M. and Hanley, J.R. (2001) 'A comparison of posthypnotic amnesia and the simulation of amnesia through brain injury', *International Journal of Psychology and Psychological Therapy*, 1:67–78.

White, R.W. (1941) 'A preface to a theory of hypnotism', *Journal of Abnormal Psychology*, 36:477–505.

Wilson, S.C. and Barber, T.X. (1982) 'The fantasy-prone personality: Implications for understanding imagery, hypnosis, and parapsychological phenomena', in A.A. Sheikh (ed.), *Imagery: Current Theory, Research and Application* (pp. 340–87), New York: Wiley.

Woody, E.Z. and Bowers, K.S. (1994) 'A frontal assault on dissociated control', in S. Lynn and J. Rhue (eds), *Dissociation: Theoretical and Research Perspectives* (pp. 52–79), New York: Guilford Press.

Zamansky, H.S. (1977) 'Suggestion and countersuggestion in hypnotic behavior', *Journal of Abnormal Psychology*, 86:346–51.
—— and Bartis, S.P. (1985) 'The dissociation of experience: The hidden observer observed', *Journal of Abnormal Psychology*, 94:243–8.

Chapter 5

Developmental determinants of high hypnotizability

Judith Rhue

Who is the highly hypnotizable child?

Let us begin our search for the highly hypnotizable child with what we know about the imaginative skills of young children. Imaginative skills, rather than a single activity, are likely to involve a spectrum of fantasy and imagination-based behaviors. Singer (1973) helped us understand more about children's use of daydreaming and fantasy. He noted that children as young as 2 to 5 are capable of fantasy and spend much time in various forms of imaginative play. As children grow and develop, their use of imagination and fantasy increases. We observe this in their daydreaming, their conversations with dolls and action figures, their recreations of superheroes and villains, their drawings, and their love of fantasy and storytelling. Those children who exhibit the most obvious capacity for these skills were described by J.R. Hilgard as being 'high in imaginative involvement'. Hilgard's highly imaginative children were likely to be involved in dance or music, to love imaginative play, and to be encouraged in these activities by adults.

Wilson and Barber (1981) might have described these same children as 'fantasy-prone' (see later). They noted that they were likely to have imaginary friends, to prefer their fantasy play to play with other children, to imagine things 'as real as real', and perhaps to come from difficult and aversive environments. Josephine Hilgard (1970) and Gail Gardner (1974) might have also described them as high in hypnotic responsiveness and to be appropriate candidates for hypnotherapy.

As we proceed with our look at the highly hypnotizable child, we shall examine in further detail the writings of these researchers and others. We shall attempt to understand the link between imagination, fantasy and hypnotizability, their development and functions, and the life circumstances that foster their growth and maintenance. We shall also examine briefly the relationship between psychopathology and high fantasy-proneness and hypnotizability. Let us begin with a look at the development and use of early childhood fantasy and imagination, since these elements seem to be the earliest forerunners and concomitants of later hypnotizability in childhood.

Fantasy, play and imagination as developmental forerunners of hypnotizability

Fantasy, imagination, and absorption have long been cited as correlates of high hypnotizability in college students and other adults by many researchers (Lynn and Rhue, 1986; see also Chapter 8). While their presence is not a one-to-one predictor of hypnotizability, they represent factors that appear important in understanding and assessing the highly hypnotizable person. These correlates have also been applied to research on the highly hypnotizable child. As part of their normal growth and development, children engage in varying states of fantasy and awareness throughout the day.

In view of their relationship to hypnotic ability during later childhood, it seems important to examine when and how fantasy and play begin for young children and what factors play a role in their development. To address this question, let us turn to some ideas about the origins of fantasy, imaginative play and daydreaming. Since these factors later correlate with hypnotic responsiveness in children, it is perhaps best to consider them separately from those theories that more directly attempt to track the development of hypnotic ability.

Carl Groos (1901 as cited in Singer, 1973) viewed play as the child's way of developing skills that later ensure survival. In other words, pretend play is a way of practicing adult roles that enhance adaptive living. Psychoanalytic views of fantasy postulated that play is a mechanism to deal with the conflicts between the child's unconscious instinctual desires and the demands of reality. Thus, the child's Oedipal conflicts, sibling rivalries and instinctual drives foster the use of fantasy, play, daydreaming and imaginative activities in order to process and control the associated desires without physically attempting to implement them.

More congruent with some recent theories of the development of hypnotic responsiveness is Piaget's work on cognitive development in children. Piaget stresses the very young child's need for

accommodation and assimilation. Accommodation involves track-
ing and grasping objects and imitating adults' communication and
movement. Assimilation builds on the process of accommodation,
allowing the child to develop a cognitive scheme for storing, recognizing and utilizing the imitations and memories of accommodation.
Fantasy and make-believe play begin as a tool for the child to assimilate and integrate the external environment. While very young children verbally and behaviorally act out much of their fantasy and
imaginative play, these behaviors become more internalized and
covert as the child conforms to the demands of society. As children's
cognitive abilities unfold, so too do the range of feelings, conflicts,
and events experienced, stored and replayed covertly in fantasy.
Singer (1973) hypothesized that the persistence of fantasy and daydreaming into adulthood may be related to the encouragement and
reinforcement that occurs from within the child's environment.

Similar to the views of Singer regarding the use of fantasy and
daydreaming are those of J.R. Hilgard. She felt that given children's
predilection for fantasy and imaginative involvement, children can
easily understand hypnosis as similar to those behaviors that they
do naturally. Hilgard's seminal work (1970, 1974, 1979) at Stanford
University provided the first links between imaginative involvement
and hypnosis. It also focused attention on the role of parental interest and encouragement of behaviors that were associated with the
development of hypnotic ability, imagination, and creativity in children. She reported that childhood involvement in drama and acting
characterized many individuals who were high in hypnotizability.
The plateau of hypnotizability and then gradual decline during adolescence is often explained in terms of maturation and societal pres-
sures that result in decreased imaginative involvement and increased
focus on rational goal-oriented behavior (Hilgard, 1970).

Hilgard then built on the childhood period of fantasy and high
hypnotic ability in her work with using hypnotherapy techniques
with children. Storytelling, which involves imaginative involvement
and absorption, can use metaphors combining direct and indirect
suggestions. Traditional induction techniques are often omitted with
storytelling procedures, and the emphasis on trance and measuring
hypnotizability is minimized or absent altogether. The use of metaphors in storytelling as a hypnotherapeutic technique was documented in the 1970s by J.R. and E.R. Hilgard and reviewed and
elaborated upon by Olness and Gardner (1988) and Olness and
Kohen (1996).

Gardner and her colleagues (Gardner, 1974; Gardner and Hinton, 1980; Gardner and Olness, 1981) also explored the correlates of children's hypnotizability. Based on their findings, the authors hypothesized that the reason that children are more hypnotizable than adults (London, 1965; Morgan and Hilgard, 1973) may be the natural occurrence of fantasy play and daydreaming that children experience in their everyday waking environment. These behaviors tend to parallel hypnotic behaviors. Cognitively through focused concentration, limited reality testing, and concrete thinking, and emotionally through openness to new experiences (including regressive states), and intensity of feeling, children are natural subjects for experiencing hypnosis. Their acceptance of adult authority figures may also affect their responsiveness, as well as parental attitude toward hypnosis, the hypnotist's skill with children, and situational factors.

LeBaron (LeBaron et al., 1988) assessed the relationship between hypnotic susceptibility in children and their involvement in fantasy-related activities in early childhood. In a series of two studies, LeBaron and his colleagues administered the Stanford Hypnotic Clinical Scale for Children and a structured interview scale based on previous work by Singer (1973). The first study used 30 medical patients from 6 to 18 years of age, while the second study used schoolchildren from 6 to 12 years of age. Across the two studies, hypnotic ability correlated modestly with the extent of involvement in fantasy-related activity. LeBaron et al.'s findings were consistent with Allen's (1985) and Plotnick et al.'s (1991) research which found that highly hypnotizable children tend to engage in more fantasy play than children with low hypnotic ability, buttressing the link between a fantasy orientation and hypnotic ability in children.

Congruent with children's natural involvement with fantasy and absorption, is children's love of mastery. It has been reported that children's responsiveness to hypnosis is directly related to their desire for mastery of skills and their understanding and active involvement in their environment (Erickson, 1959; Gardner, 1974). Being able to perform hypnotic phenomena, such as warming a hand, enhances children's feelings of power and mastery. Thus, hypnotherapy with school-age children has proved effective for a variety of problems (Brown et al., 1996).

Measuring hypnotic responsiveness
in children

While much of the work on assessing hypnotic responsiveness in children involves scales and reflects group findings rather than an individual focus on the highly hypnotizable child, it is relevant to review this body of work. These standardized scales for children are used to assess the skills of many who are identified as 'highly hypnotizable', making their strengths and weaknesses of importance in the investigation of the highly hypnotizable child.

In the past 40 years, two hypnosis scales for children have been developed and validated and have become widely used in research on the hypnotizability of children. The first of these is London's (1962, 1963) Children's Hypnotic Susceptibility Scale (CHSS). The CHSS is a two-part scale that rates both quantitative and qualitative aspects of the child's experience. Part I parallels the Stanford Hypnotic Susceptibility Scales: Form A (used for adults) with the difference that the items are adapted for children. Part II has items that focus on 'depth'. Hence both ideomotor and cognitive items (see Chapter 2) are presented to the child. The administration of both parts of the scale requires approximately 50 minutes. Three scores are derived from the scale: overt behavior, subjective involvement and a total score that is a weighted combination of the two scales.

In the late 1970s, Morgan and Hilgard (1978–9) developed the Stanford Hypnotic Clinical Scale for Children (SHCS:C) expressly for clinical use. This takes only about 20 minutes to administer and there are versions for younger children (4–8 years old) and for older children (6–16 years old). The SHCS:C does not directly assess the child's subjective involvement in hypnosis, and it has limited ability to discriminate the child's level of hypnotic responsiveness.

During the second half of the twentieth century, research using these scales to explore the hypnotic ability of children has yielded some consistent findings. From the early studies onward, there has been a consensus in results suggesting that children show more hypnotic ability than adults (Barber and Calverley, 1963; London, 1962; Morgan and Hilgard, 1973). There has also been a consistent finding of a peak in hypnotic susceptibility in the preadolescent years (8 to 12), followed by a decline during adolescence (London, 1965; Morgan and Hilgard, 1978–9; Weitzenhoffer and Hilgard, 1959).

Preschool children have consistently shown little hypnotizability using the scales that currently measure hypnotic ability. In fact, the short scale developed by Morgan and Hilgard (1978–9) measures from age 4 upward. Since children of 5 and 6 are less responsive than their older counterparts, it is often assumed that children younger than this are even lower in hypnotic ability. Around the age of 7 children show measurable hypnotic ability, which appears to increase until around the age of 12, where it seems to peak. It then appears to plateau for about two years, decrease moderately during adolescence, and then remain stable during early and middle adulthood. Thus, using a standardized measurement scale, there is no way to identify the highly hypnotizable child before age 4. The result of this is that the hypnotic ability of very young children remains unclear, with research and scale data for children aged 3 and under lacking.

Controversies concerning childhood hypnotic ability

Over the past 25 years, controversy has emerged over the hypnotic ability of very young children and Gardner and Olness (1981) suggested that it was underestimated. However, as previously noted, available scales do not show children of 4 to 6 to be as hypnotizable as older children and the SHCS:C scales are not applicable for children younger than 4. Hilgard and Morgan (1978) have used the term 'protohypnosis' to describe the external distraction (i.e. listening to a story) experienced by children under 4 (in contrast to self-controlled fantasy).

However, this controversy has been fueled by the reports of successful clinical applications of hypnotherapeutic techniques with preschool children (Olness and Gardner, 1988). For example, hypnotherapy has been successfully used to treat a variety of problems in preschool children including enuresis and encopresis (Olness, 1975, 1976), and behavior disorders (Williams and Singh, 1976) and to provide anesthesia (Antitch, 1967).

Reports of successful therapeutic outcomes in very young children suggest two thought-provoking explanations. The first is that positive therapeutic outcomes are related to some aspect of the therapeutic setting beyond the hypnotic procedures. This line of reasoning is congruent with the idea that hypnotizability simply has not developed in very young children to a degree sufficient to measure and/or account for therapeutic change. A second explanation is that for some young children hypnosis is sufficient to facilitate therapeutic change. These may be children who can use their skills in daydreaming, fantasy and imaginative involvement to respond to direct or indirect suggestions. Their responsiveness may not be appropriately tapped or measured by the current scales because of the child's inability to comply due to the demands of the items used. Many of these items are based on ideas of adult hypnotizability and adapted as markers of responsiveness in children. Perhaps these same children are individuals who measure as high in hypnotic ability when it can be validated by scales in later childhood.

In an attempt to better understand the peak in hypnotizability scores for children between the ages of 8 and 12, London (1962) conducted an intriguing study. The study was designed to evaluate the use of role-playing or simulation by children during this peak period of hypnotizability. Using 40 children between the ages of 5 and 11, London gave simulating instructions based on the motivation instructions designed by Orne (1959) for simulation paradigms with adults. Results indicated that the children below 8 years of age were poor simulators with lower scores on the CHSS Part II. For the older children in the study, simulation was indistinguishable from hypnotic performance. London theorized that the peak in hypnotic performance seen in the 8-to-12-year-olds could be partly related to their abilities to simulate hypnosis. In an effort to follow instructions, to comply with adult wishes, and to demonstrate mastery, children can successfully simulate hypnosis. Unfortunately, it seems that no follow-up research using a simulation paradigm was conducted by London, nor has it been followed up by others since. Based on London's study, it could be questioned as to whether the highly hypnotizable children, as identified by the available scales, are all truly 'high' in hypnotic ability or whether the peaking of hypnotizability scores between the ages of 8 and 12 reflects increased simulation ability combined with the motivation to please and to succeed at the task at hand.

In attempting to explain the adolescent decline in hypnotizability, Hilgard (1970) posited the adolescent's need to develop reality-based competencies and achievements as a factor in reducing the imaginative involvement important in hypnotizability. Thus, it may also be that the playful abilities of childhood are replaced by societal pressure for learning and living with reality. However, if London's (1962) findings of greater simulation in the 8-to-12-year-olds prove to be replicable, an alternative hypothesis is simply that as children move into adolescence their need to please and follow adult instructions diminishes, leading to reduced simulation of hypnosis, and this may account for their decline in hypnotizability.

Theoretical views of the development of hypnotic ability during childhood

Genetic theory

In order to explore the role of genetics in hypnotic ability, Morgan et al. (1970) undertook a study that examined families (both twin and non-twin families) and the correlation of hypnotizability scores between family members. Although the number of families in the preliminary report was limited (80 families), the methodology was rigorous. Children (age 5 and over) were tested separately from parents and siblings. Parents completed rating scales for each child.

Interestingly, while this study found mothers to be more susceptible than fathers, there were no sex differences in susceptibility between their sons and daughters. When the researchers compared the hypnotizability of monozygotic twins to that of dizygotic twins and siblings, the correlation of the monozygotic pairs was significantly higher than the correlation of dizygotic pairs and siblings. Despite the higher correspondence of hypnotic ability, the mean hypnotizability score was lower for the monozygotic pairs than for the dizygotic pairs. Fathers' and sons' hypnotizability scores were positively correlated, but there was no clear evidence for a simple genetic theory of hypnotizability.

Inherited abilities theory

An inherited abilities view of hypnotic ability has recently been postulated by Vandenberg (1998a, 1998b). This theory differs from the genetic theory in that it does not address the mode of transmission of hypnotic ability. Rather, it focuses on an earlier emergence of evidence of hypnotic ability and attempts to identify these precursors.

It has traditionally been believed that hypnotic responsiveness emerges some time after the age of 3 (Hilgard and LeBaron, 1984). Vandenberg cites newer research on infant communication as evidence that possible precursors of hypnotic ability are identifiable in the first years of life. He undertakes this task by first using current research to demonstrate that infants possess capacities on the non-verbal plane of communication that are analogous to those required for hypnosis. He notes that infants are able to engage in primitive, nonverbal exchanges and that this inter-subjectivity involves an impetus to be with others and to be influenced by others. Thus, adult caregivers control much of the communication with infants, influence the infant's experiences, and set the rules for communicative exchanges.

Vandenberg then identifies situations in infancy where the infant's communicative capacities are used in a manner paralleling the hypnotic context. These communicative features are viewed as analogous to those found in hypnosis, where one person establishes the agenda, shapes the pattern of exchanges and orients and influences another's perceptions and responses. Continuing along this line, Vandenberg notes that the demands of the hypnotic setting are often indirectly expressed through the use of voice tone, pacing, eye gaze, posture, and so on, as is the case with the growing infant's communication. By controlling discourse, the adult caregiver holds sway over what is important and how reality is defined, as does the hypnotist.

As the infant develops greater communicative skill during the second year of life, issues of complex emotions such a guilt, shame, and pride come into play. These may be the developmental precursors of the desire to please and to avoid embarrassment, the need for internal consistency, and performance appraisal, all associated with hypnotic responding. Similarly, the emergence of play, the implicit understanding of paradoxical intention, and the ability to dissociate behavior from its usual intention (e.g. should a nip be considered playful or aggressive?) have hypnotic parallels in amnesia, hallucination, hidden observer, and anesthesia.

Finally, Vandenberg postulates that identification of the factors that contribute to different responses from infants in these early communicative exchanges with adult caretakers may provide clues to the developmental precursors of individual differences in hypnotic responsiveness in later life. He cites attachment and temperament research (Kagan, 1989; Sroufe et al., 1993), identifying these as relatively stable attributes that influence a variety of psychological outcomes. While it is clear that the relationship between the infant's attributes and hypnotic responding is not linear, research on these factors may provide some insight into their roles. Greater understanding of the role of a variety of developmental factors in hypnotic responsiveness will require consideration of the transactional context in development.

Existential–phenomenological model

An existential–phenomenological model of hypnotizability during childhood emphasizes the child's uncritical experience of events to account for the greater hypnotic ability of children (Cowles, 1998). This view utilizes Piaget's work, which suggests that children do not develop a cognitive framework or schema until they reach the formal operational thinking stage at about age 11 or 12 (Piaget and Inhelder, 1969). Prior to that time, events are experienced without the filtration and evaluation of cognitive schemas that organize, classify and categorize information that characterizes adolescent and adult thinking. It is postulated that the phenomenon of hypnosis in children is the same phenomenon studied in adults (Plotnick et al., 1991). This view is based on using various correlates that predict hypnotizability in adults (absorption, creativity, vividness of imagery, social desirability, dissociative capacity, etc.) and applying them to children. The greater hypnotic responsiveness found with children is then attributed to the child's experience of the hypnotic state. While this view is intriguing and intuitively logical, it does not address individual differences in hypnotizability in adulthood. In order for this view to be sustained, it requires a mechanism to explain why the decline in hypnotizability during adolescence varies, leaving some with high hypnotizability as they enter adulthood and others with low or moderate hypnotizability. To date, it appears that the issues of individual differences remain unaddressed.

Developmental events and fantasy-proneness

In 1981 Wilson and Barber identified a 'personality type', which they identified as 'fantasy-prone personalities' (see also discussions of this in Chapters 3 and 8). These individuals were characterized by extensive and deep fantasy involvement, and were also excellent hypnotic subjects. During intensive interviews of their subjects, Wilson and Barber found that fantasizers reported finding several childhood pathways that appeared to facilitate high hypnotizability and fantasy involvement. Fantasizers often described encouragement to fantasize from a parent, grandparent, teacher or other significant adult. They reported childhood involvement in activities such as ballet, piano or dramatics. Many perceived themselves as having been lonely and isolated as children. They reported that fantasy helped them to cope with feeling alone and provided companionship and entertainment. Finally, a number of the women interviewed by Wilson and Barber reported a difficult childhood that included physical abuse, parental mental illness or desertion of the family by a parent.

Despite the importance of Wilson and Barber's findings, the absence of quantitative measures of their constructs of punishment, loneliness, parental encouragement of imaginative activities, and the use of fantasy for coping, as well as other methodological issues limited the generalizabililty of their findings. To address these shortcomings and to better understand fantasy-proneness and its relationship to hypnotizability, Rhue and Lynn (1987) undertook a large-scale construct validation study of fantasy-proneness.

Subjects were divided into high fantasy-prones (21), medium fantasy-prones (20), and low fantasy-prones (18), based on the screening of over 1400 subjects using the Inventory of Childhood Memories and Imaginings (ICMI) of Wilson and Barber (1981). The high and low fantasy groups represented the upper and lower 4 percent, respectively, of the population tested. These criteria were based on Wilson and Barber's contention that their high fantasizers represented the upper 4 percent of the population.

In addition to securing strong support for the construct of fantasy-proneness, Rhue and Lynn (1987) explored the developmental antecedents of fantasy-proneness and examined its relationship to hypnotizability in young adulthood. The high-fantasy-prone subjects differed from the comparison groups on their recollections of punishment, their interpretation of their punishment, and their reported fantasy activities related to punishment. Severe physical punishment (e.g. bruises, bleeding or broken bones) was reported by six of the fantasy-prone subjects, while no other subjects reported such abuse. The fantasy-prone subjects also reported more frequent and severe physical punishment than did the comparison groups. These findings are congruent with the results reported by Wilson and Barber (1981) and Hilgard (1974) using subjects that were chosen based on hypnotizability.

Beyond the measures of physical punishment, high fantasy subjects reported being hit more during childhood even if they were good, greater use of their imaginations to block the pain of punishment, and having more thoughts of revenge toward the person who punished them. They also reported that they would punish their own children less severely than the comparison groups. Fantasy-prones did know why they were punished as much as did the medium and low fantasy-prones, possibly indicating that parents supplied a rationale to their children across the levels of punishment. Surprisingly, high fantasy-prones were as positive about their early home environments as the comparison groups. Perhaps, their fantasy involvement provided a tool to rationalize a positive view of a punishing childhood environment. The overall pattern of results is congruent with the view that fantasy may serve an adaptive, adjustive function for individuals who have experienced aversive and punishing environments as children.

In looking at other aspects of the childhood of high fantasy subjects, Rhue and Lynn found that the fantasizers reported greater loneliness, enjoyed imaginary games and enjoyed playing alone more, and with friends less, than did subjects in the other groups. These findings suggest that, as children, high fantasizers differed in their fantasy use and that it served as a preferred play outlet as well as providing a compensatory and adaptive function. In another phase of the study (Rhue and Lynn, 1986), fantasy-prones were found to project greater hostility on the Rorschach, although they did not differ from others on projected anxiety and reality testing. Minnesota Multiphasic Personality Inventory profiles of fantasy-prones suggested greater conflict alienation and more unusual experiences than the comparison groups. The fact that these subjects were college students whose grade point did not differ from the comparison groups and who exhibited no obvious psychopathology is supportive of Kris's (1952) adaptive regression view. That is, Kris hypothesized that some individuals may regularly use fantasy and imagination adaptively to cope effectively and to channel unwanted impulses. It may be that fantasy and imagination, which are prevalent during childhood, are first tools and then become a lifestyle that extends from childhood through adulthood.

Less congruent with previous work (Hilgard, 1974) was Rhue and Lynn's finding that high fantasy-prones reported no greater parental encouragement than others to fantasize or special life situations that might foster extensive involvement in fantasy. While fantasy-prones did report greater encouragement to read than others, it was unclear what in particular they were reading. Despite the group findings, *some* of Rhue and Lynn's high fantasy-prones did report histories of parental encouragement of imaginative involvement.

Rhue and Lynn's findings on fantasy-proneness suggest largely separate pathways from childhood into adult fantasy-proneness and the likelihood of high hypnotizability, although they are not mutually exclusive. One of these pathways is parental encouragement and the other is severe punishment. Among the fantasy-prones who endorsed parental encouragement to imagine (eight subjects), only two reported severe punishment. Of the fantasy-prones (six subjects) who reported abuse, only two endorsed parental encouragement to imagine. Despite strongly emphasized requests for honesty in the Rhue and Lynn study, the reliability of their data is limited by the retrospective nature of the study. It will be important to identify children high in fantasy and hypnotizability and to better understand the factors that facilitate and sustain the development of these skills.

Practical applications of hypnosis with children

Aside from the conceptual challenge of understanding the developmental antecedents of hypnotizability for the sake of pure knowledge, it is important to understand these antecedents for pragmatic reasons. Over the past 35 to 40 years, increasing recognition has been given to the clinical application of hypnotic procedures to the treatment of children and adolescents. In the past dozen years, a number of books have devoted chapters or entire volumes to child hypnosis issues (Olness and Kohen, 1996; Rhue et al., 1993; Wester and O'Grady, 1991). Much of this has occurred in response to the increasing recognition of the value of hypnotic procedures in the treatment of childhood psychopathologies and medical problems.

Unfortunately, the emerging interest in the application of clinical hypnotic procedures with children has not been partnered with an array of well-controlled studies that would support its efficacy. In a review of the research on clinical hypnosis with children, Milling and Costantino (2000) examined a number of studies broken down into five content areas: (a) learning problems, (b) basic physiological processes, (c) general medical problems, (d) nausea and emesis from chemotherapy, and (e) acute pain. Findings from studies cited in each of the above areas suggested that hypnotic techniques were associated with positive results in reducing test anxiety (Stanton, 1994), in controlling skin temperature (Dikel and Olness, 1980), in increasing the presence of immunoglobulin IgA (when combined with relaxation) (Olness et al., 1989), in increasing lung functioning and adjustment in paediatric cystic fibrosis patients, in treating nocturnal enuresis (Banerjee et al., 1993; Edwards and van der Spuy,

1985), in controlling nausea and emesis (Jacknow et al., 1994; Zeltzer et al., 1984), and in pain control (Kutter et al., 1988; Smith et al., 1996).

Despite these overall positive findings, many of these studies did not meet the empirically supported therapies (EST) criteria set forth by Chambless and Hollon (1998). More specifically, the failure to use treatment manuals was a problem in otherwise impressive studies, and appears to be a problem throughout the child hypnosis literature. Surprisingly, much of the literature available for the above review related to the treatment of acute pain and chemotherapy distress, with virtually no controlled studies of hypnotic techniques for children's emotional or behavioral problems. It appears valid to conclude that research on the use of clinical hypnosis with children is in an early stage of development and that increased methodological rigor will be important in future research if conclusions as to its efficacy are to be reached.

Summary perspective

During the preparation of this chapter on the highly hypnotizable child, I encountered exciting and stimulating hypotheses and well-designed and carefully conducted studies, many of which were conducted 25 years ago or more. Childhood hypnotizability and imagination has always been a topic of personal interest. The impetus to examine the available research on hypnotizability in children, with particular attention to the highly hypnotizable child, and then to present it to you, the reader, in a useful and organized way has proved to be an enlightening, meaningful, and sometimes frustrating journey. The attention to careful interpretation of the results of that research followed by the presentation of thought-provoking hypotheses has deepened my respect for the work of J.R. Hilgard, Gardner, Olness, London, Morgan, E.R. Hilgard, and many others. However, the overall result of my research journey has led me to present you with many more unanswered questions and tantalizing possibilities than definitive deductions.

It is clear that there is a pressing need for additional research to buttress and expand our understanding of the developmental pathways to high hypnotizability. The causes of the paucity of new hypnosis studies with children may reflect the notable hurdles encountered by the researcher rather than any lack of interest in the topic. Faced with stringent research review boards, consent forms that continue for pages, and the myths of hypnosis as a form of mind-control, many young researchers are reluctant to shoulder the burden of a well-meaning but rigorous system of safeguards. Additionally, many parents' knowledge of hypnosis is based on misconceptions fostered by stage shows and movies where the hypnotized individual is depicted as a weak, zombie-like figure, controlled by others. Given these perspectives, most parents initially refuse to have their children participate in hypnosis studies without considerable education as to value and positive aspects of hypnosis.

It is my hope that you take away from this chapter a newfound interest in how we identify, research and conceptualize hypnotic ability in children. The applications of our understanding hold the potential to provide more widely accepted techniques for medical treatments for children, positive pathways for dealing with stress and trauma during childhood, and greater recognition of the positive aspects of fantasy, imagination, and hypnotizability

References

Allen, D. (1985) 'Hypnotic responsiveness in children', unpublished doctoral dissertation, University of Wyoming, *Dissertation Abstracts International*, 46:2451B.

Antich, J.L.S. (1967) 'The use of hypnosis in pediatric anesthesia', *Journal of the American Society of Psychosomatic Dentistry and Medicine*, 14:70–5.

Banerjee, S., Srivastav, A. and Palan, B.M. (1993) 'Hypnosis and self-hypnosis in the management of nocturnal enuresis: A comparative study with Imipramine therapy', *American Journal of Clinical Hypnosis*, 36:113–19.

Barber, T.X. and Calverley, D.S. (1963) ' "Hypnotic-like" suggestibility in children', *Journal of Abnormal and Social Psychology*, 66:589–97.

Brown, G.W., Summers, D., Coffman, B., Riddell, R. and Poulsen, B. (1996) 'The use of hypnotherapy with school-age children: Five case studies', *Psychotherapy in Private Practice*, 15:53–65.

Chambless, D.L. and Hollon, S.D. (1998) 'Defining empirically supported therapies', *Journal of Consulting and Clinical Psychology*, 66:7–18.

Cowles, R.S. (1998) 'The magic of hypnosis: Is it child's play?', *The Journal of Psychology*, 132:357–66.

Dikel, W. and Olness, K. (1980) 'Self-hypnosis, biofeedback, and voluntary peripheral temperature control in children', *Pediatrics*, 66:335–40.

Edwards, S.D. and van der Spuy, H.I. (1985) Hypnotherapy as a treatment for enuresis', *Journal of Child Psychology and Psychiatry*, 26:161–70.

Erickson, M.H. (1959) 'Further techniques of hypnosis: Utilization techniques', *American Journal of Clinical Hypnosis*, 2:3–21.

Gardner, G.G. (1974) 'Hypnosis with children', *International Journal of Clinical and Experimental Hypnosis*, 22:20–38.

—— and Hinton, R.M. (1980) 'Hypnosis with children', in G.D. Burrows and L. Dennerstein (eds), *Handbook of Hypnosis and Psychosomatic Medicine*, New York: Elsevier/North-Holland Biomedical Press.

—— and Olness, K. (1981) *Hypnosis and Hypnotherapy with Children*, New York: Grune and Stratton.

Groos, K. (1901) *The Play of Man*, New York: Appleton. Cited in J.L. Singer (1973) *The Child's World of Make-believe*, New York: Academic Press.

Hilgard, J.R. (1970) *Personality and Hypnosis: A Study of Imaginative Involvement*, Chicago: University of Chicago Press.

—— (1974) 'Imaginative involvement: Some characteristics of the highly hypnotizable and nonhypnotizable', *International Journal of Clinical and Experimental Hypnosis*, 22:138–56.

—— (1979) 'Imaginative and sensory-affective involvements: In everyday life and hypnosis', in E. Fromm and R. Shor (eds), *Hypnosis: Developments in Research and New Perspectives*, New York: Aldine.

—— and LeBaron, S. (1984) *Hypnotherapy of Pain in Children with Cancer*, Los Altos, CA: W. Kaufmann.

—— and Morgan, A.H. (1978) 'Treatment of anxiety and pain in childhood cancer through hypnosis', in F.H. Frankel and H.S. Zamansky (eds), *Hypnosis at its Bicentennial: Selected Papers*, New York: Plenum Press.

Jacknow, D.S., Tschann, J.M., Link, M.P. and Boyce, W.T. (1994) 'Hypnosis in the prevention of chemotherapy-related nausea and vomiting in children: A prospective study', *Developmental and Behavioral Pediatrics*, 15:258–64.

Kagan, J. (1989) *Unstable Ideas: Temperament, Cognition, and Self*, Cambridge, MA: Harvard University Press.

Kris, E. (1952) *Psychoanalytic Explorations in Art*, New York: International Universities Press.

Kutter, L., Bowman, M. and Teasdale, M. (1988) 'Psychological treatment of distress, pain, and anxiety for young children with cancer', *Journal of Developmental and Behavioral Pediatrics*, 9:374–81.

LeBaron, S., Zeltzer, L. and Fankurik, D. (1988) 'Imaginative involvement and hypnotic susceptibility in childhood', *International Journal of Clinical and Experimental Hypnosis*, 36:284–95.

London, P. (1962) 'Hypnosis in children: An experimental approach', *International Journal of Clinical and Experimental Hypnosis*, 10:79–91.

—— (1963) *Children's Hypnotic Susceptibility Scale*, Palo Alto, CA: Consulting Psychologists Press.

—— (1965) 'Developmental experiments in hypnosis', *Journal of Projective Techniques and Personality Assessment*, 29:189–99.

Lynn, S. and Rhue, J.W. (1986) 'The fantasy-prone person: Hypnosis, imagination, and creativity', *Journal of Personality and Social Psychology*, 51:404–8.

Milling, L. and Costantino, C (2000) 'Clinical hypnosis with children: First steps toward empirical support', *International Journal of Clinical and Experimental Hypnosis*, 48:113–37.

Morgan, A.H. and Hilgard, E.R. (1973) 'Age differences in susceptibility to hypnosis', *International Journal of Clinical and Experimental Hypnosis*, 21:78–85.

—— and Hilgard, J.R. (1978–9) 'The Stanford Hypnotic Clinical Scale for Children', *American Journal of Clinical Hypnosis*, 21:148–69.

—— Hilgard, E.R. and Davert, E.C. (1970) 'The heritability of hypnotic susceptibility of twins: A preliminary report', *Behavior Genetics*, 1:213–24.

Olness, K. (1975) 'The use of self-hypnosis in the treatment of childhood nocturnal enuresis: A report on forty patients', *Clinical Pediatrics*, 14:273–9.

—— (1976) 'Autohypnosis in functional megacolon in children', *American Journal of Clinical Hypnosis*, 19:28–32.

—— and Gardner, G.G. (1988) *Hypnosis and Hypnotherapy with Children*, 2nd edn, Philadelphia: Grune and Stratton.

—— and Kohen, D.J. (1996) *Hypnosis and Hypnotherapy with Children*, 3rd edn, New York: Guilford Press.

—— Culbert, T. and Uden, D. (1989) 'Self-regulation of salivary immunoglobulin A by children', *Pediatrics*, 83:66–71.

Orne, M.T. (1959) 'The nature of hypnosis: Artifact and essence', *Journal of Abnormal and Social Psychology*, 58:277–99.

Piaget, J. and Inhelder, B. (1969) *The Psychology of the Child*, New York: Basic Books.

Plotnick, A.B., Payne, P.A. and O'Grady, D.J. (1991) 'Correlates of hypnotizability in children: Absorption, vividness of imagery, fantasy play and social desirability', *American Journal of Clinical Hypnosis*, 34:51–58.

Rhue, J.W. and Lynn, S.J. (1986) 'Fantasy-proneness and psychopathology', *Journal of Personality and Social Psychology*, 53:327–36.

—— and Lynn, S.J. (1987) 'Fantasy-proneness: Developmental antecedents', *Journal of Personality*, 55:121–37.

—— Lynn, S.J. and Kirsch, I. (eds) (1993) *Handbook of Clinical Hypnosis*, Washington, DC: American Psychological Association.

Singer, J.L. (1973) *The Child's World of Make Believe*, New York, Academic Press.

Smith, J.T., Barabasz, A. and Barabasz, M. (1996) 'Comparison of hypnosis and distraction in severely ill children undergoing painful medical procedures', *Journal of Counseling Psychology*, 43:187–95.

Sroufe, L.A., Carlson, E. and Shulman, S. (1993) 'The development of individuals in relationships: From infancy through adolescence', in D.C. Funder, R. Parke, C. Tomlinson-Keesey and K. Widaman (eds), *Studying Lives through Time: Approaches to Personality and Development* (pp. 315–42), Washington, DC: American Psychological Association.

Stanton, H. (1994) 'Self-hypnosis: One path to reduced test anxiety', *Contemporary Hypnosis*, 11:14–18.

Vandenberg, B. (1998a) 'Infant communication and the development of hypnotic responsiveness', *International Journal of Clinical and Experimental Hypnosis*, 46:334–50.

—— (1998b) 'Hypnosis and human development: Interpersonal influence of intrapersonal processes', *Child Development*, 69:262–7.

Weitzenhoffer, A.M. and Hilgard, E.R. (1959) *Stanford Hypnotic Susceptibility Scales, Forms A and B*, Palo Alto, CA: Consulting Psychologists Press.

Wester, W.C. and O'Grady, D.J. (eds) (1991) *Clinical Hypnosis with Children*, New York: Brunner/Mazel.

Williams, D.T. and Singh, M. (1976) 'Hypnosis as a facilitating therapeutic adjunct in child psychiatry', *Journal of the American Academy of Child Psychiatry*, 15:326–42.

Wilson, S.C. and Barber, T.X. (1981) 'Vivid fantasy and hallucinatory abilities in the life histories of excellent hypnotic subjects ("somnambules"): Preliminary report with female subjects', in E. Klinger (ed.), *Imagery (Vol. 2): Concepts, Results, and Applications* (pp. 133–49), New York: Plenum.

Zeltzer, L., LeBaron, S. and Zeltzer, P.M. (1984) 'The effectiveness of behavioral intervention for reducing nausea and vomiting in children and adolescents receiving chemotherapy', *Journal of Clinical Oncology*, 2:683–90.

Chapter 6

Neurophysiological and genetic determinants of high hypnotizability

James E. Horton and Helen J. Crawford

Introduction

The purpose of this chapter is to review what is known about the neurophysiological and genetic bases of hypnotic susceptibility, with an emphasis on the highly hypnotizable individual. We draw from studies of behavioral genetics, attentional processing and electrophysiological functioning (electroencephalographic and event-related potentials). We also cite hemodynamic evidence from positron emission tomography (PET) and functional magnetic resonance imaging (fMRI) studies, but do not consider this in detail. Much like other general reviews (Crawford, 1994a, 1994b, 1996, 1999, 2001; Crawford and Gruzelier, 1992; Crawford et al., 1998a, 1998b, 1999; Gruzelier, 1998; Raz and Shapiro, 2002), we hope it encourages new researchers to pursue this fascinating field.

The concentration of this edited book upon the *highly* hypnotizable individual is important. E.R. Hilgard called the highly hypnotizable individual a 'virtuoso', indicating a potential uniqueness about him or her in comparison to the moderate or low hypnotizable individual. Several studies (Green et al., 1992; Register and Kihlstrom, 1986) point out the unique responding of the very highly hypnotizable (those who score 11 or 12 on the cognitively oriented Stanford Hypnotic Susceptibility Scale, Form C; SHSS:C; Weitzenhoffer and Hilgard, 1962) and the importance of screening for and including such individuals in research.

We are in agreement with others that hypnotic responding involves at least two mechanisms (e.g. Hilgard, 1965, 1977/1986; Tellegen, 1979; Weitzenhoffer, 1962). There is a 'social suggestibility' which is influenced by expectations, context effects and other influences; this is most obvious among those who are low responders to hypnotic suggestions. Furthermore, there is a 'true' hypnotic responsiveness which is the essence of hypnosis (e.g. Hilgard, 1973). As the Hilgards (1975/1983/1994) pointed out in their classic book, *Hypnosis in the Relief of Pain*, suggestions for hypnotic analgesia have a relaxing, distress-reducing component available to both low and high hypnotizable individuals. However, the ability to reduce or eliminate the perception of sensory pain and distress is more uniquely limited to highly hypnotizable individuals. Similarly, Balthazard and Woody (1992) demonstrated that absorption is correlated with only the most difficult hypnotic items on standardized scales, the ones only highly hypnotizable individuals are able to experience. More recently, Woody et al. (1997) showed that 'easy hypnotic performances depend on some kind of social suggestibility not unique to hypnosis, and this factor becomes less important as the difficulty of the hypnotic performances increases' (p. 399). Thus, the more difficult hypnotic tasks are more dependent on the neurophysiological and genetic substrates of 'true' hypnotic responsiveness rather than those of 'social suggestibility'.

Given these caveats, it is crucial that studies of the behavioral and neurophysiological correlates of hypnotic responsiveness include highly hypnotizable virtuosos within their sample, as well as moderate to low hypnotizable individuals. The extra effort taken to screen one's participants adequately with appropriate hypnotic susceptibility scales and to include the rarer hypnotic virtuosos ensures a methodologically sound study (Barabasz and Barabasz, 1992; Crawford and Gruzelier, 1992; Hilgard, 1965).

A genetic basis to hypnotic susceptibility

Hypnotic responsiveness is as stable as personality or intelligence (Morgan et al., 1974), even over a 25-year period (Piccione et al., 1989). This stability suggests an underlying genetic factor. A twin study by Morgan et al. (1970; see also Morgan, 1973), using the standardized Stanford hypnotic susceptibility scales, found compelling support for this hypothesis. In this study, an intraclass correlation of $r_i = 0.63$ ($n = 35$, $p = 0.001$) for the hypnotizability of monozygotic twins was obtained, although no significant correlation was found for same-sexed dizygotic twin pairs and other fraternal pairs. Similarly, in a Russian study, Bauman and Bul' (1981) found a hypnotizability concordance rate of 78.3 per cent in 60 pairs of twins, using a measure derived from participants' responses to three different 'stages' of hypnosis.

In a recent Israeli study (Lichtenberg et al., 2000), the genetic underpinnings of hypnotic susceptibility was examined by evaluating catechol O-methytransferase (COMT), a genotype that predicts performance on prefrontal executive cognition and working memory tasks (for review, see Weinberger et al., 2001) and is involved in dopaminergic and noradrenergic (but not serotonergic) metabolism (Karoum et al., 1994). Several studies of attention deficit/ hyperactivity disorder (ADHD) (Eisenberg et al., 1999) and obsessive-compulsive disorder (Karayiorgou et al., 1997), both disorders of attention, have found associations with COMT. When participants were tested for the high/low enzyme activity COMT polymorphisms, Lichtenberg et al. (2000) found a significant difference between the COMT val/val, val/met and met/met genotypes on hypnotizability.[1] Individuals with COMT val/val genotypes were significantly lower in hypnotizability than those with val/met or met/ met COMT genotypes. This was observable among women but not men and therefore deserves replication. Interestingly, Fossella et al. (2002) found that individuals who carry the val/val genotype along with a certain monoamine oxidase genotype (4/4) score significantly lower on a measure of executive attention. Since genetic modeling studies propose that many genes may underlie complex traits, as seen in Fossella et al., future hypnosis work needs to examine simultaneously various candidate genes that appear to be associated with attentional networks, particularly those associated with executive control.

Further evidence of a familial component in hypnotizability is provided by the work of Wallace and Persanyi (1989). They found that college students with left-handed relatives were significantly lower in hypnotic responsiveness than those with immediate right-handed relatives. Interestingly, the left-handed relatives were lower in responsiveness when tested than the right-handed relatives.

Even from a genetic perspective, socio-environmental factors are important in our understanding of the predictors of hypnotizability. Black and Greenough (1991) emphasized the importance of socio-environmental influences on genetic predispositions, and

[1] Two genetic forms of the enzyme are found in humans, one with the amino acid valine (val). The other with the amino acid methionine (met). As all individuals have two genes for each of their proteins, there are three possible forms of COMT: val/val, val/met, or met/met.

suggested that genetic predispositions, as evidenced by genomes, 'expect' to encounter certain types of environmental stimuli and are subsequently dependent on those stimuli for development. If these socio-environmental influences are not encountered, neural development may proceed in another direction. If one applies this analysis here, it may be concluded that heritability factors in hypnotizability are plastic and can be influenced by each individual's unique physical and social environment (e.g. J.R. Hilgard, 1970/1979; Nadon et al., 1989; Woody et al., 1992).

High hypnotizability and enhanced attentional processing

Although perception is commonly thought of as being conscious, it is clear that much information processing is done outside of awareness (Hilgard, 1977/1986; James, 1890; Velmans, 2000). Experiments on the timing of conscious awareness suggest that consciousness does not arise until at least 200 ms after a stimulus arrives at the cortex (Libet, 1996). In the time window between the arrival of a stimulus at the cortex (9 ms for an auditory sound) and the actual conscious perception of a stimulus, complex inhibitory and excitatory processes have worked in concert in various cortical and subcortical brain systems. In this way, the system is able to select some sources of information for conscious processing, while preventing others from entering conscious awareness. These processes of selection and inhibition are controlled by the attentional systems of the brain. It is quite apparent that there are individual differences in the abilities to focus or divide attention, sustain vigilance over time, or be diffuse in one's scanning of the environment. The relationship between individual differences in attentional abilities and hypnotizability, as well as shifts in attentional processing strategies during hypnosis, have been addressed in a number of studies using a diverse range of methodologies.

Given that hypnosis involves often readjusting one's attentional and/or disattentional state, diffusely or selectively, it is not surprising that hypnotic susceptibility is a cognitive trait that correlates with sustained and focused attentional abilities (Crawford, 1982; Crawford et al., 1993a; Hoyt et al., 1989; Lyons and Crawford, 1997; Roche and McConkey, 1990; Tellegen and Atkinson, 1974; Zachariae et al., 2000). At the behavioral level, attentional performance differences are noted in waking (Atkinson and Crawford, 1992; Crawford, 1982;

Crawford et al., 1993a; Wallace, 1986, 1988, 1990; Wallace and Patterson, 1984; Wallace et al., 1994) and hypnotic conditions (e.g. Crawford, 1996; Crawford and Allen, 1983; Crawford et al., 1983, Walker et al., 1976; Wallace, 1979). In the absence of a hypnotic induction, high hypnotizables show a greater susceptibility to visual illusions and reversible figures such as the Necker cube (Crawford et al., 1993a; Wallace, 1988; Wallace and Priebe, 1985), increased after-image persistence (Atkinson and Crawford, 1992; Wallace, 1979), and a greater ability to detect embedded words among a letter array (Wallace et al., 1994).

In factor-analytic studies, hypnotic susceptibility loads most strongly on a 'deeply involved and absorptive sustained attentional' factor (e.g. Crawford et al., 1993a; Lichtenberg et al., 2004; Lyons and Crawford, 1997). Attentional abilities loading on this factor are assessed by the Tellegen Absorption Scale, known to assess 'a disposition for having episodes of "total" attention that fully engage one's representational (i.e. perceptual, enactive, imaginative, and ideational) resources' (Tellegen and Atkinson, 1974, p. 268), and the Differential Attentional Processes Inventory's subscale of extremely focused attention (Crawford et al., 1993a; Lyons and Crawford, 1997). Recently, Lichtenberg et al. (2004) found that the persistence trait personality dimension from Cloninger's (1987) Tridimensional Personality Questionnaire also loaded on this factor and was related to hypnotic susceptibility. This dimension is characterized by a tendency to persevere despite frustration, and not to become discouraged and give up when expectations are not immediately satisfied. Persistence is thought to have a biological basis (Cloninger, 1994).

We suggest that the enhanced attentional abilities of highly hypnotizable individuals are underpinned by the involvement of a more effective 'executive control' anterior fronto-limbic system, which interacts with parietal and other brain regions (Crawford, 1996; Crawford and Gruzelier, 1992; Crawford et al., 1998a, 1998b, 1998c, 1999, 2000). During hypnosis, shifts of attention and disattention, as well as sustained attentional or disattentional processing, may be due to differences in the anterior fronto-limbic system. Crawford (1996), for example, proposed that hypnotic analgesia involves the anterior frontal cortex in an 'inhibitory feedback circuit that cooperates in the regulation of thalamo-cortical activities' (pp. 269).

Neuroimaging studies demonstrate that, during hypnotic analgesia, highly hypnotizable individuals have more physiological flexibility involving an active inhibitory process of supervisory, executive control by the anterior frontal cortex, which interacts with and modulates the anterior cingulate and other parts of the brain. Although this proposal goes beyond the scope of this chapter, it should be noted that support is found for this proposal in studies using fMRI (Crawford et al., 1998a, 1998c, 2000), PET (Faymonville et al., 2000; Maquet et al., 1999; Rainville et al., 1997, 1999; Wik et al., 1999), and regional cerebral blood flow (Crawford et al., 1993b), and in electrophysiological studies (e.g. Crawford et al., 1998a, 1998b, 1998d; De Pascalis and Perrone, 1996; Kropotov et al., 1997; Spiegel et al., 1989).

If our proposal is correct, reaction times should be faster among highly hypnotizable individuals, since the frontal attention system is important in guiding or inhibiting future responses (e.g. Stuss et al., 1995). Indeed, G. Stanley Hall (1883) found that reaction time became faster and more uniform during hypnosis, and he concluded this was due to enhanced focused attention. Highs may demonstrate faster reaction times than lows in simple response (Braffman and Kirsch, 2001). In a successive visual memory discrimination task, Crawford and Allen (1983) found highs exhibited faster responses than lows, both with and without a hypnotic induction. Similarly, Mészáros and his associates (e.g. Mészáros et al., 1989) found that, when identifying differences in visuo-spatial stimuli, high hypnotizables were faster. When engaged in a complex decision-making task involving the identification of faces portraying positive or negative emotions presented to either the right or left visual fields, highs were similarly faster in waking and hypnosis conditions than lows (Crawford et al., 1995).

Interestingly, however, highs are actually slower when performing dual tasks in which one task is accomplished out of awareness (Stevenson, 1976). Similarly, using the classic foreperiod paradigm (where a warning tone precedes a visual stimulus), when instructed to ignore the tone and concentrate on the visual stimulus, highs demonstrated slower reaction times to subsequent visual stimuli than lows (Horton et al., 1998a). This was observed in both the waking condition and following a hypnotic suggestion for deafness. These latter findings support Hilgard's (1977/1986) proposal that keeping a task (or stimuli) out of awareness requires additional attentional resources and cognitive effort.

While brain nerve conduction velocity and brain glucose metabolic rates have yet to be examined, features of brain-evoked potentials have been considered as possible evidence for neural efficiency differences associated with hypnotic susceptibility. Compared to low hypnotizables, highs have demonstrated more effective information processing and faster neural transmission, as indicated by shorter latencies for certain components of auditory, visual and somatosensory evoked potentials (Crawford et al., 1998e; De Pascalis, 1994; Horton et al., 1998b; Lamas and Crawford, 1997; Norby et al., 1999).

Neural systems mediating executive control, such as attention switching and focusing, may involve dopaminergic influences. For instance, a disrupted inhibitory dopaminergic effect at a striatal/ prefrontal level may be involved in some disorders of attention (e.g. Solanto, 2002). Of importance, Spiegel and King (1992) found that cerebrospinal fluid levels of homovanillic acid (HVA), a metabolite of dopamine, correlated with hypnotizability. Lichtenberg et al. (2000) suggested that when the COMT polymorphism that produces less functional enzyme is present, leading to a slower metabolism and higher levels of dopamine, hypnotizability scores tend to be higher.

Electroencephalographic evidence

The capacity to deliberately control attention is critical to higher cognitive functions, and is related to certain aspects of electro-encephalographic (EEG) activity (for a review, see Crawford et al., 1996). A robust finding in the literature is that high hypnotizable individuals generate more theta (3–7 Hz) EEG activity in waking conditions, and even more so during hypnosis, than low hypnotiza-bles (e.g. Akpinar et al., 1971; Crawford, 1990; Galbraith et al., 1970; Graffin et al., 1995; Sabourin et al., 1990; Tebecis et al., 1975; Ulett, et al., 1972a, 1972b; for reviews, see Crawford, 1994a, 1994b, and Crawford and Gruzelier, 1992; but see Williams and Gruzelier, 2001). Increased theta activity in highly hypnotizable individuals has been reported during rest (Graffin et al., 1995; Sabourin et al., 1990), hypnotic suggestions (Sabourin et al., 1990), experiences of pain when focusing on it or under conditions of hypnotic analgesia (Crawford, 1990), and positive and negative emotional states (Crawford et al., 1996). Since increased theta has been associated with cognitive effort and sustained attentional tasks (e.g. Schacter, 1977), increased theta activity among highly hypnotizable individuals is interpreted as reflecting their deeper attentive and absorptive involvement in the assigned task during EEG recordings.

As individuals enter hypnosis, EEG theta power often increases, sometimes in both lows and highs. Thereafter, highs often continue to generate more theta than lows in various brain regions including frontal, central, parietal and occipital (e.g. Crawford, 1990; Graffin et al., 1995; Sabourin et al., 1990). Sabourin et al. (1990) noted theta power increases in *both* hemispheres of the frontal, central and occipital regions during a hypnotic induction and a subsequent series of standardized hypnotic suggestions from the SHSS:C (Weitzenhoffer and Hilgard, 1962). By contrast, Graffin et al. (1995) reported that theta power increased in the posterior areas during an induction, while theta decreased for highs during a subsequent passive hypnotic condition. Within hypnosis, Crawford (1990) found highly hypnotizable persons generated significantly more high theta (5.5–7.5 Hz) than did lows at frontal, temporal, parietal and occipital regions. Highs showed asymmetrical EEG high theta power shifts, particularly in the temporal region. During cold pressor pain, there was a left temporal dominance when focusing on pain, whereas there was a right temporal dominance of theta activity during hypnotic analgesia. Originally, Crawford (1990) suggested a differential involvement of possibly the hippocampal system from which theta may be generated, particularly during vigilant conditions (e.g. Crowne et al., 1972; Michel et al., 1992). We may need to re-evaluate this proposal in light of recent research. For instance, midline frontal theta generated during different mental tasks has been found to have two sources, prefrontal–medial superficial cortex and anterior cingulate cortex (Asada et al., 1999). Furthermore, Asada et al., observed that there was an alternation of neural activity between these two regions, both of which are concerned with attention and allocation of attentional resources.

Hypnosis is not a unitary state and therefore should show different patterns of EEG activity depending upon the task being experienced. In our evaluation of the literature, enhanced theta is observed during hypnosis when there is task performance or concentrative hypnosis (e.g. Crawford, 1990; Graffin et al., 1995; Sabourin et al., 1990), but not when the highly hypnotizable individuals are passively relaxed, somewhat sleepy and/or more diffuse in their attention (Graffin et al., 1995; Williams and Gruzelier, 2001). Further support for this distinction comes from meditation. Like hypnosis, the concentrative state of meditation has long been associated with enhanced theta activity (for review, see Delmonte, 1984). In support of our argument, enhanced theta was observed to a greater extent in concentrative compared to non-concentrative Qigong meditative states (Pan et al., 1994).

In a study of self-generated positive and negative emotional states, Crawford et al. (1996) found that highly hypnotizable individuals showed significantly greater hemispheric asymmetries (right greater than left) in the parietal region in high theta (5.5–7.45 Hz). By contrast, low hypnotizable individuals showed no significant hemispheric differences. Following Heller's (1993) model, greater right parietal activation may reflect greater involvement in emotional states among high hypnotizable individuals than low hypnotizables. Furthermore, they found that high alpha (11.5–13.45 Hz) and beta activity (16.5–25 Hz) were also enhanced in highs. In their review of the literature, they pointed out that these particular frequency bands are associated with sustained attentional processing.

Highs often display greater EEG hemispheric asymmetries and hemispheric specificity for tasks than lows, which may be interpreted as evidence for differences in interhemispheric transfer of information and/or cognitive flexibility. MacLeod-Morgan and Lack (1982; see also De Pascalis and Palumbo, 1986) reported asymmetries in EEG activity, referred to as 'hemispheric specificity', in high but not low hypnotizables while performing tasks during waking and hypnosis. Karlin et al. (1980) reported hemispheric shifts in total EEG power during hypnotic analgesia that were interpreted as greater overall right-hemisphere involvement at the bipolar parieto-occipital region. Also using cold pressor pain, Crawford (1990) found only highly hypnotizable individuals exhibited hemispheric asymmetries of high theta when attending (left greater than right) and ignoring pain (right greater than left) in the anterior temporal region; low hypnotizable participants, in contrast, showed no hemispheric asymmetries and no shifts between conditions (Crawford, 1990, 1994b). Other studies reported greater asymmetries in EEG activity among highly hypnotizable individuals during rest and hypnotic suggestions (Sabourin et al., 1990), self-generated emotional states (Crawford et al., 1996) and painful stimulation (Crawford, 1990; DePascalis and Perrone, 1996).

Implications for future research

An understanding of the neurophysiological bases of hypnotic response is likely to be furthered by interdisciplinary research that bridges the fields of cognitive neuroscience, behavioral genetics, and clinical neuroscience with one another and with social and personality psychology. Increased understanding of the underlying processes involved during hypnotic conditions, through an evaluation of individuals from extremely high to extremely low in hypnotizability, will be obtained from concomitant neuroimaging, neurochemical and behavioral investigations. We must re-emphasize that it is crucial that future research into the neurophysiological correlates of hypnotizability include the highly hypnotizable virtuosos as well as moderate and low hypnotizable individuals. Only then will we be able to understand what Hilgard (1973) referred to as the 'true' hypnotic responsiveness that is the essence of hypnosis.

Attention is pivotal to our understanding highly hypnotizable individuals and how they may differ in their volitional control over behavior from those who are moderately or not at all hypnotizable. William James (1890) noted, 'Everyone knows what attention is. It is the taking possession of the mind in clear and vivid form of one out of what seem several simultaneous objects or trains of thought.' Since then, particularly in the last 30–40 years, studies have pointed out the complexities of attention and that there are attentional networks which orchestrate orienting, engagement and disengagement, and executive control (e.g. Posner and Peterson, 1990; Pribram, 1991; Pribram and McGuinness, 1975). The efficiency of these attentional networks clearly differs across individuals.

We believe that an understanding of the complexities of executive attentional control and the accompanying individual differences that appear to be strongly genetically controlled will assist us in understanding individual differences in hypnotic responsiveness. Furthermore, the studies of hypnotic responsiveness will contribute to our general understanding of individual differences in attentional efficiency. As reviewed in this chapter, there is a tremendous amount of neurophysiological evidence associating sustained and focused attentional abilities with hypnotic susceptibility (Crawford, 1982; Crawford et al., 1993a; Hoyt et al., 1989; Lyons and Crawford, 1997; Roche and McConkey, 1990; Tellegen and Atkinson, 1974; Zachariae et al., 2000), and behavioral evidence of attentional differences in waking (Atkinson and Crawford, 1992; Crawford, 1982; Crawford et al., 1993a; Wallace, 1986, 1988, 1990; Wallace and Patterson, 1984; Wallace et al., 1994) and in hypnotic conditions (e.g. Crawford, 1996; Crawford and Allen, 1983; Crawford et al., 1983; Walker et al., 1976; Wallace, 1979). Additionally, neuroimaging studies with fMRI (Crawford et al., 1998a, 1998c, 2000) and PET (Faymonville et al., 2000; Maquet et al., 1999; Rainville et al., 1997, 1999; Wik et al., 1999) indicate that highly hypnotizable individuals demonstrate more active inhibitory processes of supervisory, executive control during hypnotic analgesia than other individuals and support the proposed involvement (Crawford, 1996; Crawford and Gruzelier, 1992; Crawford et al., 1998a, 1998b, 1998c, 1999, 2000) of a more effective anterior fronto-limbic system that interacts with other brain regions in highly hypnotizable individuals and contributes to their enhanced attentional abilities.

Finally, the efficiency of the executive attention network appears to be highly heritable (e.g. Fan et al., 2001). The work by Lichtenberg et al. (2000) is but the first of many which will evaluate directly the genetic underpinnings of hypnotic susceptibility. Since genetic modeling studies propose that many genes may underlie complex traits, future hypnosis work needs to examine simultaneously various candidate genes that appear to be associated with attentional networks, particularly those associated with executive control.

References

Akpinar, S., Ulett, G.A. and Itil, T.M. (1971) 'Hypnotizability predicted by computer analyzed EEG pattern', *Biological Psychiatry*, 3:387–92.

Asada, H., Fukuda, Y., Tsunoda, S., Yamaguchi, M. and Tonoike, M. (1999) 'Frontal midline theta rhythms reflect alternative activation of prefrontal cortex and anterior cingulate cortex in humans', *Neuroscience Letters*, 274:29–32.

Atkinson, R.P. and Crawford, H.J. (1992) 'Individual differences in afterimage persistence: relationships to hypnotic susceptibility and visuospatial skills', *American Journal of Psychology*, 105:527–39.

Balthazard, C.G. and Woody, E.Z. (1992) 'The spectral analysis of hypnotic performance with respect to "absorption"', *International Journal of Clinical and Experimental Hypnosis*, 40:21–43.

Barabas, A.F. and Barabasz, M. (1992) 'Research designs and considerations', in E. Fromm and M. Nash (eds), *Contemporary Perspectives in Hypnosis Research* (pp. 173–200), New York: Guilford Press.

Bauman, D.E. and Bul', P.I. (1981) ['Human heritability of hypnotizability'], *Genetika*, 17:352–6.

Black, J.E. and Greenough, W.T. (1991) 'Developmental approaches to the memory process', in J.L. Martinez, Jr. and R.P. Kesner (eds), *Learning and Memory: A Biological View*, 2nd edn (pp. 61–91), San Diego: Academic Press.

Braffman, W. and Kirsch, I. (2001) 'Reaction time as a predictor of imaginative suggestibility and hypnotizability', *Contemporary Hypnosis*, 18:107–19.

Cloninger, C.R. (1987) 'A systematic method for clinical description and classification of personality variants', *Archives of General Psychiatry*, 44:573–88.

Cloninger, C.R. (1994) 'Temperament and personality', *Current Opinions in Neurobiology*, 4: 266–73.

Crawford, H.J. (1982) 'Hypnotizability, daydreaming styles, imagery vividness, and absorption: A multidimensional study', *Journal of Personality and Social Psychology*, 42:915–26.

—— (1990) 'Cognitive and psychophysiological correlates of hypnotic responsiveness and hypnosis', in M.L. Fass and D. Brown (eds), *Creative Mastery in Hypnosis and Hypnoanalysis: A Festschrift for Erika Fromm* (pp. 155–68), Hillsdale, NJ: Erlbaum.

—— (1994a) 'Brain dynamics and hypnosis: Attentional and disattentional processes', *International Journal of Clinical and Experimental Hypnosis*, 52: 204–32.

—— (1994b) 'Brain systems involved in attention and disattention (hypnotic analgesia) to pain', in K. Pribram (ed.), *Origins: Brain and Self-organization* (pp. 661–79), Hillsdale, NJ: Erlbaum.

—— (1996) 'Cerebral brain dynamics of mental imagery: Evidence and issues for hypnosis', in R.G. Kunzendorf, N. Spanos and B. Wallace (eds), *Imagination and Hypnosis* (pp. 253–81), New York: Baywood Press.

—— (1999) 'Cerebral brain dynamics of pain and hypnotic analgesia', in C. Taddei-Farretti and C. Musio (eds), *Neuronal Bases and Psychological Aspects of Consciousness* (pp. 236–55), Singapore: World Scientific.

—— (2001) 'Neuropsychophysiology of hypnosis: Towards an understanding of how hypnotic interventions work', in G.D. Burrows, R.O. Stanley and P.B. Bloom (eds), *International Handbook of Clinical Hypnosis* (pp. 61–84), New York: Wiley.

—— and Allen, S.N. (1983) 'Enhanced visual memory during hypnosis as mediated by hypnotic responsiveness and cognitive strategies', *Journal of Experimental Psychology: General*, 112:662–85.

—— and Gruzelier, J.H. (1992) 'A midstream view of the neuropsychophysiology of hypnosis: Recent research and future directions', in E. Fromm and M. Nash (eds), *Contemporary Perspectives in Hypnosis Research* (pp. 227–66), New York: Guilford Press.

—— Nomura, K. and Slater, H. (1983) 'Spatial memory processing: Enhancement during hypnosis', in J.C. Shorr, J. Conella, G. Sobel and T. Robin (eds), *Imagery: Theoretical Aspects and Applications* (pp. 209–16), New York: Human Sciences Press.

—— Brown, A.M. and Moon, C.E. (1993a) 'Sustained attentional and disattentional abilities: Differences between low and highly hypnotizable persons', *Journal of Abnormal Psychology*, 102:534–43.

—— Gur, R.C., Skolnick, B., Gur, R.E. and Benson, D.M. (1993b) 'Effects of hypnosis on regional cerebral blood flow during ischemic pain with and without suggested hypnotic analgesia', *International Journal of Psychophysiology*, 15:181–96.

—— Kapelis, L. and Harrison, D.W. (1995) 'Visual field asymmetry in facial affect perception: Moderating effects of hypnosis, hypnotic susceptibility level, absorption, and sustained attentional abilities', *International Journal of Neuroscience*, 82:11–23.

—— Clarke, S.W. and Kitner-Triolo, M. (1996) 'Self-generated happy and sad emotions in low and highly hypnotizable persons during waking and hypnosis: Laterality and regional EEG activity differences', *International Journal of Psychophysiology*, 24:239–66.

—— Horton, J.E., McClain-Furmanski, D. and Vendemia, J. (1998a) 'Brain dynamic shifts during the elimination of perceived pain and distress: Neuroimaging studies of hypnotic analgesia', On-line Proceedings of the 5th Internet World Congress on Biomedical Sciences '98 at McMaster University, Canada (http://www.mcmaster.ca/inabis98/simantov/dus0133/index.html).

—— Knebel, T. and Vendemia, J.M.C. (1998b) 'The nature of hypnotic analgesia: Neurophysiological foundation and evidence', *Contemporary Hypnosis*, 15:22–33.

—— Horton, J.E., Harrington, G.S., Vendemia, J.M.C., Plantec, M.B., Yung, S., Shamro, C. and Downs III, J.H. (1998c) 'Hypnotic analgesia (disattending pain) impacts neuronal network activation: An fMRI study of noxious somatosensory TENS stimuli', *NeuroImage*, 7:S436.

—— Knebel, T., Kaplan, L., Vendemia, J., Xie, M., Jameson, S. and Pribram, K. (1998d) 'Hypnotic analgesia: I. Somatosensory event-related potential changes to noxious stimuli and II. Transfer learning to reduce chronic low back pain', *International Journal of Clinical and Experimental Hypnosis*, 46:92–132.

—— Horton, J.E. and Lamas, J. (1998e) 'Information processing speed is faster for highly hypnotizable than low hypnotizable persons: Evidence from behavioral reaction time and event-related potential studies', *International Journal of Psychophysiology*, 30:84.

—— Knebel, T., Vendemia, J.M.C., Horton, J.E. and Lamas, J.R. (1999) 'La naturaleza de la analgesia hipnótica: bases y evidencias neurofisiológicas', *Anales de Psicologia*, 15:133–46.

—— Horton, J.E., Harrington, G.S., Hirsch Downs, T., Fox, K., Daugherty, S. and Downs III, J.H. (2000) 'Attention and disattention (hypnotic analgesia) to noxious somatosensory TENS stimuli: fMRI differences in low and highly hypnotizable individuals', *NeuroImage*, 11:S44.

Crowne, D.P., Konow, A., Drake, K.J. and Pribram, K.H. (1972) 'Hippocampal electrical activity in the monkey during delayed alternation problems', *Electroencephalography and Clinical Neurophysiology*, 33:567–77.

Delmonte, M.M. (1984) 'Electrocortical activity and related phenomena associated with meditation practice: A literature review', *International Journal of Neuroscience*, 24: 217–31.

De Pascalis, V. (1994) 'Event-related potentials during hypnotic hallucination', *International Journal of Clinical Experimental Hypnosis*, 42:9–55.

—— and Palumbo, G. (1986) 'EEG alpha asymmetry: Task difficulty and hypnotizability', *Perceptual and Motor Skills*, 62:139–50.

—— and Perrone, M. (1996) 'EEG asymmetry and heart rate during experience of hypnotic analgesia in high and low hypnotizables', *International Journal of Psychophysiology*, 21:163–75.

Eisenberg, J., Mei-Tal, G., Steinberg, A., Tartakovshy, E., Zohar, A., Gritsenko, I., Nemanov, L. and Ebstein, R.P. (1999) 'Haplotype relative risk study of catechol-*O*-methyltransferase (COMT) and attention deficit hyperactivity disorder (ADHD): Association of the high-enzyme activity Val allele with ADHD impulsive–hyperactive phenotype', *American Journal of Medical Genetics*, 88:497–502.

Fan, J., McCandliss, B.D., Sommer, T., Raz, A. and Posner, M.I. (2001) 'Testing the efficiency and independence of attentional networks', *Journal of Cognitive Neuroscience*, 14:340–7.

Faymonville, M.E., Laureys, S., Degueldre, C., DelFiore, G., Luxen, A., Franck, G., Lamy, M. and Maquet, P. (2000) 'Neural mechanisms of antinociceptive effects of hypnosis', *Anesthesiology*, 92:1257–67.

Fossella, J., Sommer, T., Fan, J., Wu, Y., Swanson, J.M., Pfaff, D.W. and Posner, M.I. (2002) 'Assessing the molecular genetics of attention networks', *BMC Neuroscience*, 3:14 (http://www.biomedcentral.com/1471–2202/3/14).

Galbraith, G.C., London, P., Leibovitz, M.P., Cooper, L. M. and Hart, J.T. (1970) 'EEG and hypnotic susceptibility', *Journal of Comparative and Physiological Psychology*, 72:125–31.

Graffin, N.F., Ray, W.J. and Lundy, R. (1995) 'EEG concomitants of hypnosis and hypnotic susceptibility', *Journal of Abnormal Psychology*, 104:123–31.

Green, J.P., Lynn, S.J. and Carlson, B.W. (1992) 'Finding the hypnotic virtuoso – another look: A brief communication', *International Journal of Clinical and Experimental Hypnosis*, 40:68–73.

Gruzelier, J. (1998) 'A working model of the neurophysiology of hypnosis: a review of the evidence', *Contemporary Hypnosis*, 15:3–21.

Hall, G.S. (1883) 'Reaction-time and attention in the hypnotic state', *Mind*, 8:170–82.

Heller, W. (1993) 'Neuropsychological mechanisms of individual differences in emotion, personality, and arousal', *Neuropsychology*, 7:476–89.

Hilgard, E.R. (1965) *Hypnotic Susceptibility*, New York: Harcourt, Brace and World.

—— (1973) 'The domain of hypnosis, with some comments on alternative paradigms', *American Psychologist*, 28:972–82.

—— (1977/1986) *Divided Consciousness: Multiple Controls in Human Thought and Action*, New York: Wiley-Interscience.

—— and Hilgard, J.R. (1975/1983/1994) *Hypnosis in the Relief of Pain*, Los Altos, CA: William Kaufmann. (Revised edn, New York: Brunner/ Mazel, 1994.)

Hilgard, J.R. (1970/1979) *Personality and Hypnosis: A Study of Imaginative Involvement*, Chicago: University of Chicago Press.

Horton, J.E., Lamas, J., Valle-Inclán, F. and Crawford, H.J. (1998a) 'Intending to ignore in waking and hypnosis: Influence of hypnotizability, sex, state and hand used on classic foreperiod reaction time effect', *International Journal of Psychophysiology*, 30:238.

—— McClain-Furmanski, D., Mészáros, I. and Crawford, H.J. (1998b) 'To inhibit pain is to actively shift conscious awareness: Somatosensory event-related potential evidence during hypnotic analgesia', *International Journal of Psychophysiology*, 30:234–5.

Hoyt, I.P., Nadon, R., Register, P.A., Chorny, J., Fleeson, W., Grigorian, E.M., Otto, L. and Kihlstrom, J.F. (1989) 'Daydreaming, absorption and hypnotizability', *International Journal of Clinical and Experimental Hypnosis*, 37:332–42.

James, W. (1890) *Principles of Psychology* (Vols 1–2), New York: Holt. (See also the authorized scholarly edition [Vols 1–3]. Cambridge, MA: Harvard University Press, 1981.)

Karayiorgou, M., Altemus, M., Galke, B.L., Goldman, D., Murphy, D.L., Ott, J. and Gogos, J.A. (1997) 'Genotype determining low catechol-*O*-methyltransferase activity as a risk factor for obsessive-compulsive disorder', *Proceedings of the National Academy of Sciences USA*, 94:4572–5.

Karlin, R., Morgan, D. and Goldstein, L. (1980) 'Hypnotic analgesia: A preliminary investigation of quantitated hemispheric electroencephalographic and attentional correlates', *Journal of Abnormal Psychology*, 89:591–4.

Karoum, F., Chrapusta, S.J. and. Egan, M.F. (1994) '3-Methoxytyramine is the major metabolite of released dopamine in the rat frontal cortex: Reassessment of the effects of antipsychotics on the dynamics of dopamine release and metabolism in the frontal cortex, nucleus accumbens, and striatum by a simple two pool model', *Journal of Neurochemistry*, 63:972–9.

Kropotov, J.D., Crawford, H.J. and Polyakov, Y.I. (1997) 'Somatosensory event-related potential changes to painful stimuli during hypnotic analgesia: Anterior cingulate cortex and anterior temporal cortex intracranial recordings', *International Journal of Psychophysiology*, 27:1–8.

Lamas, J.R. and Crawford, H.J. (1997) 'Auditory event-related potentials and attention: Effects of posthypnotic suggested deafness and hypnotizability level', *International Journal of Psychophysiology*, 25:72.

Libet, B. (1996) 'Neural processes in the production of conscious experience', in M. Velmans (ed.), *The Science of Consciousness: Psychological, Neuropsychological, and Clinical Reviews* (pp. 96–119), London: Routledge.

Lichtenberg, P., Bachner-Melman, R., Gritsenko, I. and Ebstein, R.P. (2000) 'Exploratory association study between catechol-*O*-methyltransferase (COMT) high/low enzyme activity polymorphism and hypnotizability', *American Journal of Medical Genetics*, 96:771–4.

—— Bachner-Melman, R., Ebstein, R.P. and Crawford, H.J (2004) 'Hypnotic susceptibility: Multidimensional relationships with biologically relevant personality, COMT, polymorphism, absorbtion, and attentional characteristics'. *International Journal of Clinical and Experimental Hypnosis*, 52:47–72.

Lyons, L. and Crawford, H.J. (1997) 'Sustained attentional and disattentional abilities and arousability: Factor analysis and relationships to hypnotic susceptibility', *Personality and Individual Differences*, 23:1071–84.

MacLeod-Morgan, C. and Lack, L. (1982) 'Hemispheric specificity: A physiological concomitant of hypnotizability', *Psychophysiology*, 19:687–90.

Maquet, P., Faymonville, M.E., Degueldre, C., Delfiore, G., Franck, G., Luxen, A. and Lamy, M. (1999) 'Functional neuroanatomy of hypnotic state', *Biological Psychiatry*, 45:327–33.

Mészáros, I., Crawford, H.J., Szabó, Cs., Nagy-Kovács, A. and Révész, M.A. (1989) 'Hypnotic susceptibility and cerebral hemisphere preponderance', in V. Gheorghiu, P. Netter, H. Eysenck and R. Rosenthal (eds), *Suggestion and Suggestibility: Theory and Research* (pp. 191–203), Heidelberg and New York: Springer-Verlag.

Michel, C.M., Lehmann, D., Henggeler, B. and Brandeis, D. (1992) 'Localization of the sources of EEG delta, theta, alpha and beta frequency bands using the FFT dipole approximation', *Electroencephalography and Clinical Neurophysiology*, 82: 3844.

Morgan, A.H. (1973) 'The heritability of hypnotic susceptibility in twins', *Journal of Abnormal Psychology*, 82:55–61.

—— Hilgard, E.R. and Davert, E.C. (1970) 'The heritability of hypnotic susceptibility of twins: A preliminary report', *Behavior Genetics*, 1:213–24.

—— Johnson, D.L. and Hilgard, J.R. (1974) 'The stability of hypnotic susceptibility: A longitudinal study', *International Journal of Clinical and Experimental Hypnosis*, 22:249–57.

Nadon, R., Laurence, J. and Perry, C. (1989) 'Interactionism: Cognition and context in hypnosis', *British Journal of Experimental and Clinical Hypnosis*, 6:141–50.

Norby, H., Hugdahl, K., Jasiukaitis, P. and Spiegel, D. (1999) 'Effects of hypnotizability on performance of a Stroop task and event-related potentials', *Perceptual and Motor Skills*, 88:819–30.

Pan, W., Zhang, L. and Zia, Y. (1994) 'The difference in EEG theta waves between concentrative and non-concentrative qigong states – a power spectrum and topographic mapping study', *Journal of Traditional Chinese Medicine*, 14:212–18.

Piccione, C., Hilgard, E.R. and Zimbardo, P.G. (1989) 'On the degree of stability of measured hypnotizability over a 25-year period', *Journal of Personality and Social Psychology*, 56:289–95.

Posner, M.J. and Peterson, S.E. (1990) 'The attention span of the brain', *Annual Review of Neuroscience*, 13–42.

Pribram, K.H. (1991) *Brain and Perception: Holonomy and Structure in Figural Processing*, Hillsdale, NJ: Laurence Erlbaum Associates.

—— and McGuinness, D. (1975) 'Arousal, activation, and effort in the control of attention', *Psychological Review*, 82:116–49.

Rainville, P., Duncan, G.H., Price, D.D., Carrier, B. and Bushnell, M.C. (1997) 'Pain affect encoded in human anterior cingulate but not somatosensory cortex', *Science*, 277:968–71.

—— Hofbauer, R.K., Paus, T., Duncan, G.H., Bushnell, M.C. and Price, D. (1999) 'Cerebral mechanisms of hypnotic induction and suggestion', *Journal of Cognitive Neuroscience*, 11:110–25.

Raz, A. and Shapiro, T. (2002) 'Hypnosis and neuroscience', *Archives of General Psychiatry*, 59:85–90.

Register, P.A. and Kihlstrom, J.F. (1986) 'Finding the hypnotic virtuoso', *International Journal of Clinical and Experimental Hypnosis*, 41:112–23.

Roche, S.M. and McConkey, K. (1990) 'Absorption: Nature, assessment and correlates', *Journal of Personality and Social Psychology*, 59:91–101.

Sabourin, J.M., Cutcomb, S.D., Crawford, H.J. and Pribram, K. (1990) 'EEG correlates of hypnotic susceptibility and hypnotic trance: Spectral analysis and coherence', *International Journal of Psychophysiology*, 10:125–42.

Schacter, D.L. (1977) 'EEG theta waves and psychological phenomena: A review and analysis', *Biological Psychology*, 5:47–82.

Solanto, M.V. (2002) 'Dopamine dysfunction in AD/HD: Integrating clinical and basic neuroscience research', *Behavioural Brain Research*, 130:65–71.

Spiegel, D. and King, R. (1992) 'Hypnotizability and CSF HVA levels among psychiatric patients', *Biological Psychiatry*, 31:95–8.

—— Bierre, P. and Rootenberg, J. (1989) 'Hypnotic alteration of somatosensory perception', *American Journal of Psychiatry*, 146:749–54.

Stevenson, J.H. (1976) 'Effect of posthypnotic dissociation on the performance of interfering tasks', *Journal of Abnormal Psychology*, 85:398–407.

Stuss, D.T, Shallice, T., Alexander, M.P. and Picton, T.W. (1995) 'A multidisciplinary approach to anterior attentional functions', in J. Grafman and K.J. Holyoak (eds), *Structure and Functions of the Human Prefrontal*

Cortex. Annals of the New York Academy of Sciences, vol. 769 (pp. 191–211), New York: New York Academy of Sciences.

Tebecis, A.K., Provins, K.A., Farnbach, R.W. and Pentony, P. (1975) 'Hypnosis and the EEG: A quantitative investigation', *Journal of Nervous and Mental Disease*, 161:1–17.

Tellegen, A. (1979) 'On measures and conceptions of hypnosis', *American Journal of Clinical Hypnosis*, 21:219–36.

—— and Atkinson, G. (1974) 'Openness to absorbing and self-altering experiences ("absorption"), a trait related to hypnotic susceptibility', *Journal of Abnormal Psychology*, 83:268–77.

Ulett, G.A., Akpinar, S. and Itil, T.M. (1972a) 'Quantitative EEG analysis during hypnosis', *Electroencephalography and Clinical Neurophysiology*, 33:361–8.

—— Akpinar, S. and Itil, T.M. (1972b) 'Hypnosis: Physiological, pharmacological reality', *American Journal of Psychiatry*, 128:799–805.

Velmans, M. (2000) *Understanding Consciousness*, Florence, KY: Taylor and Francis/Routledge.

Walker, N.S., Garrett, J.B. and Wallace, B. (1976) 'Restoration of eidetic imagery via hypnotic age regression: A preliminary report', *Journal of Abnormal Psychology*, 85:335–7.

Wallace, B. (1979) 'Hypnotic susceptibility and the perception of after-images and dot stimuli', *American Journal of Psychology*, 92:681–91.

—— (1986) 'Latency and frequency reports to the Necker cube illusion: Effects of hypnotic susceptibility and mental arithmetic', *Journal of General Psychology*, 113:187–94.

—— (1988) 'Hypnotic susceptibility, visual distraction, and reports of Necker cube apparent reversals', *Journal of General Psychology*, 115:389–96.

—— (1990) 'Imagery vividness, hypnotic susceptibility, and the perception of fragmented stimuli', *Journal of Personality and Social Psychology*, 58:354–9.

—— and Patterson, S.L. (1984) 'Hypnotic susceptibility and performance on various attention-specific cognitive tasks', *Journal of Personality and Social Psychology*, 47:175–81.

—— and Persanyi, M.W. (1989) 'Hypnotic susceptibility and familial handedness', *Journal of Genetic Psychology*, 116:345–50.

—— and Priebe, F.A. (1985) 'Hypnotic susceptibility, interference, and alternation frequency to the Necker cube illusion', *Journal of General Psychology*, 11:271–7.

—— Allen, P.A. and Weber, T.A. (1994) 'Hypnotic susceptibility, imaging ability, and the detection of embedded words within letters', *International Journal of Clinical and Experimental Hypnosis*, 42:20–38.

Weinberger, D.R., Egan, M.F., Bertolino, A., Callicott, J.H., Mattay, V.S., Lipska, B.K., Berman, K.F. and Goldberg, T.E. (2001) 'Prefrontal neurons and the genetics of schizophrenia', *Biological Psychiatry*, 50:825–44.

Weitzenhoffer, A.M. (1962) 'The nature of hypnosis: Part I', *American Journal of Clinical Hypnosis*, 5:295–321.

—— and Hilgard, E.R. (1962) *Stanford Hypnotic Susceptibility Scale, Form C*, Palo Alto, CA: Consulting Psychologists Press.

Wik, G., Fischer, H., Bragée, B., Finer, B. and Fredrikson, M. (1999) 'Functional anatomy of hypnotic analgesia: A PET study of patients with fibromyalgia', *European Journal of Pain*, 3:7–12.

Williams, J.D. and Gruzelier, J.H. (2001) 'Differentiation of hypnosis and relaxation by analysis of narrow band theta and alpha frequencies', *International Journal of Clinical and Experimental Hypnosis*, 49:185–206.

Woody, E.Z., Bowers, K.S. and Oakman, J.M. (1992) 'A conceptual analysis of hypnotic responsiveness: Experience, individual differences, and context', in E. Fromm and M. Nash (eds), *Contemporary Perspectives in Hypnosis Research* (pp. 3–33), New York: Guilford Press.

—— Drugovic, M. and Oakman, J.M. (1997) 'A reexamination of the role of nonhypnotic suggestibility in hypnotic responding', *Journal of Personality and Social Psychology*, 72:399–407.

Zachariae, R., Jorgensen, M.M. and Christensen, S. (2000) 'Hypnotizability and absorption in a Danish sample: Testing the influence of context', *International Journal of Clinical and Experimental Hypnosis*, 48:306–14.

Chapter 7

An integrative cognitive theory of hypnosis and high hypnotizability

Richard J. Brown and David A. Oakley

Introduction

Cognitive concepts have been central to hypnosis research and theory since the advent of the information processing revolution in psychology. Models based on cognitive principles (e.g. Bowers, 1990; E.R. Hilgard, 1986; Kirsch and Lynn, 1997; Spanos and Chaves, 1989; Spiegel, 1990; Woody and Bowers, 1994) have grown in sophistication in recent years, offering important insights into the mechanisms of hypnotic phenomena. Despite this progress, mainstream psychology has largely failed to capitalize on the wealth of information that has amassed since hypnosis research began over two centuries ago. In retrospect, this seems like a remarkable oversight. Hypnotic phenomena provide a window on some of the most fascinating and entrenched mysteries of the mind, including the nature of will and consciousness, and the relationship between psyche and soma. Hypnosis also has clear instrumental value (Reyher, 1962) as a tool to facilitate the investigation of various psychological phenomena, including pain (Rainville et al., 1997), auditory hallucinations (Szechtman et al., 1998), dissociative amnesia (Barnier, 2002), unexplained neurological illness (i.e. conversion hysteria; Halligan et al., 2000; Oakley, 1999a) and voluntary control of movement (Blakemore et al., 2003).

Despite such instrumental interest, it is likely that 'intrinsic' hypnosis research (where hypnosis itself is the primary focus; Reyher, 1962) will remain on the fringes of psychology until there is greater theoretical consensus within the field (Dixon and Laurence, 1992a; Nadon, 1997). In this chapter, we draw on further material from cognitive psychology to address the question of how such consensus might be achieved. We begin by summarizing two recent approaches to hypnosis – dissociated control theory (Bowers, 1990, 1992; Woody and Bowers, 1994) and response set theory (Kirsch and Lynn, 1997) – that are based on contemporary cognitive principles. We then consider how these approaches can be combined and extended using a heuristic model of the mechanisms underlying perception, attention and consciousness. In this way, we aim to demonstrate how several different approaches to hypnosis can be unified within a single conceptual framework firmly based within cognitive psychology. The resulting model provides a novel perspective on the nature of hypnosis and hypnotizability, as well as a clear agenda for future research. We discuss in particular possible processes underlying high hypnotic suggestibility and hypnotizability.

Hypnosis and automaticity

Both dissociated control theory and response set theory address the issue of hypnotic involuntariness by reference to cognitive research and theory concerning the concept of *automaticity*.

Dissociated control theory

The foundation for dissociated control theory is the Norman and Shallice (1986) model of action control described in Chapter 1. According to Norman and Shallice, routine behaviours are controlled by the competitive activation of low-level control structures or 'schemata'. Schemata are hierarchically organized, nested representations describing the sequence of processing operations involved in the execution of well-learned behaviours. These schemata are triggered 'automatically' by environmental input, and therefore do not draw on central processing resources (i.e. attention). Novel behaviours, in contrast, require intervention from a high-level executive or supervisory attentional system (SAS). Behaviours managed by the SAS consume central resources and are therefore viewed as 'controlled'. Norman and Shallice suggest that the phenomenological sense of *will* results from the operation of the SAS, with greater levels of SAS involvement leading to a more intense experience of willing. This assumption provides the basis for dissociated control theory. In this account, suggested phenomena result from the automatic activation of low-level schemata by the words of the hypnotist. As such, the experience of hypnotic involuntariness reflects an absence of SAS involvement in the creation of the suggested act.

This is made possible by the hypnotic induction, which inhibits the SAS to create a reliance on environmental input for the activation of behaviour. Thus, dissociated control theory proposes that hypnotic behaviours are perceived as involuntary because they are executed and maintained automatically, that is, without volitional control. This contrasts with the neodissociation and sociocognitive approaches, both of which assume that hypnotic behaviours are executed voluntarily but have involuntariness attributed to them (Kirsch and Lynn, 1997).

One apparent limitation of dissociated control theory is its reliance on an altered state account of hypnotic phenomena. In Chapter 1 we saw that most, if not all, hypnotic phenomena can be suggested successfully without a prior induction procedure (e.g. Barber, 1969; Barber and Calverley, 1965), and that the induction itself produces only modest increases in suggestibility (Kirsch, 1997). According to Kirsch and Lynn (1998), this invalidates dissociated control theory, which assumes that the induction is required to produce a state of executive inhibition conducive to suggested responding. Woody and Sadler (1998), in contrast, suggest that weakened executive control may be a useful explanation for some, but not all, instances of hypnotic behaviour. By this view, the fact that responses to suggestions can be produced successfully without a hypnotic induction need not invalidate dissociated control theory, although its explanatory power is clearly reduced.

Response set theory

The dissociated control account of hypnotic involuntariness relies on the assumption that automatic behaviours are perceived as involuntary. According to Norman and Shallice, however, all routine behaviour is automatic, and yet we rarely feel as though our actions are outside our control.[1] Clearly, the feeling of involuntariness reflects more than just the systems involved in the production of an act (see Blakemore et al., 2003). This concept is central to response set theory (Kirsch and Lynn, 1997), which assumes that the experience of volition is an *attribution* derived from beliefs about the causes of actions. By this view, attributions of volition depend on the kinds of 'response set' that have been put in place for the execution of a given behaviour. Response sets are representations specifying

---

[1] Although we often feel as though they are *effortless*.

the relationship between an individual's actions and events in his or her environment. An *implementation intention* is a representation of the form 'When *x* happens, I will do *y*' (e.g. 'When the number 47 bus arrives, I will get on it'). The creation of implementation intentions allows behaviour to be readied for automatic activation in response to specific environmental events. Behaviours that are consistent with the prior generation of an implementation intention are perceived as voluntary. *Response expectancies*, in contrast, are representations of the form 'When *x* happens, *y* will occur' (e.g. 'When I am hypnotized, I will feel out of control'). Response expectancies are identical to implementation intentions except that they label the predicted response as non-deliberate.[2] Acts triggered following the generation of a response expectancy are perceived as involuntary.

According to Kirsch and Lynn (1997), subjects enter the hypnotic situation with the *generalized response expectancy* that they will follow the hypnotist's instructions and produce behaviours that are experienced as involuntary. As a result, subjects attribute hypnotic responses to external causes and experience a sense of involuntariness. The hypnotic behaviour itself is triggered by subjective experiences that are consistent with the content of the suggestion; in arm levitation, for example, the upward movement of the arm is triggered by the experience of its becoming lighter. The subject may facilitate this process by engaging in strategies (e.g. goal-directed imaging) that help produce experiences consistent with the suggestion. Importantly, alterations in consciousness or information processing are not necessary for this to occur. Indeed, in this account, hypnotic responses are triggered by the same mechanisms as normal voluntary behaviours; the only difference is the way in which the two are experienced. This is in marked contrast to dissociated control theory, which asserts that hypnotic behaviours are involuntary responses reflecting an alteration in information processing.

Empirical evidence

A number of studies have used the so-called dual-task paradigm to investigate whether hypnotic behaviours are executed automatically.

---

[2] The difference between implementation intentions and response expectancies is similar to that between instructions and suggestions. Instructions imply that the response should be performed intentionally, whereas suggestions imply that the response will happen by itself.

Dual-task methodology is based on the finding that two tasks performed concurrently often interfere with one another, producing decrements in performance on both tasks. Historically, dual-task interference has been attributed to the operation of an attentional system with limited resources (e.g. Kahneman, 1973), akin to the executive systems described in neodissociation theory, dissociated control theory and response set theory. As such, the dual-task paradigm would appear to offer a useful means of investigating predictions made by these theories (Kirsch and Lynn, 1998). According to these authors, dissociated control theory predicts that there will be a smaller interference effect if one of the tasks is completed in response to hypnotic suggestion, based on the assumption that it is performed automatically (i.e. without SAS involvement). In contrast, response set theory predicts that interference will increase, based on the assumption that generating the subjective experiences necessary for the activation of expected responses is attentionally demanding. Several studies using variants of the dual-task paradigm indicate that the interference between competing tasks increases during hypnosis for high susceptibles, apparently supporting response set theory (Green and Lynn, 1995; Hull, 1933; Knox et al., 1975; Stevenson, 1976; cf. Bowers and Brenneman, 1981).

In our view, there are fundamental problems with the dual-task methodology as it is used here. In each case, the method is premised on the idea that one of the two tasks can be performed without the individuals being aware of his or her performance, that is, 'subconsciously'. Although this may be true for easier tasks, such as that adopted by Bowers and Brenneman (1981), this is less likely for the more difficult tasks used in other studies (e.g. Hull, 1933; Knox et al., 1975; Stevenson, 1976). In such cases, suggesting that the individual perform the task sub-consciously can only lead to a decrement in performance and the pattern of results observed in these studies. This is true regardless of whether the subject performs the task sub-consciously by erecting an amnesic barrier, by relinquishing executive control, or by engaging in concurrent strategic processing. As such, these studies say more about the nature of the tasks involved than the validity of the theories they are purporting to assess (cf. Kihlstrom, 1998).

Other cognitive methodologies have been used to investigate the automaticity of hypnotic phenomena. Kirsch et al. (2000), for example, investigated the effect of concurrent cognitive load on responses to different hypnotic suggestions. According to these authors, dissociated control theory predicts that hypnotic responses will not be impeded by cognitive load, based on the assumption that they do not consume attentional resources. Kirsch et al. (2000) found that cognitive load disrupted subjective responses to ideomotor, challenge and hallucination suggestions, seemingly contrary to the predictions of dissociated control theory. These findings were interpreted as evidence for response set theory, which predicts that attention is required for the generation of hypnotic responses. Also consistent with this view is recent research by Barnier and McConkey (1996, 1998, 1999), which demonstrates that post-hypnotic suggestions require attention to the environment to be triggered successfully. Importantly, subjects in these studies had compelling suggested experiences regardless of the amount of attention required to generate the response.

Despite these findings, there is some evidence to suggest that hypnotic responses consume fewer cognitive resources, and hence are *relatively* more automatic, than comparable non-hypnotic behaviours. Miller and Bowers (1993), for example, found that hypnotic analgesia produced less interference on a cognitively demanding task than a non-hypnotic stress inoculation procedure, despite similar reductions in cold-pressor pain in the two conditions. In addition, there is evidence to suggest that suggested responses may bypass strategic cognitive processing. Bowers and Woody (1996), for example, found that the paradoxical thought suppression effect (Wegner, 1989) was reduced for high hypnotizables when amnesia for to-be-suppressed material was suggested during hypnosis. This was interpreted as evidence for the idea that hypnotic amnesia is produced by an automatic cognitive process, rather than strategic thought suppression.

These observations are difficult to reconcile with the traditional idea that automaticity involves processing without attention, intention, effort or awareness (e.g. Bargh, 1994; Brown, 1999a; Logan, 1988), a concept that is inherent to the Norman and Shallice model. This research demonstrates that hypnotic phenomena require attention to operate but may be more automatic than comparable non-suggested behaviours. In addition, it indicates that the sense of involuntariness is independent of the amount of effort involved in creating a suggested effect (Barnier, 2001). Overall, these results add to other evidence indicating that automatic processes vary in the degree to which they involve attention, intention, awareness and control, which to some extent are independent qualities (see e.g. Bargh,

1994; Brown, 1999a; Logan, 1988). This is a powerful demonstration of how hypnosis research can contribute to our understanding of normal cognitive processes, as well as the value of synchronizing hypnosis theory with mainstream psychological concepts. In these respects, the dissociated control and response set theories represent a significant step forward in our understanding of will and voluntariness, both in hypnosis and elsewhere.

In the remainder of this chapter, we address how mainstream cognitive theory can contribute to our understanding of other aspects of suggestion, particularly altered experiences such as hallucinations, analgesia, sensory loss and the like. Our account incorporates insights from both the dissociated control and response set theories. Thus, we endorse both the dissociated control concept that suggested responses may be facilitated by an inhibition of high-level attention, and the response set idea that suggested involuntariness is an interpretation or attribution about the causes of behaviour. Compared to these previous approaches, however, we place much greater emphasis on the nature of perception and consciousness to explain hypnotic phenomena.

A heuristic model of the cognitive system

Central to this approach is the idea that suggestion and hypnosis can be understood by reference to normal cognitive principles. To this end, we begin by outlining a heuristic model of perception, attention, control and awareness informed by contemporary cognitive theory; we then consider how it can account for the phenomena of suggestion, hypnosis and hypnotizability. The model is an amalgamation of ideas from several different sources, most notably Brown (1999a, 2002), Halligan and Oakley (2000), Kemler (1983), Kosslyn (1996), Logan (1988), Marcel (1983), Norman and Shallice (1986), Oakley (1985, 1999a, 1999b), Rumelhart et al. (1986), Sloman (1996), and Velmans (2000). For further information about the model's theoretical origins, see Brown (1999a). A summary of the model is presented in Figure 7.1.

Pre-attentive processing

Research suggests that incoming information is extensively analysed prior to the operation of attentional mechanisms which determine what information will provide the basis for further processing and

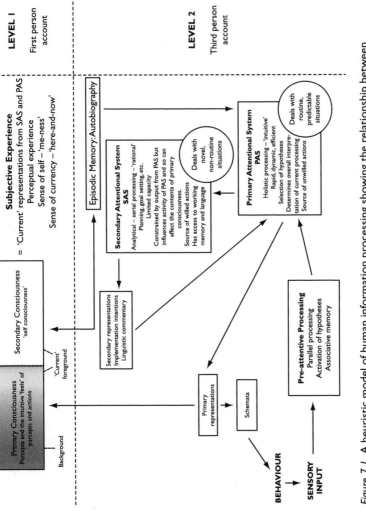

Figure 7.1 A heuristic model of human information processing showing the relationship between underlying processes (Level 2) and subjective experience (Level 1). See text for further explanation.

action (Marcel, 1983; Posner and Snyder, 1975; Velmans, 2000).[3] In the first instance, stimulus information is received by the sensory apparatus, triggering early perceptual processes that represent the basic features of the stimulus array (Marr, 1982). Once early sensory analyses have been performed, the resulting sensory representations are encoded in associative memory providing a basis for recognition (Kosslyn, 1996). The encoding process generates patterns of activation across the memory network corresponding to stored representations of the stimulus acquired during previous learning episodes (Rumelhart et al., 1986). This activation then spreads in parallel throughout related representations within associative memory until the overall activation level of the network stabilizes (Marcel, 1983; Neely, 1977; Posner and Snyder, 1975; Rumelhart et al., 1986; Sloman, 1996). Following Marcel (1983) and Sloman (1996), we suggest that this spread of activation within associative memory acts as an inferential process, generating possible interpretations of the environment for the subsequent control of action. Activation within the memory network also feeds back to basic perceptual systems, allowing prior knowledge to facilitate the acquisition of relevant sensory information (cf. Neisser, 1976)

Attentional selection

Following this pre-attentive spread of activation, a subset of the information activated in representational systems is selected as a basis for behaviour (cf. Allport, 1987). In this model, selection is modulated by a centralized control structure or *primary attentional system* (PAS) that performs two basic functions. First, it establishes the most meaningful interpretation of the environment out of the available alternatives (cf. Crick and Koch, 1990; Halligan and Oakley, 2000; Marcel, 1983). Second, it uses this interpretation to integrate information from a number of different sources producing representations that allow for behavioural control (cf. Allport, 1987; Marcel, 1983; Velmans, 2000). Following Marcel (1983), we assume that the PAS iteratively samples representational activity within associative

---

[3] We acknowledge evidence demonstrating that the locus of attentional selection varies according to the amount of information being processed at any one time (Lavie, 1995), and the nature of the material being selected (Styles, 1997). For current purposes, we have chosen to ignore these subtleties: the general idea that extensive processing often occurs prior to attentional selection suffices.

memory, continually selecting processing 'hypotheses' that provide the best-fitting interpretation of current activity in the light of previous experience. During the selection process, the best-fitting hypotheses in memory are used to organize sensory information to form integrated multi-modal units that we term *primary representations* (cf. Marcel, 1983; Taylor, 2001).

In addition to the nature of incoming information, a number of other factors determine which hypotheses are selected by the PAS for the generation of primary representations. First, the probability of selection is closely related to the resting activation threshold of hypotheses within associative memory. Hypotheses with relatively low activation thresholds, such as those that have been well learned through repeated use, require less activation for their selection by primary attention. Selection is also a relatively self-perpetuating process, as previously selected hypotheses direct the acquisition of information that confirms their validity (Neisser, 1976), influencing activation levels and thresholds accordingly. Second, selection is influenced by the lateral activation of complementary representations within associative memory (cf. Norman and Shallice, 1986; Rumelhart et al., 1986). Third, selection is influenced by current processing goals, with information related to those goals being selected preferentially over goal-irrelevant information. Finally, the selection process is influenced by secondary processing (see below).

Automatic behavioural control

We assume that primary representations serve as triggering input to a network of cognition and action schemata that are executed automatically in accordance with a competitive scheduling mechanism governed by relative activation values (corresponding to contention scheduling in the model by Norman and Shallice, 1986; see Chapter 1). In this model, actions governed by this single-step activation of schemata are regarded as automatic (Logan, 1988). This contrasts with the traditional approach to automaticity, which defines a process as automatic if it does not require attention, awareness, intention or control to operate. In the current model, all actions (automatic or otherwise) require attentional selection to operate.[4] Nevertheless, automatic actions do not require secondary attentional

---

[4] It is for this reason that we choose not to describe pre-attentive processing as automatic (Logan, 1992).

input (see below) to proceed and therefore may not interfere with concurrent tasks conducted solely by secondary systems. Moreover, automatic actions exhibit many of the properties traditionally associated with automaticity, such as rapidity, efficiency and perceived effortlessness. However, we assume that automatic behaviours vary in the degree to which they exhibit these qualities (cf. Logan, 1988).

This automatic activation of schemata by the products of attentional selection provides the system with a means of controlling behaviour in situations with which it is at least relatively familiar. The operation of these low-level processes is viewed as a default mode of behavioural control that is rapid, dynamic and highly efficient, providing that the system possesses the relevant representations in memory.

High-level behavioural control

In cases where existing knowledge is insufficient to underpin adaptive behavioural management, such as in novel situations, an additional means of control is required (Norman and Shallice, 1986). We propose that the control of novel situations is managed by a high-level *secondary attentional system* (SAS), a complex set of sub-systems operating via general-purpose serial-processing algorithms (cf. Logan, 1988). This system broadly corresponds to the supervisory attentional system in the model offered by Norman and Shallice (1986).[5] The SAS is a limited-capacity system that manages a number of high-level processes including trouble-shooting, behavioural inhibition, planning, goal setting, decision making and problem solving (see e.g. Burgess and Shallice, 1996; Shallice and Burgess, 1996). The SAS has privileged access to language systems and working memory but does not have direct control over the representations underlying perception and action (Shallice, 1988): rather, the SAS influences behaviour by moderating the activation levels of schemata via the PAS. Moreover, the processing operations available to the SAS are based on, and hence constrained by, the primary representations generated by the PAS.

In this model, the SAS operates by the construction of *secondary representations* (cf. Burgess and Shallice, 1996; Shallice and Burgess, 1996). Secondary representations are high-level information struc-

---

[5] We use the term 'secondary attentional system' simply to preserve the internal consistency of the present model.

tures that are involved in goal setting, the sequencing of actions and the control of cognitive processing. Included in this category are representations akin to the implementation intentions (Gollwitzer, 1993) central to the model of Kirsch and Lynn (1997). Secondary representations indirectly affect low-level activity via the PAS. In this sense, the PAS serves as an interface between higher- and lower-level processing operations. Once generated, secondary representations may become established as primary cognition or action schemata, allowing for the automatic control of future cognitive processing when activated by internal and external stimuli.

All primary and secondary representations that are subjected to processing by the SAS are labelled as 'current' and encoded as episodic memories (Halligan and Oakley, 2000). One important aspect of this is the continual SAS re-description of low-level processing products in the form of language. As this continuous 'commentary' about the contents of processing is encoded over time, so the system develops a historical narrative or 'autobiography' about its operation (cf. Conway and Pleydell-Pearce, 2000). We suggest that this aspect of SAS processing is the source of a 'first-person' account of consciousness and the sense of self (Halligan and Oakley, 2000; Velmans, 2000).

The current model is similar to that described by Halligan and Oakley (2000), although there are important differences between the two. The most significant structural difference is our inclusion of a primary attentional system that selects information for priority processing and action, a function that is performed by the SAS in Halligan and Oakley (2000). This allows us to differentiate between the systems involved in the selection process and those that perform post-selection processing (Brown, 1999a), which is the province of the SAS in this model.

Consciousness and subjective experience

It is well established that subjective experience is closely associated with processing at a late stage in the cognitive chain (Velmans, 2000). In line with this, we assume that experience is associated with the PAS and SAS, with each having distinct phenomenological correlates. We suggest that the SAS is associated with a sense of meta-cognition or self-consciousness (i.e. an awareness of being aware), which we label *secondary consciousness*. Processing at this level is perceived as effortful and its products may be verbalized by the subject (cf. Norman and Shallice, 1986). It is clear, however, that an individual can be conscious (i.e. have subjective experience) without being aware of himself or herself as an experiencing being (Oakley, 1985). We suggest that this aspect of subjective experience is associated with the primary attentional system, which we regard as the seat of *primary consciousness*. The main component of primary consciousness is perceptual experience, which is specifically associated with the primary representations generated by the PAS during attentional selection (cf. Marcel, 1983). Perceptual experience at this level has a self-evidently valid quality to it, because the inferential processes by which it is produced are unconscious in the strict sense (i.e. entirely lacking in experiential qualities). We suggest that interpretive and behavioural processing at the level of the PAS is also associated with an *intuitive* phenomenological character – that is, the subjective impression of 'rightness' (or, equally, 'wrongness') that accompanies our everyday interactions with the world. In other words, individuals can *feel* the products of low-level cognitive activity, but typically have no awareness of the specific informational content of processing at this level (cf. Damasio, 2000).

As the question of voluntariness is so central to the phenomena of hypnosis, it is essential to describe the basic mechanisms associated with the experience of volition. Following Jahanshahi and Frith (1998), we assume that *all* actions are voluntary (by definition), but that not all are *willed*. According to Jahanshahi and Frith (1998), willed actions are defined by their association with (i) attention and conscious awareness, (ii) choice and control, and (iii) intentionality. On this basis, we suggest that all actions and processes directly controlled by the SAS can be regarded as willed actions, which are typically experienced as voluntary[6] (cf. Norman and Shallice, 1986). In contrast, we regard actions triggered automatically by PAS selection as voluntary but unwilled behaviours. Phenomenologically, such actions constitute 'ideo-motor' acts (James, 1890), although whether they are perceived as volitional depends on the type of information available about the act in the cognitive system. In most cases, such actions are perceived as intentional as they are consistent with system plans, and hence previous intentions (Kirsch and Lynn, 1997). Even in the absence of such intentions, actions at this level will be perceived as voluntary if they are triggered by primary representations

---

[6] Although not always. See Blakemore et al. (2002).

that are consistent with such an interpretation. We discuss this issue in more detail below, when we consider the nature of the classic suggestion effect.

Although we assume that subjective experience correlates highly with processing by the PAS and SAS, we do not assume that the two are ontologically identical (Velmans, 2000). Similarly, we follow Velmans (2000) and Halligan and Oakley (2000) in rejecting the idea that subjective experience serves an information-processing function or has any other causal properties. This contrasts with dissociated control theory, which identifies consciousness as serving an integrative function that imposes order on lower-level processing (Woody and Bowers, 1994). In our account, conscious experience *reflects* the integration imposed on lower systems by the SAS and PAS, rather than performing an integrative function itself. In general, we assume that all conscious contents are generated by non-conscious mental processes and that conscious experience arises *after* the processing to which it relates (Halligan and Oakley, 2000; Velmans, 2000).

The current approach is similar to the model by Halligan and Oakley (2000) in its assumption that only the products of PAS selection, as well as subsequent post-selection analyses, are represented in subjective experience. Moreover, both models agree that subjective experience lacks causal properties. Halligan and Oakley (2000) use the term 'level 1' as a label for the subjective aspects of processing and 'level 2' for the specific processes involved in the generation of these subjective contents. This distinction between level 1 and level 2 is commensurate with Velmans's (2000) distinction between first- and third-person accounts of consciousness. In the present model, Velmans's first-person account (and Halligan and Oakley's level 1) corresponds to the current contents of primary and secondary consciousness. Our description of the PAS and SAS (and therefore the mechanisms involved in generating subjective experience) is a third-person account of consciousness and therefore corresponds to level 2 in the model by Halligan and Oakley (see Figure 7.1).

A model of suggestion, hypnosis and hypnotizability

Having provided a basic description of the cognitive system, we now turn to the phenomena of suggestion, hypnosis and hypnotizability. Our starting point is the assumption that responses to hypnotic and non-hypnotic suggestions are governed by the same causal mechanisms, based on the strong correlation between suggestibility in the two contexts and the fact that most 'hypnotic' phenomena can be suggested successfully without an induction (see Kirsch, 1997). We therefore reject the idea that suggested responses require the creation of an altered state of processing, and hence adopt a broadly sociocognitive stance. Nevertheless, we draw a distinction between the mechanisms underpinning suggested phenomena and other factors that influence the operation of those mechanisms. Included in the latter category are 'non-state' variables such as context, motivation, expectation and strategy use, as well as 'state' variables such as changes in information processing resulting from the hypnotic induction (Brown, 1999b). In this sense, we also endorse a 'neo-state' view of hypnosis (Oakley, 1998), which separates 'trance' from suggestion in the generation of 'hypnotic' phenomena.

This account draws a distinction between the classic suggestion effect and other changes in experience associated with suggestion. We propose that slightly different, although related, mechanisms can account for these different aspects of suggested responding. In both cases, the mechanisms involved are fundamental to the everyday control of perception and action. In this sense, suggested phenomena can be regarded as the product of normal psychological processes, which are altered to produce unusual results. We begin by describing the mechanisms underlying suggested alterations in experience in general. We then consider suggested behaviour and the classic suggestion effect. We conclude by addressing factors that moderate the occurrence of suggested phenomena, such as 'trance' and contextual features.

Mechanisms I: Suggested alterations in experience

Suggested experiences are one of a range of phenomena (e.g. dreams, hallucinations and certain illusions) that demonstrate how the contents of awareness often contradict sensory stimulation. In the current model, this is a predictable consequence of the mechanisms involved in the creation of experience. By this view, the contents of awareness are a construction or interpretation of reality (Marcel, 1983), jointly determined by sensory information and existing knowledge in the cognitive system. Although there is normally a close correspondence between experience and information provided by the senses, experience is often shaped by material stored in memory

(Gregory, 1970). In our view, suggested phenomena provide a compelling demonstration of this process in action.

In the first instance, suggestions serve to activate perceptual hypotheses corresponding to their experiential intent.[7] If the activation of a suggestion-related hypothesis exceeds its selection threshold, it is selected by the PAS as the best-fitting interpretation of current processing activity and used to generate corresponding primary representations. As the SAS has no direct access to this process, it misinterprets these primary representations as a reliable account of current processing within the system. The result is a convincing perceptual distortion that is experienced as self-evidently valid (i.e. 'real'). One important aspect of this process is the top-down effect of the suggested hypothesis (or *rogue representation*) on basic perceptual processing. In the case of positive hallucinations and other sensory experiences (e.g. dreams and regressions), the rogue representation activates basic perceptual systems to create a brain state that is very similar to the actual sensory event being suggested. This process is comparable to that involved in normal imagining (Kosslyn, 1996), although suggestion tends to produce a more compelling perceptual experience than imagery alone. Neuroimaging data from Derbyshire et al. (under review), Kosslyn et al. (2000) and Szechtman et al. (1998), indicate that this may be because suggestions are more effective at activating basic perceptual systems than imagery, producing a brain state that corresponds more closely with the genuine sensory event. That is, suggestions create a 'virtual reality' experience (Walters and Oakley, 2003).

In the case of negative hallucinations and sensory experiences (e.g. blindness, deafness, and anaesthesia), the rogue representation inhibits the primary representation of certain objects, modalities or bodily systems. Here, basic perceptual systems are relatively unaffected by the suggestion process; rather, it is the output from these systems and/or its selection by the PAS that is mainly affected. As this process operates at a late stage in the processing chain, pre-attentive processes remain relatively unaffected by the suggestion. This is consistent with evidence demonstrating the preservation of implicit processing in suggested sensory loss (e.g. Kihlstrom, 1987). In this respect, the current model embraces the idea that suggested phenomena often involve 'dissociations' between different cognitive

---

[7] This process is likely to be particularly effective when mediated by language, which is commonly used by the SAS to activate low-level schemata (cf. Luria, 1973).

systems (see Kihlstrom, 1998). Similar representations inhibiting the operation of certain memory retrieval routines are responsible for amnesia (see David et al., 2000).

Mechanisms II: Suggested behaviour and the classic suggestion effect

The classic suggestion effect also demonstrates the interpretive nature of subjective experience, in this case the experience of volition. In the current model, suggested actions reflect the automatic activation of low-level behavioural schemata, triggered when their activation threshold is reached. In this sense, there is no difference between suggested phenomena and normal routine behaviours in terms of basic control mechanism. The major difference between the two is how the behaviour is experienced. We assume that this reflects information about the act within the system, particularly surrounding the circumstances in which the behaviour was triggered. As an active interpretation of current processing, primary representations are of central importance in this respect. Under normal circumstances, primary representations indicate that behaviour is being generated internally; as a result, it is experienced as voluntary. In the case of suggested phenomena, representations indicate that the behaviour is being triggered by external factors, creating an experience of involuntariness (Kirsch and Lynn, 1997). An arm levitation, for example, may be triggered by primary representations corresponding to lightness in the arm and/or images of an external source of lift (e.g. a balloon). This is consistent with research indicating that imagining a movement activates the motor systems involved in creating that movement (Jeannerod, 1997). Similar mechanisms are operating in challenge suggestions, although the underlying schemata specify movement inhibition rather than initiation. In the case of post-hypnotic suggestions, the underlying representation is a response expectancy (Kirsch and Lynn, 1997). The actual source of perceived involuntariness may be the absence of an advance prediction about the sensory consequences of the suggested movements (Blakemore et al., 2002, 2003).[8] It is possible that this aspect

---

[8] Blakemore et al. (2002, 2003) propose a similar mechanism for the experience of passivity in schizophrenia. Although these mechanisms are comparable, this should not be taken as implying that hypnotic and psychotic phenomena are necessarily related (cf. Woody and Sadler, 1998).

of motor processing is inhibited by the content of the primary representation.

We assume that the primary representation need not be perceptual, in line with evidence indicating that imagery is not necessary to produce suggested phenomena (Hargadon et al., 1995). A simple verbal representation consistent with the experience of involuntariness (e.g. 'Your arm is rising' rather than 'You are raising your arm'; Spanos and Gorassini, 1984) may be enough to trigger the schema and the corresponding experience. This may occur directly via the PAS or indirectly via the SAS; the latter may be particularly important in a 'constructive' response mode (see below) or self-hypnosis.

Moderating factors

Having identified the basic mechanisms mediating suggested phenomena, we now consider the factors that moderate them. In this account, suggestion is related to the PAS selection process responsible for the creation of experience and the automatic control of action; thus, any factor that influences PAS selection will moderate suggested responding. PAS selection is influenced by a number of factors other than sensory stimulation, including the activation levels and selection thresholds of representations in associative memory, processing goals, and input from the SAS. Each of these factors is relevant in understanding why suggestibility typically increases in the hypnotic situation. From the outset, we assume that there is more than one route to successful responding, with individuals often differing in the way that they activate the suggestion process (Brown, 1999b). We begin by describing two common routes to suggestion. We then consider how aspects of the hypnotic situation interact with these different routes to increase the likelihood of successful responding.

Routes to suggestion

We distinguish between two main routes to suggestion, broadly comparable to the concentrative and constructive response styles identified by Sheehan and McConkey (1982). The first route involves the automatic activation of low-level schemata by external input (see Figure 7.2a). In our account, schemata may be directly activated without prior inhibition of the SAS, although schema activation may be facilitated by such inhibition (see below). This process is also facilitated by focusing attention on the suggestion content and

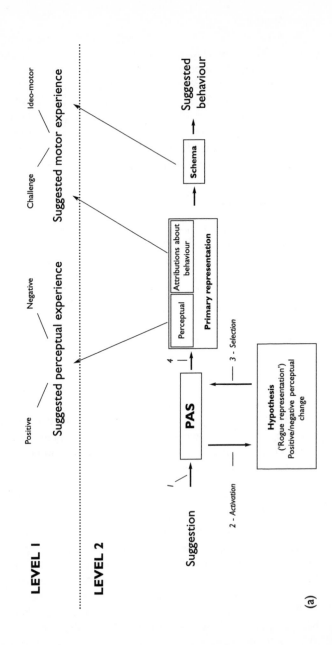

(a)

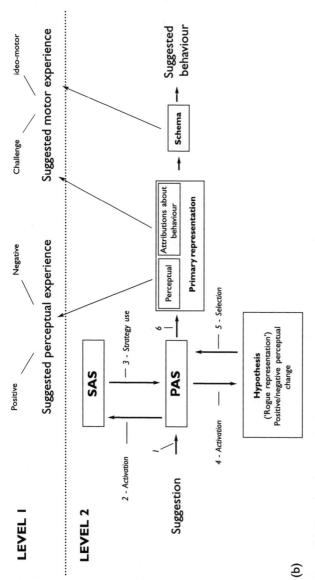

Figure 7.2 Processing stages involved in 'concentrative' (a) and 'constructive' (b) modes of responding to suggestion. See text for further explanation.

disattending to extraneous stimuli; in this sense, the style may be regarded as 'concentrative'. The second route involves the indirect activation of low-level schemata by SAS processing (see Figure 7.2b). This encompasses the use of deliberate SAS strategies, such as 'thinking with' suggestions or engaging in goal-directed imaging, that influence PAS activity and hence suggested responding; this might be regarded as a 'constructive' style of responding. This particular aspect of our account is similar to response set theory and other sociocognitive approaches to hypnosis. These two routes to responding may be associated with different experiences during the creation of suggested effects. Thus, subjects using a constructive style may report using a range of strategies to create the suggested experience, whereas concentrative responders are more likely to report that the experience simply occurred (McConkey et al., 1989). The processes involved in these two routes to suggestion are summarized in Figure 7.2. These different routes to suggestion are available in all contexts, hypnotic and otherwise. Nevertheless, we identify certain features associated with the hypnotic context that may facilitate suggested responding, some of which may relate differently to these two response routes.

The hypnotic context

In this model, any existing representations about hypnosis within associative memory, particularly beliefs and expectations, are pre-attentively activated[9] when the individual enters the hypnotic situation. Typical beliefs pertain to the relationship between hypnosis and sleep, relaxation, alterations in consciousness, responding to suggestions and the loss of control over one's behaviour (e.g. McConkey, 1986; McConkey and Jupp, 1986). The pattern of activity in associative memory is also influenced by contextual features relating to the surrounding environment, the hypnotist, and the demands placed on the individual as part of the interaction (e.g. to remain motivated and cooperative, or to adopt a particular strategy). This process can be conceived as a simple form of suggestion, which creates a pattern of representational activity in associative memory that colours all subsequent behaviour and experience in the hypnotic context; we assume that this facilitates the selection of rogue representations and the automatic activation of suggested behaviours.

---

[9] Some degree of post-attentive belief activation by the SAS is also likely.

Following Sarbin (1950), we label this frame of mind *the hypnotic role*. Rather than being a conscious mind-set as suggested in classical role-theory, the hypnotic role in this account is generated simply by being in the hypnotic situation. Sociocognitive theorists often allude to such a process when they discuss the subject's *implicit* or *tacit* perceptions of the role requirements during hypnosis (e.g. Lynn and Rhue, 1991; Spanos and Coe, 1992).

Absorption

In addition to these non-state factors, we assume that the hypnotic context is often associated with certain changes in information processing that facilitate suggested responding. One such change is the creation of an *absorbed* state during hypnosis, an idea that has been endorsed by researchers from across the theoretical spectrum (see Chapters 1 and 3; also Spanos and Barber, 1974). Absorption has been described as a state of highly focused or 'total' attention 'involving a full commitment of available perceptual, motoric, imaginative and ideational resources to a unified representation of the attentional object' (Tellegen and Atkinson, 1974, p. 274). The language of the induction typically encourages subjects to achieve such a state, instructing them to focus their attention on the voice of the hypnotist to the exclusion of other stimuli. The absorbed individual reports being completely involved in his or her experience, often with little or no awareness of competing information. Similar states have been reported in contexts other than hypnosis (J.R. Hilgard, 1979; Maslow, 1968; Nakamura and Csikszentmihalyi, 2002; Roche and McConkey, 1990); everyday examples include the highly focused states experienced when one is engrossed in a good book or film (see e.g. Baum and Lynn, 1981). The marked time distortion (underestimation) frequently seen in hypnosis is also common to these 'everyday' focused and absorbed states (Naish, 2003).

The inclusion of instructions to focus one's attention and become absorbed in the hypnotic experience appears to enhance suggestibility (Brown et al., 2001). Cognitive and neurophysiological evidence is also consistent with the idea that hypnotic procedures promote a state of highly focused attention (Graham, 1975, cited in Graham and Evans, 1977; Gruzelier, 1998; see Chapter 6 of this volume), as is the relationship between hypnotizability and sustained attentional abilities discussed previously. In the current model, a state of absorption facilitates suggested responding by maximizing the amount of representational activation produced by the words of the suggestion. In this respect, the creation of an absorbed state may be an important component of the concentrative response style. Absorption may also facilitate constructive responding, however, by increasing the potency of certain strategies such as imagery.

Changes in level of processing

The creation of an absorbed state may have additional cognitive consequences that influence suggestive responding. In particular, absorption may serve to inhibit the SAS and bias the system towards PAS-level processing; this is akin to inhibiting critical thought and 'going with the flow' during the hypnotic session. This leads to an increased reliance on automatic processes for the control of behaviour, facilitating the direct activation of suggestion-related schemata by the words of the hypnotist. Such a process may be an important component of the concentrative route to suggestion. This is the same mechanism identified in dissociated control theory, although in this account SAS inhibition is not *required* for successful responding to take place: rather, it makes it more likely. Most special process theories support a variation on this theme (see Chapter 1; also Brown and Oakley, 1997). According to ego-psychological theory, for example, hypnosis is characterized by a suspension of rational secondary processes, with an accompanying shift towards more primitive primary process mentation (e.g. Fromm, 1992). In neodissociation theory, hypnosis serves to inhibit and fractionate high-level executive systems, allowing voluntary behavioural sequences to be initiated without conscious awareness (e.g. E.R. Hilgard, 1986). In Gruzelier's neurophysiological theory (e.g. Gruzelier, 1998), the hypnotic subject 'lets go' of high-level attentional functions and becomes absorbed in passive imagery and daydreaming. The idea is also consistent with Tellegen and Atkinson's (1974) original description of absorption as a state precluding 'salient qualifying "meta-cognitions", that is, thoughts about the primary representation, such as "this is only my imagination" or "this is not really happening" ' (p. 274). Even certain sociocognitive theorists have endorsed a variant on this position (e.g. Sarbin, 1950; see Spanos and Barber, 1974). Indeed, although this state of absorption and high-level inhibition corresponds broadly to the traditional concept of trance, it is very much the product of 'normal' psychological processes.

The language of the induction often conveys the idea that the subject should inhibit critical thought during hypnosis, encouraging him or her not to think about what is happening during the session and to 'go with the flow' (see e.g. Shor and Orne, 1962). Evidence suggests that such instructions contribute significantly to the suggestibility-enhancing effects of the induction (Brown et al., 2001). Studies indicating that the hypnotized individual sometimes displays a tolerance for logical incongruities, so-called 'trance-logic' (Orne, 1959), are also consistent with this idea (cf. Spanos, 1986). Other studies are consistent with the idea that hypnotized individuals experience a shift towards more imaginal, holistic and emotional forms of thinking (Crawford et al., 1989; Fromm et al., 1970; Hammer et al., 1978; J.R. Hilgard, 1979; Levin and Harrison, 1976; Pinnell et al., 1998; for a brief review see Nash, 1991). Evidence pertaining to the neurophysiological correlates of 'traditional' hypnotic inductions is also consistent with this hypothesis (Gruzelier, 1998; see Chapter 1).

Suggestibility, hypnotic suggestibility and hypnotizability

Following Kirsch (1997), we draw a distinction between *suggestibility, hypnotic suggestibility* and *hypnotizability*. Suggestibility and hypnotic suggestibility are defined as an individual's responsivity to suggestions in non-hypnotic and hypnotic contexts respectively. There is considerable overlap between these two forms of responsivity, reflecting our assumption that the basic mechanisms of suggestion are the same in both hypnotic and non-hypnotic contexts (Kirsch, 1997). Hypnotizability is defined as the *change* in suggestibility associated with testing in the hypnotic context; by this view, therefore, traditional measurement scales assess hypnotic suggestibility rather than hypnotizability *per se*.

Although individuals skilled in concentrative and constructive routes to suggestion will have comparable levels of hypnotic suggestibility (i.e. similar scores on traditional scales), we anticipate that the two groups may differ in terms of suggestibility and hypnotizability. As the same strategies are available to constructive responders both in and outside hypnosis, it is likely that this group will show comparable levels of suggestibility in the two contexts. Concentrative responders, in contrast, may benefit more from increased absorption and SAS inhibition, resulting in higher suggestibility scores in hypnotic compared to non-hypnotic context. As such, high hypnotizability may be a characteristic of concentrative but not constructive responders. Moreover, as the two groups differ in the way that they respond to suggestions during hypnosis, it is meaningful to speak of two different types of high hypnotic suggestibility. Despite considerable evidence for different types of responsive subject, few theories of hypnosis have even considered this issue (see Chapter 3).

By this view, a concentrative form of high hypnotic suggestibility may be associated with skills in focused attention, disattention and possibly SAS inhibition, whereas a constructive form may be associated with skills in the flexible use of effortful strategies. Thus, individuals skilled in a concentrative response style may process language more automatically than non-concentrators (Dixon et al., 1990; Dixon and Laurence, 1992b; cf. Sheehan et al., 1988), have greater sustained attentional abilities (Crawford et al., 1993; Van Nuys, 1973; Wallace et al., 1976; also Chapter 6 of this volume; cf. also Jamieson and Sheehan, 2002; Kallio et al., 2001; Sigman et al., 1985), and inhibit to-be-ignored material more efficiently (David and Brown, 2002; David et al., 2001). As such skills are difficult to train, it is unlikely that suggestibility could be modified by adopting this mode of responding. Individuals skilled in a constructive response style may be more able to shift from one kind of cognitive strategy to another and therefore exhibit greater cognitive flexibility (Aikins and Ray, 2001; Priebe and Wallace, 1986; Wallace, 1988, 1990; Wallace et al., 1994; Wallace and Patterson, 1984).[10] A constructive style may also be more closely associated with empathy, social conformity, high motivation and a positive response set (cf. Barber, 1999). It is therefore likely that suggestibility could be modified by training individuals in this mode of responding (see Chapter 9).

Although we draw a distinction between styles of responding, it is likely that these styles will overlap in practice. Moreover, some individuals may adopt one style under some circumstances and another style when the situation changes (see Chapter 3). It is also likely that other styles of responding are possible. Indeed, it is worth considering how the current model might account for other kinds of highly suggestible individuals, such as Barrett's (1990) fantasy-prone and amnesia-prone subjects (see Chapters 4 and 8). One possibility is that

---

[10] It is possible that such flexibility is also characteristic of a concentrative style, due to its relationship with attentional ability. This is an empirical question.

fantasy-prone and amnesia-prone subjects are virtuoso sub-types of constructive and concentrative responders respectively.

Are hypnotic responses automatic?

Given the theoretical origins of this model, it seems appropriate to say more about the automaticity of suggested phenomena. In the current model, behaviours are regarded as automatic if they are governed by the direct activation of a cognition or action schema by the products of PAS selection. As suggested behaviours involve precisely this mechanism at the point of execution, they can be viewed as automatic responses (cf. Kirsch and Lynn, 1997; Woody and Bowers, 1994). In the case of suggested alterations in experience, however, the locus of suggestion is the process of PAS selection; as such, they may be more appropriately viewed as pre-attentive (or, perhaps, *peri*-attentive) rather than automatic phenomena. In both cases, the response is closely associated with the operation of attention and may therefore consume processing resources. It is also important to bear in mind that responding to suggestion is a process that occurs over time. Although suggested behaviours are automatic at the point of execution, the subject may have engaged in a range of non-automatic behaviours to facilitate and maintain the process of responding. This is particularly true in the case of individuals who adopt a constructive response mode, whose *overall* response to the suggestion may be regarded as relatively less automatic than that of a concentrative responder. One obvious prediction from this is that concentrative responders will exhibit less interference than constructive responders on concurrent tasks performed alongside suggested responses.

Summary and conclusions

The model presented here combines several existing theories of hypnosis into a single explanatory framework based on well-established principles from cognitive psychology. On the one hand, it embraces the idea that hypnosis often involves becoming absorbed in suggested experiences and 'letting go' of high-level, critical processes. These concepts are central to the ego-psychological, neodissociation, dissociated control and neuropsychophysiological theories of hypnosis. In this sense, the model adopts a variation on the state or special-process view of hypnotic responding. On the other hand, although the model proposes that absorption and critical inhibition facilitate suggested responding, they are not necessary for this to take place. Moreover, both hypnotic and non-hypnotic suggestions are produced by the same normal psychological mechanisms. This aspect of the model is consistent with a non-state or sociocognitive account of hypnosis. Also consistent with the sociocognitive approach is the proposal that the suggested experience of involuntariness results from a process of misattribution. In so doing, the current model demonstrates that these apparently disparate approaches to hypnosis are more compatible than traditionally conceived (cf. Kihlstrom, 1997).

Unlike most previous approaches, the present model incorporates evidence demonstrating that there are different routes to suggested responding and therefore different types of high hypnotic suggestibility. Indeed, the model goes further than this in suggesting that not all individuals who score high on traditional scales are actually high in hypnotizability. In particular, we suggest that concentrative responders are more likely than constructive responders to benefit from hypnotic induction procedures and are therefore more highly hypnotizable. We have also identified the different characteristics possessed by successful concentrative and constructive responders that make them more able to respond to suggestions than their less suggestible counterparts.

This integration of different theoretical approaches and its implications for suggestibility and hypnotizability provides clear directions for future research with novel predictions, underlining the value of basing hypnosis research and theory in mainstream psychology. In turn, this approach provides an explanatory platform for the instrumental use of hypnosis as a cognitive tool, and demonstrates how research in this area can inform mainstream cognitive psychology.

References

Aikins, D. and Ray, W.J. (2001) 'Frontal lobe contributions to hypnotic susceptibility: A neuropsychological screening of executive functioning', *International Journal of Clinical and Experimental Hypnosis*, 49:320–9.

Allport, A. (1987) 'Selection for action: Some behavioural and neurophysiological considerations of attention and action', in H. Heuer, and A.F. Sanders (eds), *Perspectives on Selection and Action* (pp. 395–419), Hillsdale, NJ: Lawrence Erlbaum Associates.

Barber, T.X. (1969) *Hypnosis: A Scientific Approach*, New York: Van Nostrand Reinhold.

—— (1999) 'Hypnosis: A mature view', *Contemporary Hypnosis*, 16:123–7.

—— and Calverley, D.S. (1965) 'Empirical evidence for a theory of "hypnotic" behavior: Effects on suggestibility of five variables typically included in hypnotic induction procedures', *Journal of Consulting Psychology*, 29:98–107.

Bargh, J.A. (1994) 'The four horsemen of automaticity: Awareness, intention, efficiency, and control in social cognition', in R.S. Wyer Jr. and T.K. Srull (eds), *Handbook of Social Cognition, Volume 1: Basic Processes* (pp. 1–40), Hillsdale, NJ: Lawrence Erlbaum Associates.

Barnier, A.J. (2001) 'Posthypnotic suggestion: Attention, awareness and automaticity', *Sleep and Hypnosis*, 1:57–63.

—— (2002) 'Post-hypnotic amnesia for autobiographical episodes: A laboratory model of functional amnesia?', *Psychological Science*, 13:232–7.

—— and McConkey, K.M. (1996) 'Action and desire in post-hypnotic responding', *International Journal of Clinical and Experimental Hypnosis*, 44:120–39.

—— and McConkey, K.M. (1998) 'Post-hypnotic responding away from the hypnotic setting', *Psychological Science*, 9:256–62.

—— and McConkey, K.M. (1999) 'Hypnotic and post-hypnotic suggestion: Finding meaning in the message of the hypnotist', *International Journal of Clinical and Experimental Hypnosis*, 47:192–208.

Barrett, D. (1990) 'Deep trance subjects: A schema of two distinct subgroups', in R.G. Kunzendorf (ed.), *Mental Imagery* (pp. 101–12), New York: Plenum Press.

Baum, D. and Lynn, S.J. (1981) 'Hypnotic susceptibility level and reading involvement', *International Journal of Clinical and Experimental Hypnosis*, 29:366–74.

Blakemore, S.-J., Wolpert, D.M. and Frith, C.D. (2002) 'Abnormalities in the awareness of action', *Trends in Cognitive Sciences*, 6:237–42.

—— Oakley, D.A. and Frith, C.D. (2003) 'Delusions of alien control in the normal brain', *Neuropsychologia*, 41:1058–67.

Bowers, K.S. (1990) 'Unconscious influences and hypnosis', in J.L. Singer (ed.), *Repression and Dissociation: Implications for Personality Theory, Psychopathology and Health* (pp. 143–78), Chicago: University of Chicago Press.

—— (1992) 'Imagination and dissociation in hypnotic responding', *International Journal of Clinical and Experimental Hypnosis*, 40:253–75.

—— and Brenneman, H.A. (1981) 'Hypnotic dissociation, dichotic listening, and active versus passive modes of attention', *Journal of Abnormal Psychology*, 90:55–67.

—— and Woody, E.Z. (1996) 'Hypnotic amnesia and the paradox of intentional forgetting', *Journal of Abnormal Psychology*, 105:381–90.

Brown, R.J. (1999a) *An Integrative Cognitive Theory of Suggestion and Hypnosis*, Unpublished PhD thesis, University College London.

—— (1999b) 'Three dimensions of hypnosis or multiple routes to suggested responding?', *Contemporary Hypnosis*, 16:128–31.

—— (2002) 'The cognitive psychology of dissociative states', *Cognitive Neuropsychiatry*, 7:221–35.

—— and Oakley, D.A. (1997) 'Hypnosis and cognitive-experiential self-theory: A new conceptualization for hypnosis?', *Contemporary Hypnosis*, 14:94–9.

—— Antonova, E., Langley, A. and Oakley, D.A. (2001) 'The effects of absorption and reduced critical thought on suggestibility in a hypnotic context', *Contemporary Hypnosis*, 18:62–72.

Burgess, P.W., and Shallice, T. (1996) 'Confabulation and the control of recollection', *Memory*, 4:359–412.

Conway, M.A. and Pleydell-Pearce, C.W. (2000) 'The construction of auto-biographical memories in the self–memory system', *Psychological Review*, 107:261–88.

Crawford, H. J., Clarke, S.N., Kitner-Triolo, M. and Olesko, B. (1989) 'EEG correlates of emotions: Moderated by hypnosis and hypnotic level', Paper presented at the meeting of the American Psychological Association, New Orleans.

—— Brown, A.M. and Moon, C.E. (1993) 'Sustained attentional and dis-attentional abilities: Differences between low and highly hypnotizable individuals', *Journal of Abnormal Psychology*, 102:534–43.

Crick, F., and Koch, C. (1990) 'Towards a neurobiological theory of consciousness', *Seminars in the Neurosciences*, 2:263–75.

Damasio, A. (2000) *The Feeling of What Happens*, London: Heinemann.

David, D. and Brown, R.J. (2002) 'Suggestibility and negative priming: Two replication studies', *International Journal of Clinical and Experimental Hypnosis*, 50:215–28.

—— King, B.J. and Borkardt, J.J. (2001) 'Is a capacity for negative priming correlated with hypnotizability? A preliminary study', *International Journal of Clinical and Experimental Hypnosis*, 49:30–7.

—— Brown, R.J., Pojoga, C. and David, A. (2000) 'The impact of posthypnotic amnesia and directed forgetting on implicit and explicit memory: New insights from a modified process dissociation procedure', *International Journal of Clinical and Experimental Hypnosis*, 48:267–89.

Derbyshire, S.W.G., Whalley, M.G., Stenger, U.A. and Oakley, D.A. (under review) 'Cerebral activation during hypnotically induced and imagined pain', NeuroImage.

Dixon, M. and Laurence, J.-R. (1992a) 'Two hundred years of hypnosis research: Questions resolved? Questions unanswered!', in E. Fromm and M.R. Nash (eds), *Contemporary Hypnosis Research* (pp. 34–66), New York: Guilford Press.

—— and Laurence, J.-R. (1992b) 'Hypnotic susceptibility and verbal automaticity: Automatic and strategic processing differences in the Stroop color-naming task', *Journal of Abnormal Psychology*, 101:344–7.

—— Brunet, A. and Laurence, J.-R. (1990) 'Hypnotizability and automaticity: Toward a parallel distributed processing model of hypnotic responding', *Journal of Abnormal Psychology*, 99:336–43.

Fromm, E. (1992) 'An ego-psychological theory of hypnosis', in E. Fromm and M.R. Nash (eds), *Contemporary Hypnosis Research* (pp. 131–48), London: Guilford Press.

—— Oberlander, M.I. and Gruenewald, D. (1970) 'Perceptual and cognitive processes in different states of consciousness: The waking state and hypnosis', *Journal of Projective Techniques and Personality Assessment*, 34:375–87.

Gollwitzer, P.M. (1993) 'Goal achievement: The role of intentions', in W. Stroebe and M. Hewstone (eds), *European Review of Social Psychology*, Vol. 4 (pp. 141–85), Chichester: Wiley.

Graham, C. and Evans, F.J. (1977) 'Hypnotizability and the deployment of waking attention', *Journal of Abnormal Psychology*, 86:631–8.

Green, J.P. and Lynn, S.J. (1995) 'Hypnosis, dissociation, and simultaneous-task performance', *Journal of Personality and Social Psychology*, 69:728–35.

Gregory, R.L. (1970) *The Intelligent Eye*, London: Weidenfeld and Nicolson.

Gruzelier, J.H. (1998) 'A working model of the neuropsychophysiology of hypnosis: A review of evidence', *Contemporary Hypnosis*, 15:5–23.

Halligan, P.W. and Oakley, D.A. (2000) 'Greatest myth of all', *New Scientist*, 168:35–49.

—— Athwal, B.S., Oakley, D.A. and Frackowiak, R.S.J. (2000) 'Imaging hypnotic paralysis: Implications for conversion hysteria', *The Lancet*, 355:986–7.

Hammer, A.G. Walker, W. and Diment, A.D. (1978) 'A nonsuggested effect of trance induction', in F.H. Frankel and H.S. Zamansky (eds), *Hypnosis at its Bicentennial: Selected Papers* (pp. 91–100), New York: Plenum.

Hargadon, R., Bowers, K.S. and Woody, E.Z. (1995) 'Does counterpain imagery mediate hypnotic analgesia?', *Journal of Abnormal Psychology*, 104:508–16.

Hilgard, E.R. (1986) *Divided Consciousness: Multiple Controls in Human Thought and Action*, 2nd edn, New York: Wiley.

Hilgard, J.R. (1979) *Personality and Hypnosis: A Study of Imaginative Involvement*, 2nd edn, Chicago: University of Chicago Press.

Hull, C.L. (1933) *Hypnosis and Suggestibility*, New York: Appleton-Century-Crofts.

Jahanshahi, M. and Frith, C.D. (1998) 'Willed action and its impairments', *Cognitive Neuropsychology*, 15:483–533.

James, W. (1890) *The Principles of Psychology*, London: Macmillan.

Jamieson, G.A. and Sheehan, P.W. (2002) 'A critical evaluation of the relationship between sustained attentional abilities and hypnotic susceptibility', *Contemporary Hypnosis*, 19:62–74.

Jeannerod, M. (1997) *The Cognitive Neuroscience of Action*, Oxford: Blackwell.

Kahneman, D. (1973) *Attention and Effort*, Englewood Cliffs, NJ: Prentice-Hall.

Kallio, S., Revonsuo, A., Haemaelaeinen, H., Markela, J. and Gruzelier, J. (2001) 'Anterior brain functions and hypnosis: A test of the frontal hypothesis', *International Journal of Clinical and Experimental Hypnosis*. 49:95–108.

Kemler, D.G. (1983) 'Holistic and analytic modes in perceptual and cognitive development' in R. Tighe and B.E. Shepp (eds), *Perception, Cognition and Development: Interaction Analysis* (pp. 77–102), Hillsdale, NJ: Erlbaum.

Kihlstrom, J.F. (1987) 'The cognitive unconscious', *Science*, 237:1445–51.

—— (1997) 'Convergence in understanding hypnosis? Perhaps, but perhaps not quite so fast', *International Journal of Clinical and Experimental Hypnosis*, 45:324–32.

—— (1998) 'Dissociations and dissociation theory in hypnosis: Comment on Kirsch and Lynn (1998)', *Psychological Bulletin*, 123:186–91.

Kirsch, I. (1997) 'Suggestibility or hypnosis: What do our scales really measure?', *International Journal of Clinical and Experimental Hypnosis*, 45:212–25.

—— and Lynn, S.J. (1997) 'Hypnotic involuntariness and the automaticity of everyday life', *American Journal of Clinical Hypnosis*, 40:329–48.

—— and Lynn, S.J. (1998) 'Dissociation theories of hypnosis', *Psychological Bulletin*, 123:100–15.

—— Milling, L.S. and Burgess, C. (2000) 'Suggestion difficulty as a hypothesized moderator of the relation between absorption and suggestibility: A new spectral analysis', *International Journal of Clinical and Experimental Hypnosis*, 48:32–43.

Knox, V.J., Crutchfield, L. and Hilgard, E.R. (1975) 'The nature of task interference in hypnotic dissociation: An investigation of hypnotic behavior', *International Journal of Clinical and Experimental Hypnosis*, 30:305–23.

Kosslyn, S.M. (1996) *Image and Brain*, Cambridge, MA: MIT Press.

—— Thompson, W.L., Costantini-Ferrando, M.F., Alpert, N.M. and Spiegel, D. (2000) 'Hypnotic visual illusion alters color processing in the brain', *American Journal of Psychiatry*, 157:1279–84.

Lavie, N. (1995) 'Perceptual load as a necessary condition for selective attention', *Journal of Experimental Psychology: Human Perception and Performance*, 21:451–68.

Levin, L.A. and Harrison, R.H. (1976) 'Hypnosis and regression in the service of the ego', *International Journal of Clinical and Experimental Hypnosis*, 24:400–18.

Logan, G.D. (1988) 'Toward an instance theory of automatization', *Psychological Review*, 95:492–527.

—— (1992) 'Attention and pre-attention in theories of automaticity', *American Journal of Psychology*, 105:317–39.

Luria, A.R. (1973) *The Working Brain*, London: Penguin.

Lynn, S.J. and Rhue, J.W. (1991) 'An integrative model of hypnosis', in S.J. Lynn and J.W. Rhue (eds), *Theories of Hypnosis: Current Models and Perspectives* (pp. 397–438), New York: Guilford Press.

Marcel, A.J. (1983) 'Conscious and unconscious perception: An approach to the relations between phenomenal experience and perceptual processes', *Cognitive Psychology*, 15:238–300.

Marr, D. (1982) *Vision*, San Francisco: Freeman.

Maslow, A.H. (1968) *Toward a Psychology of Being*, 2nd edn, Princeton, NJ: Van Nostrand.

McConkey, K.M. (1986) 'Opinions about hypnosis and self-hypnosis before and after hypnotic testing', *International Journal of Clinical and Experimental Hypnosis*, 34:311–19.

—— and Jupp, J.J. (1986) 'A survey of opinions about hypnosis', *British Journal of Experimental and Clinical Hypnosis*, 3:87–93.

—— K.M., Glisky, M.L. and Kihlstrom, J.F. (1989) 'Individual differences among hypnotic virtuosos: A case comparison', *Australian Journal of Clinical and Experimental Hypnosis*, 17:131–40.

Miller, M.E. and Bowers, K.S. (1993) 'Hypnotic analgesia: Dissociated experience or dissociated control?', *Journal of Abnormal Psychology*, 102:29–38.

Nadon, R. (1997) 'What this field needs is a good nomological network', *International Journal of Clinical and Experimental Hypnosis*, 45:314–23.

Naish, P.L.N. (2003) 'The production of hypnotic time distortion: Determining the necessary conditions', *Contemporary Hypnosis*, 20:3–15.

Nakamura, J. and Csikszentmihalyi, M. (2002) 'The concept of flow', in C.R. Snyder, and S.J. Lopez (eds), *Handbook of Positive Psychology* (pp. 89–105), London: Oxford University Press.

Nash, M.R. (1991) 'Hypnosis as a special case of psychological regression', in S.J. Lynn and J.W. Rhue (eds), *Theories of Hypnosis: Current Models and Perspectives* (pp. 171–94), New York: Guilford Press.

Neely, J.H. (1977) 'Semantic priming and retrieval from lexical memory: Roles of inhibitionless spreading activation and limited capacity attention', *Journal of Experimental Psychology: General*, 106:226–54.

Neisser, U. (1976) *Cognition and Reality*, San Francisco: W.H. Freeman.

Norman, D.A., and Shallice, T. (1986) 'Attention to action: Willed and automatic control of behavior', in R.J. Davidson, G.E. Schwartz and

D. Shapiro (eds), *Consciousness and Self-regulation. Advances in Research and Theory*, Vol. 4 (pp. 1–18), New York: Plenum.

Oakley, D.A. (1985) 'Animal awareness, consciousness and self-image', in D.A. Oakley (ed.), *Brain and Mind* (pp. 217–51), London: Methuen.

—— (1998) 'Editorial commentary', *Contemporary Hypnosis*, 15:1–2.

—— (1999a) 'Hypnosis and conversion hysteria: A unifying model', *Cognitive Neuropsychiatry*, 4:243–65.

—— (1999b) 'Hypnosis and consciousness: A structural model', *Contemporary Hypnosis*, 16:215–23.

Orne, M.T. (1959) 'The nature of hypnosis: Artifact and essence', *Journal of Abnormal and Social Psychology*, 58:277–99.

Pinnell, C.M., Lynn, S.J. and Pinnell, J.P. (1998) 'Primary process, hypnotic dreams, and the hidden observer: Hypnosis versus alert imagining', *International Journal of Clinical and Experimental Hypnosis*, 46:351–62.

Posner, M.I. and Snyder, C.R.R. (1975) 'Facilitation and inhibition in the processing of signals', in P.M.A. Rabbitt and S. Dornick (eds), *Attention and Performance V* (pp. 669–82), New York: Academic Press.

Priebe, F.A. and Wallace, B. (1986) 'Hypnotic susceptibility, imaging ability and the detection of embedded objects', *International Journal of Clinical and Experimental Hypnosis*, 34:320–9.

Rainville, P., Duncan, G.H., Price, D.D., Carrier, B. and Bushnell, C. (1997) 'Pain affect encoded in human anterior cingulated but not somatosensory cortex', *Science*, 277:968–71.

Reyher, J. (1962) 'A paradigm for determining the clinical relevance of hypnotically induced psychopathology', *Psychological Bulletin*, 59:34–52.

Roche, S.M. and McConkey, K.M. (1990) 'Absorption: Nature, assessment and correlates', *Journal of Personality and Social Psychology*, 59:91–101.

Rumelhart, D.E., McClelland, J.L. and the PDP Research Group (1986) *Parallel Distributed Processing. Explorations in the Microstructure of Cognition. Volume 1: Foundations*, Cambridge, MA: MIT Press.

Sarbin, T.R. (1950) 'Contributions to role-taking theory: I. Hypnotic behavior', *Psychological Review*, 57:255–70.

Shallice, T. (1988) *From Neuropsychology to Mental Structure*, Cambridge: Cambridge University Press.

—— and Burgess, P.W. (1996) 'The domain of supervisory processes and temporal organization of behaviour', *Philosophical Transactions of the Royal Society of London*, 351:1405–12.

Sheehan, P.W. and McConkey, K.M (1982) *Hypnosis and Experience: The Exploration of Phenomena and Process*, Hillsdale, NJ: Erlbaum.

—— Donovan, P. and MacLeod, C.M. (1988) 'Strategy manipulation and the Stroop effect in hypnosis', *Journal of Abnormal Psychology*, 97:455–60.

Shor, R.E. and Orne, E.C. (1962) *The Harvard Group Scale of Hypnotic Susceptibility*, Palo Alto, CA: Consulting Psychologists Press.

Sigman, A., Phillips, K.C. and Clifford, B. (1985) 'Attentional concomitants of hypnotic susceptibility', *British Journal of Experimental and Clinical Hypnosis*, 2:69–75.

Sloman, S.A. (1996) 'The empirical case for two systems of reasoning', *Psychological Bulletin*, 119:3–22.

Spanos, N.P. (1986) 'Hypnotic behavior. A social psychological interpretation of amnesia, analgesia and "trance logic" ', *Behavioral and Brain Sciences*, 9:449–67.

—— and Barber, T.X. (1974) 'Towards a convergence in hypnosis research', *American Psychologist*, 29:500–11.

—— and Chaves, J.F. (1989) *Hypnosis: The Cognitive-behavioral Perspective*, Buffalo, NY: Prometheus Books.

—— and Coe, W.C. (1992) 'A social-psychological approach to hypnosis', in E. Fromm and M.R. Nash (eds), *Contemporary Hypnosis Research* (pp. 102–30), London: Guilford Press.

—— and Gorassini, D.R. (1984) 'Structure of hypnotic test suggestions and attributions of responding involuntarily', *Journal of Personality and Social Psychology*, 46:688–96.

Spiegel, D. (1990) 'Hypnosis, dissociation, and trauma: Hidden and overt observers', in J.L. Singer (ed.), *Repression and Dissociation: Implications for Personality Theory, Psychopathology and Health* (pp. 121–42), Chicago: University of Chicago Press.

Stevenson, J.H. (1976) 'The effect of posthypnotic dissociation on the performance of interfering tasks', *Journal of Abnormal Psychology*, 85:398–407.

Styles, E.A. (1997) *The Psychology of Attention*, Hove, UK: Psychology Press.

Szechtman, H., Woody, E., Bowers, K.S. and Nahmias, C. (1998) 'Where the imaginal appears real: A positron emission tomography study of auditory hallucinations', *Proceedings of the National Academy of Sciences*, 95:1956–60.

Taylor, J.G. (2001) 'The central role of the parietal lobes in consciousness', *Consciousness and Cognition*, 10:379–417.

Tellegen, A. and Atkinson, G. (1974) 'Openness to absorbing and self-altering experiences ("absorption"), a trait related to hypnotic susceptibility', *Journal of Abnormal Psychology*, 83:268–77.

Van Nuys, D. (1973) 'Meditation, attention, and hypnotic susceptibility: A correlational study', *International Journal of Clinical and Experimental Hypnosis*, 21:59–69.

Velmans, M. (2000) *Understanding Consciousness*. London: Routledge.

Wallace, B. (1988) 'Imaging ability, visual search strategies, and the unvividness paradox', *Journal of Mental Imagery*, 12:173–84.

—— (1990) 'Imagery vividness, hypnotic susceptibility, and the perception of fragmented stimuli', *Journal of Personality and Social Psychology*, 58:354–9.

Wallace, B. and Patterson, S.L. (1984) 'Hypnotic susceptibility and performance on various attention-specific cognitive tasks', *Journal of Personality and Social Psychology*, 47:175–81.

—— Knight, T.A. and Garrett, J.B. (1976) 'Hypnotic susceptibility and fluency reports to illusory stimuli', *Journal of Abnormal Psychology*, 85:558–63.

—— Allen, P.A. and Weber, T.A. (1994) 'Hypnotic susceptibility, imaging ability and the detection of embedded words within letters', *International Journal of Clinical and Experimental Hypnosis*, 42:20–38.

Walters, V.J. and Oakley, D.A. (2003) 'Does hypnosis make in vitro, in vivo? Hypnosis as a possible "virtual reality" context in Cognitive-Behavioural Therapy For an environmental phobia', *Clinical Case Studies*, 2:295–305.

Wegner, D.M. (1989) *White Bears and Other Unwanted Thoughts*, New York: Viking.

Woody, E.Z. and Bowers, K.S. (1994) 'A frontal assault on dissociated control', in S.J. Lynn and J.W. Rhue (eds), *Dissociation: Clinical and Theoretical Perspectives* (pp. 52–79), New York: Guilford Press.

—— and Sadler, P. (1998) 'On reintegrating dissociated theories: Comment on Kirsch and Lynn (1998)', *Psychological Bulletin*, 123:192–7.

Chapter 8

Clinical correlates of high hypnotizability

Steven Jay Lynn, Eric Meyer and Kelley Shindler

One of the most robust findings in the literature on hypnotic suggestibility is that there are large individual differences in the extent
to which people respond to imaginative suggestions. Although
approximately 15 per cent of people respond to very few suggestions,
a comparable percentage of individuals respond to a wide range
of suggestions for changes in sensation, perception, cognition, and
action. Many highly suggestible individuals are able to experience
involuntary or automatic movements, vivid hallucinations, age
regression, anesthesia, compulsive posthypnotic behavior, and
amnesia in response to suggestions.

Observations of the dramatic effects of hypnosis led early investigators, including Charcot and Janet, to the mistaken conclusion that
hypnosis is a pathological condition, while the therapeutic potential
of hypnosis was recognized by Breuer who used hypnosis to explore
the psychological dynamics of conversion disorder (Spiegel, 1989).
The ideas that highly suggestible individuals are imbued with 'special' characteristics or abilities; that there is a link between hypnotic
suggestibility and psychopathology (and medical conditions); and
that suggestibility is associated with the ability to benefit from hypnotic procedures are very much alive today. We discuss each of these
ideas in our examination of the clinical correlates of high hypnotic
suggestibility and our discussion of the more general correlates of
hypnotic suggestibility.

T.X. Barber's three-dimensional theory of high hypnotic suggestibility

T.X. Barber (1999a, 1999b, 1999c) has recently argued that there are
actually three distinct types of highly responsive participants who

are capable of displaying the gamut of hypnotic phenomena: the fantasy-prone, the amnesia-prone, and the positively set participants. Wilson and Barber (1981, 1983) first identified the fantasy-prone person or 'fantasizer' in an intensive interview study of 27 highly hypnotically suggestible individuals. The authors discovered that virtually all of their subjects reported the ability to have very vivid and realistic fantasy-based experiences in multiple sensory modalities (e.g. seeing imagined things 'as real as real'). Their subjects also reported that they expended a great deal of time engaging in pretend play and fantasizing as children that included interacting with imaginary playmates, spirits, and guardian angels, and enjoying life-like and highly gratifying sexual fantasies. Many of the subjects could experience alterations in sensations, and more than a few experienced false or hysterical pregnancies. Often fantasizers closely guarded their secret fantasy life or they assumed that most if not all people shared their proclivities toward active fantasy.

Wilson and Barber estimated that this group of highly suggestible subjects comprised approximately 2–4 per cent of the general population, and that their high degree of hypnotic responsiveness represented a straightforward deployment of their long-standing imaginative abilities in everyday life to imaginative suggestions in the hypnotic context. Lynn and Rhue (1988) and Barrett (1991, 1996) succeeded in confirming the claim that a small percentage of individuals could be described as fantasy-prone persons, along the lines indicated by Wilson and Barber.

Barber's description of fantasizers as able to experience profound alterations in consciousness, including 'trance-like states', with no special prompting, resembles H. Spiegel's description of 'Grade 5' syndrome. According to Spiegel, certain highly hypnotizable Grade 5 individuals spontaneously enter into trance states even when they are not intended (Spiegel, 1974). The typical Grade 5 individual is trusting, easily suspends critical judgment, readily affiliates with new metaphors, emphasizes the present without too much concern for past or future perspectives, is comfortable with incongruities, has an excellent memory, and is capable of intense concentration. Spiegel also contended that Grade 5s are prone toward dramatic presentations of somatic complaints, hysteria, or 'hysterical psychosis' under severe stress. Unfortunately, empirical work to date has not been devoted to determining (1) whether some highly hypnotizable persons can be described in terms of a Grade 5 syndrome; (2) whether and how much overlap exists between the characteristics of Grade 5 and fantasy-prone persons; and (3) what percentage of highly hypnotizable persons can be characterized in terms of Spiegel's 'Grade 5 description'.

Whereas research confirms Wilson and Barber's observation that certain highly suggestible persons are fantasy-prone, it is not the case that there is a close association between hypnotic suggestibility and fantasy-proneness in general. Indeed, there is generally a small relationship (0.24–0.26) between scores on an inventory of fantasy-proneness, the Inventory of Creative Memories and Imaginings (ICMI; Wilson and Barber, 1983) and standardized hypnotic suggestibility scales (see Lynn and Rhue, 1988). Moreover, fantasy-prone subjects are not necessarily distinguishable from subjects in the medium range of fantasy-proneness on measures of hypnotic suggestibility (Council and Huff, 1990; Lynn and Rhue, 1988; Lynn et al., 1988; Rhue and Lynn, 1989; Siuta, 1990). Additionally, Green et al. (1989) failed to confirm Wilson and Barber's finding that the majority of highly suggestible individuals are highly fantasy-prone. Green et al., tested 12 individuals who scored in the upper 5 per cent of hypnotic suggestibility based on their positive responses to two tests of hypnotic suggestibility, the Harvard Group Scale of Hypnotic Susceptibility, Form A (HGSHS:A) and the Stanford Hypnotic Susceptibility Scale, Form C (SHSS:C). Contrary to Wilson and Barber's finding that 96 per cent of their highly suggestible subjects were fantasy-prone, Green et al., found that only 2 of the 12 highly suggestible individuals could be so classified based on their scoring in the upper 2–4 per cent of the college population on the ICMI.

Green et al.'s findings are consistent with Barber's (1999a, 1999b) latest claim that the majority of highly suggestible individuals are *not* fantasy-prone. Rather, they are 'very good or positively set' hypnotic subjects because they exhibit

(a) positive attitudes towards the idea of hypnosis, towards the specific test situation and towards the particular hypnotist; (b) positive motivation to perform well on the suggested tasks and to experience those things suggested; (c) positive expectancies that they can be hypnotized and can experience the suggested effects; and (d) a positive set to visualize, think with and not contradict the hypnotist's suggestions.

(Barber, 1999b, p. 124)

Barber claims that the positively set individuals he identified comprise the large majority of highly suggestible persons, and that only about 1 per cent of student subjects exhibit a special talent for fantasizing that accounts for their high hypnotic suggestibility.

In addition to the fantasy-prone and positively set subjects, Barber contends that a very small group of highly suggestible subjects (1 per cent of college students) are amnesia-prone. This third type of highly suggestible, 'amnesia-prone' subject, was actually first 'differentiated' by Deirdre Barrett (1990, 1996). She reported that 15 out of the 34 highly responsive subjects (total $N = 1200$) she studied reported spontaneous amnesia for events that transpired during hypnosis and seemed slow to talk after hypnosis. These subjects also reported few memories of events prior to age 5, amnesia for their dreams, histories rife with childhood trauma, and amnesia for significant events that occurred in the recent past, including traumatic life experiences such as sexual and physical abuse.

Barber draws interesting historical parallels between Barrett's amnesia-prone subjects and both 19th-century hysterics and somnabulistic subjects who were reportedly not only highly suggestible but also displayed spontaneous posthypnotic amnesia as well as forgetfulness regarding important everyday life events. Barber (1999c) also draws a number of striking parallels between amnesia-prone persons and 'Janet's hysterics' in the 100 dissociative psychiatric patients that Bliss (e.g. 1980, 1986) studied who were excellent hypnotic subjects and manifested amnesic symptoms in everyday life that extended to 'behaviors they disowned that could be attributed to an "alter ego" or an "alternative personality" ' (p. 197). Like dissociative individuals, amnesia-prone persons report histories of severe trauma (e.g. childhood sexual and physical abuse) and purportedly 'compartmentalize' and forget aversive stimuli such as severe parental criticism. In fact, Barber (1999c) goes so far as to claim that 'compartmentalized memories, feelings, emotions and cognitions have their own dynamics and potentially act as a separate center of consciousness, ego state, or personality' (p. 198).

Criticisms of Barber's model

Barber's typology of highly suggestible subjects has encountered criticism on a number of fronts. Perhaps the most trenchant criticisms revolve around the studies that Barber used to generate his model. For example, Barber cites the cluster analytic findings of

Pekala (1991) and Pekala et al. (1995) as furnishing impressive corroboration for his tripartite distinction. However, Lynn et al. (1999) noted that the results of both studies provided evidence for two, rather than three, subtypes of hypnotic subjects, only one of which replicated across both cluster analyses. Pekala (1991) found evidence for two subtypes that seemed to correspond to Barber's fantasy-prone and amnesia-prone groups, whereas Pekala et al. (1995) found evidence for two subtypes that seemed to correspond to Barber's positively set and amnesia-prone groups. Accordingly, with respect to two of Barber's putative groups (fantasy-prone and positively set), the two studies of Pekala and colleagues can best be described as amounting to a double non-replication (Lynn et al., 1999). Relatedly, Chaves (1999) observed that Pekala's studies focused on a general sample of subjects and did not (given their purported rarity) include many amnesia-prone (or fantasy-prone) persons, thereby limiting the direct relevance of the research to elucidating the characteristics of these individuals.

Barrett's studies have also come under fire for methodological shortcomings. For example, Brown (1999) commented that Barrett (1990) provided neither details of the measures used to assess fantasy and amnesia, nor the analyses performed to distinguish the subject types she identified. Moreover, Barrett is faulted for failing to provide operational criteria for her basis for distinguishing different subject types: whether or not they enter 'trance' quickly. This failure is adjudged to be problematic insofar as there are no widely accepted criteria for defining a 'trance' and for stating whether a person is 'in a trance'. Moreover, Lynn et al. (1999) noted that Barrett failed to conduct interviews blindly of knowledge concerning participants' responses to hypnosis, the extent to which interview questions were standardized across participants is unclear, inter-rater reliability for the coding of participants' responses were not reported, and participants' child abuse memories were not corroborated by external evidence. Furthermore, Lynn et al. (1999) pointed out that in several cases, Barrett interpreted questionable signs and symptoms (e.g. recurring nightmares, vomiting on being touched on the thigh) as indicative of possible or probable early abuse without additional corroborating information. Relatedly, it seems reasonable to question the reliability of amnesia-prone individuals' accounts of their personal history. Finally, Barrett's assertions regarding the association between early abuse and amnesia will need to be reconciled with the recent meta-analysis of Rind et al. (1998) which reported a very weak relation ($r = 0.09$) between self-reported childhood sexual abuse and later dissociative symptoms among college students ($N = 1324$).

Clinical implications

Even if there are difficulties in isolating distinct 'types' of highly suggestive individuals, and methodological limitations of previous research preclude firm conclusions, Barber's typology does highlight important individual differences in the presentation of highly suggestible individuals that have important implications for clinical assessment and treatment. Knowing something about clients' 'positive set' or lack of it, their imaginative abilities, and their dissociative tendencies may, for example, help therapists tailor their treatment to particular clients and maximize responsiveness to therapeutic suggestions.

Imagery-based techniques

Identifying clients who are highly suggestible and fantasy-prone is important insofar as therapists can exploit imaginative abilities to good advantage. Techniques that capitalize on imaginative and fantasy abilities have been used to treat a wide variety of psychological and medical disorders. The behavioral techniques of flooding, implosion, and systematic desensitization, used so effectively in the treatment of phobias and anxiety disorders, rely heavily on imagination-based exposure to anxiety-related stimuli (Mellinger and Lynn, 2003). Imagination-based treatments may also be useful in problem solving by rehearsing and coping with events in fantasy. Although fantasy, by itself, does not ensure successful coping, it can facilitate that objective.

There are distinct similarities between cognitive–behavioral therapy and hypnosis (Kirsch et al., 1999). Imagery-based techniques, presented in the context of hypnosis, have been used successfully in the cognitive–behavioral treatment of anxiety disorders. In fact, the outcome of imagery-based, cognitive–behavioral treatments can be improved by presenting cognitive–behavioral procedures as 'hypnosis' to clients (Kirsch et al., 1995). The mere label of 'hypnosis' seems to boost the credibility of the intervention and thereby enhance treatment gains.

Reliability of self-reports

In order to chart the course of treatment, one of the therapist's main tasks is to evaluate the meaning and credibility of the narratives that clients weave in telling the story of their life. Clients who are particularly fantasy-prone report problems differentiating fantasy and reality. Additionally, many fantasizers report memories prior to the age of 2 (Barber, 1999b), raising further questions about the veracity of their reports. Age 2 is significant insofar as it is the cutoff of infantile amnesia, a time at which cognitive scientists agree memories are unlikely to be reliable. Additionally, researchers have documented a moderate-to-high degree of association (0.40–0.65) between scores on dispositional measures of imagination, fantasy-proneness, and dissociation (Lynn et al., 1996a), traits associated with memory problems and the tendency to be misled by suggestive procedures (Eisen and Lynn, 2001). The fact that fantasy-prone people also tend to score high on measures of schizotypy, or 'psychosis proneness', which is associated with 'unreality experiences', as well as high hypnotic suggestibility (Jamieson and Gruzelier, 2001), raises further questions about the reliability of fantasizers' testimony.

Dissociation

Lynn and his colleagues (Lynn et al., 1996a) have argued that fantasizers are more likely to be diagnosed as having a dissociative identity disorder, as well as a variety of other disorders (e.g. major depression and personality disorders), than their non-fantasy-prone counterparts. The researchers caution against accepting fantasy-prone persons' reports of having multiple identities or personalities at face value. Indeed, such 'personalities' may well represent fantasy-based or imaginative creations that play a functional and perhaps defensive role in a person's life, rather than distinct indwelling entities that hold separate memories and experiences that are rigidly isolated from ordinary conscious experience. Individuals who come to be diagnosed as having a dissociative identity disorder often report a history of severe physical and sexual abuse, as do a subset of fantasy-prone individuals (Bryant, 1995; Heap, 1999; Rhue and Lynn, 1987). If the person who reports such experiences is highly fantasy-prone, there may be good reason to suspect the veracity of their reports. Nevertheless, it is incumbent on the clinician not to simply discount such reports on the basis of a history of fantasy-proneness.

Barber (1999c) claims that amnesia-prone, highly suggestive participants exhibit a propensity to dissociate. The high suggestibility and spotty memories of amnesia-prone persons, in general, warrant cautions regarding memory similar to those elucidated for fantasy-prone individuals. Indeed, there may be more overlap of these two 'types' than Barber acknowledges, given commonalities including a history of reported abuse, memory difficulties, and dissociative tendencies. A case could be made that individuals who are unable to recall or identify leading or suggestive hypnotic communications, due to dense amnesias for what transpires during hypnosis, would be particularly likely to incorporate suggested memories or imaginings into their memories because they fail to recognize the source of the suggested information. In summary, therapists should carefully weigh the plausibility of memories reported (in and apart from the hypnotic context) by fantasizers and amnesia-prone persons, as well as clients in general, and scrupulously avoid leading interview procedures.

Amnesia and session recall

Of all the putative types of highly suggestible individuals, amnesia-prone persons have been the least extensively studied. The failure to recall what occurs during hypnosis may limit what can be accomplished during therapy. For example, it is unclear whether it would be possible to benefit from techniques such as imaginative rehearsal or coping with anxiety-evoking situations with participants who do not recall what was rehearsed during hypnosis. In fact, one might ask whether amnesia-prone persons are able to transfer *any* insights or 'corrective experiences' (e.g. relaxation training) achieved during hypnosis to a non-hypnotic situation. Still unknown is whether suggestions for posthypnotic recall of hypnotic experiences are effective with amnesia-prone clients or what specific procedures, if any, are contraindicated with an amnesia-prone client.

It may not be obvious that clients do not have good recall of what occurs during hypnosis. Accordingly, therapists should routinely ask clients what they recall during hypnosis in order to assess this possibility. We recommend that therapists consider audio or video recording sessions with individuals who are amnesic for suggestions so that they can review the hypnosis session, and so that a record of the session is available for review of the presence and possible influence of unduly leading and counter-therapeutic procedures.

Facilitating a positive set: Enhancing suggestibility

Barber claims that the majority of highly suggestible individuals are neither fantasy-prone nor amnesia-prone: they are positively set to respond to hypnotic suggestions. This is not surprising in that a great deal of evidence (see Kirsch and Lynn, 1999) indicates that a person's 'set' and response expectancies are of crucial importance in determining a variety of responses to hypnosis. Research reveals that the lion's share of variability in responsivity to imaginative suggestions can be accounted for in terms of participants' expectations, motivation, beliefs, and attitudes about hypnosis, as well as their responsiveness to imaginative suggestions in general (see Braffman and Kirsch, 1998; Lynn and Rhue, 1991). These determinants are much more important than the nature or wording of the hypnotic induction, for example, or even the rapport that the hypnotist establishes with the participant (Lynn et al., 1990). Accordingly, prior to any hypnotic induction, it is imperative that the clinician acquires information concerning a particular client's set, that is, the client's agenda regarding hypnosis and suggestive procedures, as well as his or her specific beliefs, attitudes, and expectancies regarding the hypnotic experience that will follow.

Fortunately, although there is some disagreement, many believe that hypnotic suggestibility is not immutable and can be substantially modified. Even individuals who initially test in the low and medium range of suggestibility can be taught how to be 'positively set' toward hypnosis and test as 'highly suggestible' following a training program based on social learning principles (see Gorassini and Spanos, 1999; also Chapter 9). Gfeller (1994) has written perceptively on ways in which hypnotic suggestibility enhancement strategies developed in the laboratory can be transferred to clinical situations to increase responsiveness to a wide range of psychotherapeutic suggestions. This can be accomplished by establishing a positive rapport and working alliance with clients as well as by facilitating or increasing clients': (1) positive attitudes and beliefs about hypnosis; (2) motivation and response expectancies; (3) active imagining and responding to suggestions, rather than waiting for responses to 'just happen'; and (4) ability to accurately interpret suggestions.

Many individuals are likely to benefit from active interventions designed to maximize their responses to hypnosis and therapeutic suggestions. Some individuals who are highly fantasy-prone in everyday life may nevertheless harbor common misconceptions about hypnosis and be unwilling or reluctant to fully participate in the events of hypnosis. Lynn and Rhue (1988) observed that a number of the fantasy-prone subjects they tested expressed reservations and fears about being hypnotized and did not score in the high range of hypnotic suggestibility. In cases in which imaginative abilities are accompanied by negative attitudes, hypnotic suggestibility can be optimized by forging a strong therapeutic alliance and providing clients with accurate information that contradicts beliefs (e.g. that hypnotized people go into a 'trance' and lose consciousness) that interfere with achieving comfort and ease during hypnosis.

Unusual or aberrant psychology traits, symptoms or diagnoses have not, at least to date, been associated with a positive set towards hypnosis. Indeed, it is possible to speculate that individuals who are positively set are imbued with positive characteristics that are not easily captured by existing assessment instruments. For instance, positively set individuals are unlikely to entertain serious reservations about taking 'directions' from another person (i.e. the 'hypnotist') as well as relaxing in the presence of and relinquishing a modicum of 'control' to the hypnotist. It would be of considerable interest to determine whether positively set subjects evidence what Oakley and Frasquilho (1998) describe as an 'F-bias', where 'F' represents: (1) focused attention (and disattention to extraneous stimuli); (2) flexibility in switching cognitive styles appropriately to conform to the demands of suggestions; and (3) frontal cortical systems that underlie these cognitive capacities (p. 41). It would also be worthwhile to determine whether a positive set toward hypnosis generalizes to other therapeutic contexts and accounts for some of the associations between hypnotic suggestibility and treatment outcome that have been reported in the literature, which we will review below.

Suggestibility, psychopathology, and treatment outcome

Empirical studies of the relation between hypnotic suggestibility and both psychopathology and treatment outcome have not distinguished among putative types of highly suggestible persons, but instead have examined hypnotic suggestibility and treatment outcome across the entire range of hypnotic suggestibility. Nevertheless, it is clinically useful to understand how hypnotic suggestibility is related to both psychopathology and treatment outcome (see Bates,

1993; Lynn et al., 1996b; Mott, 1979; Perry et al., 1979; Spanos, 1991; Wadden and Anderton, 1982). For example, if individuals in a particular diagnostic group are especially responsive to hypnotic interventions, then it would make good sense to either define procedures as being 'hypnotic' in nature or to add a hypnotic component to a given treatment protocol. Under these circumstances, the inclusion of hypnosis as an adjunctive procedure might be expected to optimize treatment gains (Kirsch et al., 1995). In contrast, if a person were immune to the effects of hypnotic suggestions, there would appear to be little justification for incorporating hypnosis into treatment.

Unfortunately, the attempt to correlate psychopathology and hypnotic suggestibility has proven elusive. Early investigators, including Janet and Charcot, believed that hypnotic suggestibility and psychopathology were linked, and this idea, propelled by the influence of these individuals, carried over to the 20th century. However, studies specifically designed to investigate the connection between hypnotic suggestibility and a wide range of traits or characteristics, including neuroticism, repression, and symptoms measured by diverse Minnesota Multiphasic Personality Inventory scales, generally yielded negative findings and no consistent or reliable correlates of suggestibility (de Groh, 1989). Brown's (1992) review concluded that attempts to predict hypnotic suggestibility without actually attempting hypnosis by way of knowledge of patients' diagnoses and other factors including sex, introversion/extroversion, social status, ethnicity, and intelligence, have been likewise unsuccessful. By the mid-1960s, research regarding potential relationships between various forms of psychopathology and hypnotic responding yielded such inconsistent results that this line of inquiry gave way to research on more 'positive' personality variables (e.g. sociability and emotional stability; de Groh, 1989). Because studies of positive personality traits were vexingly inconsistent, researchers began to focus on cognitive variables (e.g. imaginative ability, absorption) and secured more promising, albeit inconclusive, results (Council et al., 1996; de Groh, 1989).

Despite these dour assessments, a good deal has been learned about the links among hypnotic suggestibility, treatment outcome, and various psychological and medical conditions, even if the findings are far from conclusive. In the discussion that follows, we review disorders that are either commonly treated with hypnosis, or that have garnered attention because of their association, or lack thereof, with particular symptoms, hypnotic suggestibility, and treatment outcome.

Smoking cessation

Green and Lynn's (2000) review of the literature on smoking cessation concluded that hypnosis is a promising and cost-effective smoking cessation technique. However, they note that the picture that emerges with respect to hypnotic suggestibility and treatment outcome is mixed. Whereas five studies have documented a relation between hypnotic suggestibility and abstinence, twelve studies have failed to do so (see also Lynn et al., 1993a). Interestingly, all of the studies that measured hypnotic suggestibility after treatment found no correlation between suggestibility and outcome. Schoenberger et al. (1997) contend that post-treatment measurement of hypnotic suggestibility is preferable to pre-treatment assessment in order to minimize contamination of treatment data.

Hypnotic analgesia

Recently, Montgomery and his colleagues (Montgomery et al., 2000) performed a meta-analysis on 18 studies (total number of participants > 900) of hypnoanalgesia. The reviewers concluded that hypnosis provided substantial pain relief for three-quarters of the population. An important finding was that the magnitude of pain reduction was greater for the highly suggestible than the low-suggestible participants. However, the effect sizes observed were comparable for highly suggestible and medium-suggestible participants. Although the analysis only included eight studies of clinical pain, the authors found that hypnotic suggestions seemed to be equally effective in the laboratory and medical settings. The authors concluded that 'the majority of the population (i.e. excluding people scoring in the low hypnotizability range) should benefit to a large extent from hypnotically suggested analgesia' (p. 146).

Post-traumatic stress disorder

There is only one controlled study (Brom et al., 1989) of the use of hypnosis in the treatment of post-traumatic stress disorder (PTSD). In this study, there was no advantage for using hypnosis compared with systematic desensitization and psychodynamic therapy, although the treatment groups improved relative to a waiting-list control group. At the same time, studies have shown that PTSD patients are more hypnotizable than normal controls and a variety of other populations including patients with schizophrenia, affective disorders, and anxiety disorders (see Cardeña, 2000, Spiegel, 1993 for reviews). However, these positive findings must be tempered by the fact that the most impressive findings were derived from a hospitalized Vietnam veteran population, raising the question of whether some of the individuals might have been presenting themselves as highly suggestible as a means of validating their diagnosis and thereby continuing to receive benefits.

Dissociative disorders

To date, no attempt has been made to examine the relative effectiveness of hypnotic and non-hypnotic procedures with dissociative disorder patients. However, patients with dissociative disorders score higher on measures of hypnotic suggestibility than a number of different inpatient psychiatric populations and normal college students (Bliss, 1980, 1986; Frischholz et al., 1992). Previous studies have not, however, evaluated whether these findings are attributable to the hypnotic context or to dissociative individuals' responses to imaginative suggestions more generally, given the moderate association between measures of dissociation and imagination. Additionally, if hypnosis is used to establish a diagnosis of dissociative identity disorder, for example, and if the procedures themselves are iatrogenic, and engender a presentation of 'multiple personalities', as some have argued (see Lilienfeld et al., 1999), then it would not be surprising at all that dissociative patients are very high in hypnotizability. Finally, studies of dissociation and hypnotic suggestibility have not used experimenters naive with respect to the diagnosis of the patients, raising the possibility that experimenter bias contributes significant variance to the findings obtained.

Wart remission

DuBreuil and Spanos's (1993) review of the research on the psychological treatment of warts provided strong support for the contention that hypnotic suggestions can produce wart remission that cannot be attributed to spontaneous remission or placebo effects. However, it is also likely that direct suggestions for wart removal, rather than hypnosis *per se*, is responsible for wart disappearance (Spanos et al., 1988, 1990). DuBreuil and Spanos (1993) conclude that the findings related to hypnotic suggestibility and wart remission have been mixed. However, those studies that have reported a link between the two have used non-standardized criteria, whereas the studies that have failed to find an association have used standardized measures following treatment. Additionally, well-controlled studies in Spanos's laboratory (Spanos et al., 1988, 1990) indicated that although hypnotic suggestibility failed to predict wart loss, a measure of vividness of treatment-specific imagery was significantly associated with wart regression. DuBrueil and Spanos (1993) note that these findings are ambiguous insofar as they might mean (1) that vivid suggestion-related imagery influences wart loss or (2) that imagery measures indirectly reflect participants' treatment motivation and their belief that they have been able to control their physiological processes.

Obesity

Levitt's (1993) review of 20 published reports on hypnosis and the treatment of obesity concluded that 'hypnotherapy for weight reduction is effective'. Levitt also noted that individuals who participated in hypnosis and behavior modification lost an equivalent amount of weight. However, individuals who were hypnotized continued to lose weight during the follow-up periods because they seemed more motivated to practice the behavior-change tactics they had learned. Studies since Levitt's review are consistent with his contention that treatments that include hypnosis can result in weight loss (Johnson, 1977; Johnson and Karkut, 1996).

Levitt's (1993) analysis of 11 reports on the relation between hypnotic suggestibility and outcome revealed that three out of four recent studies, published since earlier reviews that concluded that no relationship was evident, indicated that there was a relationship between hypnotic suggestibility and outcome. On the basis of these studies, Levitt concluded that 'At the very least, the issue is again open' (p. 542).

Eating disorders

Although there is limited research evidence regarding the use of hypnosis with eating disorders, a number of reviews (Baker and Nash, 1987; Hornyak, 1996; Lynn et al., 1993b; Nash and Baker,

1993) indicate that hypnotic interventions hold promise in the treatment of eating disorders. In their review, Griffiths et al. (1995) concluded that the extant evidence supports the notion that patients with bulimia nervosa as well as those with the bingeing and purging subtype of anorexia nervosa are significantly more hypnotizable than either those with restricting anorexia or non-clinical populations. In some studies, approximately half of the sample of bulimic individuals tested in the high-hypnotizable range on standardized hypnotic suggestibility scales (Griffiths and Channon-Little, 1993; Griffiths et al., 1995). However, hypnotic suggestibility was not found to be related to treatment outcome in these studies. Moreover, in a study (Vanderlinden et al., 1995) not cited in the review, patients with both mixed anorexia and bulimia were more highly suggestible than participants in the normal control group; however, subjective responding was not significantly different for any of the patient groups or the control group and all groups tested in the medium hypnotizability range. Other more recent studies with normal-weight college students have found evidence for: (1) correlations between non-hypnotic suggestibility and restrained eating (Wybraniec and Oakley, 1996); (2) higher waking suggestibility in restrained eaters than non-restrained eaters and a greater subjective response to suggestions to visualize their bodies becoming fatter rather than thinner; and (3) an association between waking suggestibility and cognitive restraint (Frasquilho and Oakley, 1997). It will be important for future researchers to disentangle the effects of waking and hypnotic suggestibility in evaluating the relation between symptoms of eating disorders and hypnotic suggestibility.

Anxiety disorders

Hypnosis has proved to be a useful adjunct to psychological treatments of phobias that span a wide range of theoretical orientations, ranging from cognitive–behavioral to insight therapies. Crawford and Barabasz's (1993) review paints a mixed picture of the relation between the presence of a phobic condition and hypnotic suggestibility. Although seven of the studies they reviewed found support for an association between hypnotic suggestibility and phobias, three studies found no evidence for an association, and one of these studies found that 68 per cent of the phobics were low in hypnotizability.

A more recent and well-controlled study by Schoenberger et al. (1997) not only failed to find a positive association between hypnotic suggestibility and treatment outcome, but the relationship was negative in direction. And, finally, Van Dyck and Spinhoven (1997) found that hypnotic suggestibility was associated with reduction of symptoms in agoraphobia in a hypnotic condition but not in an exposure-alone condition, a finding that supports the idea that hypnotic suggestibility is not associated with treatment gains in general, but is, instead, contextually dependent.

Somatization disorder

'Somatization' is a term that encompasses reports of diverse physical symptoms in the absence of detectable physical pathology. As many as 50 per cent or more of individuals who consult primary-care physicians exhibit some degree of somatization, even if the symptoms reported do not fulfill the DSM-IV criteria for the disorder (Wickramasekera, 1993).

According to Wickramasekera (1993) either very high or very low hypnotizability can predispose somatization, along with a tendency to catastrophize and high levels of negative affect. Wickramasekera contends that hypnotic suggestibility is a risk factor because highly suggestible individuals are prone to perceive automaticity or involuntariness in both hypnotic and non-hypnotic situations, and because when threatening situational or interpersonal cues are present, 'aversive changes in perception, memory, and mood' are likely to ensue in this population. Accordingly, high hypnotizability, as well as catastrophizing and negative affect, constitute a diathesis in which threat perception is maximized, particularly in the context of stressful life-events. The extent to which risk factors are present, combined with the propensity to either magnify physical symptoms or translate psychological symptoms into physical ones, dictates the way somatization is manifested, allowing for the display of a wide variety of somatization symptoms. In the absence of protective factors that are hypothesized to include strong coping skills and social support, vulnerability to a somatization disorder is increased.

Wickramasekera (1993) finds support for his high-risk model in studies (Wickramasekera, 1984, 1991) indicating that a disproportionate number of individuals with 'typical somatization symptoms' are high or low in hypnotizability compared to student controls in published reports (Kirsch et al., 1990). He also points to a similar pattern of findings in studies of insomniacs, obese patients, individuals with affective disorders, and chronic pain. However,

Wickramasekera includes disorders such as hypertension and vascular headaches as involving 'typical somatization symptoms'. These disorders can often be determined to have an organic basis, even though the exact psychophysiological mechanisms may not be well understood. Additionally, the pattern of findings in many of the studies reviewed above does not conform to the distribution of hypnotic suggestibility predicted by Wickramasekera. Nevertheless, more research is called for, with well-validated scales of hypnotic suggestibility, and clinicians would do well to evaluate individuals with somatization symptoms so that hypnotic procedures may be used to relieve symptoms where indicated. Indeed, according to the threat perception model, hypnotic suggestibility plays a critical role in the diagnosis and treatment of somatization disorder.

Depression

The relationship between depression and hypnotic suggestibility has received considerably less attention than the relationship between hypnosis and many other disorders. McCloskey et al. (1999) recently reviewed the extant research and were able to identify only five studies that investigated the relation between depression and hypnotic suggestibility. In all of these studies, depression was found to be unrelated to hypnotic suggestibility, depressed individuals were less suggestible than non-depressed persons, or depressed participants were not at all suggestible. In a sixth study, which the authors conducted (McCloskey et al., 1999), hypnotic suggestibility was not related to depression, although hypnotic suggestibility was found to be related to a measure of physical anhedonia. It does not appear that the failure to find a relationship between hypnotic suggestibility and depression can be attributable to the effects of psychotropic medications for the treatment of depression (Spiegel, 1980). Although researchers have not systematically studied the effects of hypnosis on depressed versus non-depressed patients, Yapko (1996) contends that a variety of hypnotic techniques can be useful in the treatment of depression.

Asthma

In the single study (Ewer and Stewart, 1986) that directly assessed the relation between hypnotic suggestibility as measured by a standardized scale and treatment gains, only highly suggestible patients in the hypnosis treatment achieved symptom improvement on self-report and physiological measures. Low hypnotizable patients, regardless of whether they participated in hypnosis or an attention control condition, did not improve. Findings from less well-controlled studies range from showing a substantial relation between hypnotic suggestibility and symptom improvement to no relationship at all (see Pinnello and Covino, 2000). However, these less well-controlled studies did not use standardized scales, and ratings of hypnotic suggestibility were made by the treating physician, raising the possibility that the ratings were based on the remission of symptoms.

Psychosis

Not all patient populations appear to be highly suggestible, which may account for why hypnosis is not universally employed. The paradigmatic example is that of psychosis. Early reports dating to the late 19th century estimated that only 10 per cent of psychotic patients were suggestible. Copeland and Kitching (1937) were even less optimistic regarding treatment prospects, noting that 'true cases of psychosis' were impervious to hypnosis. Several reviews (Lavoie and Sabourin, 1980; Pettinati, 1982) have confirmed the observation that psychotic individuals are generally less hypnotically suggestible than their non-psychotic counterparts, although some research indicates that psychotic individuals can respond to hypnotic suggestions and test in at least the normative range of hypnotic responsiveness (e.g. Pettinati et al., 1990). Interestingly, in the undergraduate college student population, schizotopy, characterized by the capacity for 'unreality experiences', including perceptual distortions and magical thinking, is correlated with hypnotic suggestibility ($r = 0.43$; Jamieson and Gruzelier, 2001). Unfortunately, no controlled studies have been conducted to evaluate the relation between treatment outcome and hypnotic suggestibility among psychotic patients.

Conclusions

Whereas our discussion indicates that high hypnotic suggestibility is in no case associated with a negative treatment outcome, it is not necessarily an advantage. A clear exception to this is in the area of pain management in which highly suggestible individuals are more responsive to hypnotic analgesia than low suggestible individuals.

This finding can probably be accounted for in terms of the correspondence between the experience of analgesia and the ability to
alter cognitive–perceptual–sensory processes that typify the person
who is highly responsive to hypnotic suggestion (Lynn et al., 2000).
It would therefore seem to be incumbent on clinicians to assess
hypnotic responsiveness in clients prior to administering hypnotic
suggestions for pain relief.

Other disorders or conditions in which the findings are mixed, yet
at least somewhat promising regarding the link between suggestibility and treatment outcome, include smoking cessation, obesity,
warts, anxiety, somatization, and asthma. The fact that many studies
indicate little or no relation between hypnotic suggestibility and
treatment outcome may mean that typical interventions require
little special hypnotic or imaginative abilities and instead rely on
relatively easy suggestions (e.g. relaxation, guided imagery, imaginative rehearsal) that the majority of the population can pass (Lynn
et al., 2000).

The association between hypnotic suggestibility and treatment
outcome is potentially mediated by diverse factors including positive
motivation, beliefs and expectancies about hypnosis. Clearly, clinicians should assess these factors in tandem with hypnotic suggestibility in general in order to gauge clients' readiness, preparation,
and proclivities for treatment, hypnotic or otherwise.

Kirsch (1997) has defined hypnotic suggestibility as the increment
in responding to imaginative suggestions (e.g. suggestions on standardized hypnosis scales) when they are administered in a hypnotic
context (i.e. procedures labeled as 'hypnosis') over and above when
they are administered in a 'waking' context. Conceptualizing hypnotic suggestibility in this way is important because much of the
variability in 'hypnotic responding' can be accounted for in terms of
responses to imaginative suggestions administered in non-hypnotic
situations. According to this line of reasoning, in order to
'test' for hypnotic suggestibility it is necessary to test each subject's
responsiveness to imaginative suggestions in both a hypnotic and
a non-hypnotic context. An important task for future researchers is
to investigate the clinical correlates of high suggestibility and the
link between suggestibility and treatment outcome when hypnotic
suggestibility is measured along the lines suggested by Kirsch.

More generally, it is imperative that future studies use well-
standardized hypnotic suggestibility scales, examine the correlates of
hypnotic suggestibility with outcome measures administered before

206   Lynn et al.

and after hypnosis to evaluate the potential contaminating influence
of order of scale administration, and select clients who are carefully
diagnosed with a particular condition. In this way, it will be possible
to develop empirically supported treatments that can be better
targeted to individuals of different levels of hypnotic suggestibility.

References

Baker, E.L. and Nash, M.R. (1987) 'Applications of hypnosis in the treatment of anorexia nervosa', *American Journal of Clinical Hypnosis*,
29:185–93.
Barber, T.X. (1999a) 'A comprehensive three-dimensional theory of hypnosis', in I. Kirsch, A. Capafons, E. Cardeña-Buelna and S. Amigó (eds),
Clinical Hypnosis and Self-regulation: Cognitive-behavioral Perspectives
(pp. 21–48), Washington, DC: American Psychological Association.
—— (1999b) 'Hypnosis: A mature view', *Contemporary Hypnosis*, 16:123–7.
—— (1999c) 'The essence and mechanism of superb hypnotic performances', *Contemporary Hypnosis*, 16:192–208.
Barrett, D. (1991) 'Deep trance subjects: A schema of two distinct subgroups', in R.G. Kunzendorf (ed.), *Mental Imagery* (pp. 101–11), New
York: Plenum.
—— (1996) 'Fantasizers and dissociaters: Two types of hypnotizables,
two different imagery styles', in R.G. Kundendorf, N.P. Spanos and
B. Wallace (eds), *Hypnosis and Imagination* (pp. 123–35) Amityville, NY:
Baywood.
Bates, B.L. (1993) 'Individual differences in response to hypnosis', in J.W.
Rhue, S.J. Lynn and I. Kirsch (eds), *Handbook of Clinical Hypnosis*
(pp. 23–54), Washington, DC: American Psychological Association.
Bliss, E.L. (1980) 'Multiple personalities: A report of 14 cases with implications for schizophrenia and hysteria', *Archives of General Psychiatry*,
37:1388–97.
—— (1986) *Multiple Personality, Allied Disorders, and Hypnosis*, New York:
Oxford University Press.
Braffman, W. and Kirsch, I. (1998) 'Predictors of hypnotizability, hypnotic,
and nonhypnotic suggestibility', Paper presented at the annual meeting
of the American Psychological Association, San Francisco, California.
Brom, D., Kleber, R.J. and Defare, P.B. (1989) 'Brief psychotherapy
for post-traumatic stress disorder', *Journal of Consulting and Clinical
Psychology*, 57:607–12.
Brown, D.P. (1992) 'Clinical hypnosis research since 1986', in E. Fromm
and M.R. Nash (eds), *Contemporary Hypnosis Research* (pp. 427–58),
New York: Guilford Press.
Brown, R.J. (1999) 'Three dimensions of hypnosis or multiple routes to
suggested responding?', *Contemporary Hypnosis*, 16:128–31.

Bryant, R.A. (1995) 'Fantasy-proneness, reported childhood abuse, and the relevance of reported abuse onset', *International Journal of Clinical and Experimental Hypnosis*, 43:184–93.

Cardeña, E. (2000) 'Hypnosis in the treatment of trauma: A promising, but not fully supported, efficacious intervention', *International Journal of Clinical and Experimental Hypnosis*, 48:225–38.

Chaves, J.F. (1999) 'Deconstructing hypnosis: A generative approach to theory and research', *Contemporary Hypnosis*, 16:139–43.

Copeland, C.L. and Kitching, E.H. (1937) 'Hypnosis in mental hospital practice', *Journal of Mental Science*, 83:216–329.

Council, J. and Huff, K.D. (1990) 'Hypnosis, fantasy activity, and reports of paranormal experiences in high, medium, and low fantasizers', *British Journal of Experimental and Clinical Hypnosis*, 7:9–15.

—— Kirsch, I. and Grant, D.L. (1996) 'Imagination, expectancy, and hypnotic responding', in R.G. Kunzendorf, N.P. Spanos and B. Wallace (eds), *Hypnosis and Imagination* (pp. 41–65), Amityville, NY: Baywood.

Crawford, H.J. and Barabasz, A.F. (1993) 'Phobias and intense fears: Facilitating their treatment with hypnosis', in J.W. Rhue, S.J. Lynn and I. Kirsch (eds), *Handbook of Clinical Hypnosis* (pp. 311–37), Washington, DC: American Psychological Association.

De Groh, M. (1989) 'Correlates of hypnotic susceptibility', in N.P. Spanos and J.F. Chaves (eds), *Hypnosis: The Cognitive-behavioral Perspective* (pp. 32–63), Buffalo, NY: Prometheus Books.

DuBreuil, S.C. and Spanos, N.P. (1993) 'Psychological treatment of warts', in J.W. Rhue, S.J. Lynn and I. Kirsch (eds), *Handbook of Clinical Hypnosis* (pp. 623–48), Washington, DC: American Psychological Association.

Eisen, M. and Lynn, S.J. (2001) 'Memory, suggestibility, and dissociation in children and adults', *Applied Cognitive Psychology*, 15:49–73.

Ewer, T.C. and Stewart, D.E. (1986) 'Improvement in bronchial hyper-responsiveness in patients with moderate asthma after treatment with a hypnotic technique: A randomized controlled trial', *British Medical Journal of Clinical Research Education*, 293:1129–32.

Frasquilho, F. and Oakley, D. (1997) 'Hypnotizability, dissociation and three factors of eating behaviour', *Contemporary Hypnosis*, 14:105–11.

Frischholz, E.J., Lipman, L.S., Braun, B.G. and Sachs, R.G. (1992) 'Psychopathology, hypnotizability, and dissociation', *American Journal of Psychiatry*, 149:1521–5.

Gfeller, J.D. (1994) 'Hypnotizability enhancement: Clinical implications of empirical findings', *American Journal of Clinical Hypnosis*, 37:107–16.

Gorassini, D.R. and Spanos, N.P. (1999) 'The Carleton Skill Training Program for modifying hypnotic suggestibility: Original version and variations', in I. Kirsch, A. Capafons, E. Cardeña-Bulena and S. Amigó (eds), *Clinical Hypnosis and Self-regulation: Cognitive-behavioral*

Perspectives (pp. 141–80), Washington, DC: American Psychological Association.

Green, J.P. and Lynn, S.J. (2000) 'Hypnosis and suggestion-based approaches to smoking cessation: An examination of the evidence', *International Journal of Clinical and Experimental Hypnosis*, 48:195–224.

—— Lynn, S.J., Williams, B. and Maré, C. (1989) 'Fantasy proneness in high hypnotizable subjects', Paper presented at the annual meeting of the American Psychological Association, New Orleans.

Griffiths, R.A. and Channon-Little, L.D. (1993) 'Dissociation, dieting disorders and hypnosis: A review', *European Eating Disorders Review*, 3:148–59.

—— Channon-Little, L. and Hadzi-Pavlovic, D. (1995) 'Hypnotizability and outcome in the treatment of bulimia nervosa', *Contemporary Hypnosis*, 12:165–72.

Heap, M. (1999) 'High hypnotizability: Types and dimensions', *Contemporary Hypnosis*, 16:153–6.

Hornyak, L. (1996) 'Hypnosis in the treatment of anorexia nervosa', in S.J. Lynn, I. Kirsch and J.W. Rhue (eds), *Casebook of Clinical Hypnosis*, Washington, DC: American Psychological Association.

Jamieson, G.A. and Gruzelier, J.H. (2001) 'Hypnotic susceptibility is positively related to a subset of schizotypy items', *Contemporary Hypnosis*, 18:32–7.

Johnson, D.L. (1997) 'Weight loss for women: Studies of smokers and nonsmokers using hypnosis and multicomponent treatments with and without overt aversion', *Psychological Reports*, 80:931–3.

—— and Karkut, R.T. (1996) 'Participation in multicomponent hypnosis treatment programs for women's weight loss with and without overt aversion', *Psychological Reports*, 79:659–88.

Kirsch, I. (1997) 'Suggestibility or hypnosis? What do our scales really measure?', *International Journal of Clinical and Experimental Hypnosis*, 45:212–25.

—— and Lynn, S.J. (1999) 'The automaticity of behavior and clinical psychology', *American Psychologist*, 54:504–15.

—— Council, J.R. and Wickless, C. (1990) 'Subjective scoring for the Harvard Group Scale of Hypnotic Susceptibility, Form A', *International Journal of Clinical and Experimental Hypnosis*, 38:101–11.

—— Montgomery, G. and Sapirstein, G. (1995) 'Hypnosis as an adjunct to cognitive-behavioral psychotherapy: A meta-analysis', *Journal of Consulting and Clinical Psychology*, 63:214–20.

—— Capafons, A., Cardeña-Bulena, E. and Amigó, S. (1999) *Clinical Hypnosis and Self-regulation: Cognitive-behavioral Perspectives*, Washington, DC: American Psychological Association.

Lavoie, G. and Sabourin, M. (1980) 'Hypnosis and schizophrenia: A review of experimental and clinical studies', in G.D. Burrows and L. Dennerstein (eds), *Handbook of Hypnosis and Psychosomatic Medicine* (pp. 377–419), New York: Elsevier/North Holland Biomedical.

Levitt, E.E. (1993) 'Hypnosis in the treatment of obesity', in J.W. Rhue, S.J. Lynn and I. Kirsch (eds), *Handbook of Clinical Hypnosis* (pp. 533–53), Washington, DC: American Psychological Association.

Lilienfeld, S., Lynn, S.J., Kirsch, I., Chaves, J., Sarbin, T., Ganaway, G. and Powell, R. (1999) 'Dissociative identity disorder and the sociocognitive model: Recalling the lessons of the past', *Psychological Bulletin*, 125:507–23.

Lynn, S.J. and Rhue, J.W. (1988) 'Fantasy-proneness: Hypnosis, developmental antecedents, and psychopathology', *American Psychologist*, 43:35–44.

—— and Rhue, J.W. (eds) (1991) *Theories of Hypnosis: Current Models and Perspectives*, New York: Guilford Press.

—— Rhue, J.W. and Green, J.P. (1988) 'Multiple personality and fantasy-proneness: Is there an association or disassociation?', *British Journal of Experimental and Clinical Hypnosis*, 5:138–42.

—— Rhue, J.W. and Weekes, J.R. (1990) 'Hypnotic involuntariness: A social-cognitive analysis', *Psychological Review*, 97:169–84.

—— Neufeld, V., Rhue, J.W. and Matorin, A. (1993a) 'Hypnosis and smoking cessation: A cognitive-behavioral treatment', in J.W. Rhue, S.J. Lynn and Kirsch, I. (eds), *Handbook of Clinical Hypnosis* (pp. 555–85), Washington, DC: American Psychological Association.

—— Rhue, J.W., Kvaal, S. and Maré, C. (1993b) 'The treatment of anorexia nervosa: A hypnosuggestive framework', *Contemporary Hypnosis*, 10:73–80.

—— Neufeld, V., Green, J., Rhue, J.W. and Sandberg, D. (1996a) 'Daydreaming, fantasy, and psychopathology', in R. Kunzendorf, N. Spanos and B. Wallace (eds), *Hypnosis and Imagination*, New York: Baywood Press.

—— Kirsch, I., Neufeld, J. and Rhue, J.W. (1996b) 'Clinical hypnosis: Assessment, applications, and treatment considerations', in S.J. Lynn, I. Kirsch and J.W. Rhue (eds), *Casebook of Clinical Hypnosis* (pp. 3–30), Washington, DC: American Psychological Association.

—— Lilienfeld, S. and Rhue, J.W. (1999) 'An evaluation of T.X. Barber's three-dimensional theory of hypnosis: Promise and pitfalls', *Contemporary Hypnosis*, 16:160–4.

—— Kirsch, I., Barabasz, A., Cardeña, E. and Patterson, D. (2000) 'Hypnosis as an empirically supported adjunctive technique: The state of the evidence', *International Journal of Clinical and Experimental Hypnosis*, 48:343–61.

McCloskey, M.S., Kumar, V.K. and Pekala, R.J. (1999) 'State and trait depression, physical and social anhedonia, hypnotizability and subjective experiences during hypnosis', *American Journal of Clinical Hypnosis*, 41:231–52.

Mellinger, D.I. and Lynn, S.J. (2003) *The Monster in the Cave: How to Face your Fear and Anxiety and Live your Life*, New York: Berkley.

Montgomery, G., DuHamel, K.N. and Redd, W.H. (2000) 'A meta-analysis of hypnotically induced analgesia: How effective is hypnosis?', *International Journal of Clinical and Experimental Hypnosis*, 48:138–53.

Mott, T. (1979) 'The clinical importance of hypnotizability', *American Journal of Clinical Hypnosis*, 21:263–9.

Nash, M.R. and Baker, E. (1993) 'Hypnosis in the treatment of anorexia nervosa', in J.W. Rhue, S.J. Lynn and I. Kirsch (eds), *Handbook of Clinical Hypnosis* (pp. 383–94), Washington, DC: American Psychological Association.

Oakley, D.A. and Frasquilho, F. (1998) 'Hypnotic susceptibility, or F-bias: Its relevance to eating disorders', *Contemporary Hypnosis*, 15:40–51.

Pekala, R.J. (1991) 'Hypnotic types: Evidence from a cluster analysis of phenomenal experience', *Contemporary Hypnosis*, 8:95–104.

—— Kumar, V.K. and Marcano, G. (1995) 'Hypnotic types: A partial replication concerning phenomenal experience', *Contemporary Hypnosis*, 12:194–200.

Perry, C., Gelfand, R. and Marcovitch, P. (1979) 'The relevance of hypnotic susceptibility in the clinical context', *Journal of Abnormal Psychology*, 88:592–603.

Pettinati, H.M. (1982) 'Measuring hypnotizability in psychotic patients', *International Journal of Experimental Hypnosis*, 30:404–16.

—— Kogan, L.G., Evans, F.J., Wade, J.H., Horne, R.L. and Staats, J.M. (1990) 'Hypnotizability of psychiatric inpatients according to two different scales', *American Journal of Psychiatry*, 174:69–75.

Pinnell, C.M. and Covino, N. (2000) 'Empirical findings on the use of hypnosis in medicine: A critical review', *International Journal of Clinical and Experimental Hypnosis*, 48:170–82.

Rhue, J.W. and Lynn, S.J. (1987) 'Fantasy-proneness: Developmental antecedents', *Journal of Personality*, 55:121–37.

Rhue, J.W. and Lynn, S.J. (1989) 'Fantasy-proneness, hypnotisability and absorption: A re-examination', *International Journal of Clinical and Experimental Hypnosis*, 37:100–37.

Rind, B., Tromovich, P. and Bauserman, R. (1998) 'A meta-analytic examination of assumed properties of child sexual abuse using college samples', *Psychological Bulletin*, 124:22–53.

Schoenberger, N., Kirsch, I., Gearan, P., Montgomery, G. and Pastyrnak, S.L. (1997) 'Hypnotic enhancement of a cognitive-behavioral treatment for public speaking anxiety', *Behavior Therapy*, 28:127–40.

Siuta, J. (1990) 'Fantasy-proneness: Towards cross-cultural comparisons', *British Journal of Experimental and Clinical Hypnosis*, 7:93–102.

Spanos, N.P. (1991) 'Hypnosis, hypnotizability, and hypnotherapy', in C.R. Snyder and D.R. Forsyth (eds), *Handbook of Social and Clinical*

Psychology: The Health Perspective (pp. 644–63), Elmsford, NY: Pergamon.

—— Stenstrom, R.J. and Johnson, J.C. (1988) 'Hypnosis, placebo, and suggestion in the treatment of warts', *Psychosomatic Medicine*, 50:245–60.

—— Williams, V. and Gwynn, M.I. (1990) 'Effects of hypnotic, placebo, and salicylic acid treatments on wart regression', *Psychosomatic Medicine*, 52:109–14.

Spiegel, D. (1980) 'Hypnotizability and psychoactive medication', *American Journal of Clinical Hypnosis*, 22:217–22.

—— (1989) 'Hypnosis', in J.G. Howells (ed.), *Modern Perspectives in the Psychiatry of the Neuroses*, New York: Brunner-Mazel.

—— (1993) 'Hypnosis in the treatment of posttramuatic stress disorders', in J.W. Rhue, S.J. Lynn and I. Kirsch (eds), *Handbook of Clinical Hypnosis*, Washington, DC: American Psychological Association.

Spiegel, H. (1974) 'The grade 5 syndrome: The highly hypnotizable person', *International Journal of Clinical and Experimental Hypnosis*, 22:303–19.

Van Dyck, R. and Spinhoven, P. (1997) 'Does preference for type of treatment matter?', A study of exposure in vivo with or without hypnosis in the treatment of panic disorder with agoraphobia. *Behavior Modification*, 21:172–86.

Vanderlinden, J., Spinhoven, P., Vandereycken, W. and van Dyck, R. (1995) 'Dissociative and hypnotic experiences in eating disorder patients: An exploratory study', *American Journal of Clinical Hypnosis*, 38:97–108.

Wadden, T.A. and Anderton, C.H. (1982) 'The clinical use of hypnosis', *Psychological Bulletin*, 91:215–43.

Wickramasekera, I. (1984) 'A model of people at high risk to develop chronic stress-related symptoms', in F.J. McGuigan, W. Smye and J.M. Wallace (eds), *Stress and Tension Control, 2*, New York: Plenum Press.

—— (1991) 'The unconscious, somatization, psychophysiological psychotherapy and threat perception: Footnotes to a cartography of the unconscious mind', *Biofeedback*, 19:18–23.

—— (1993) 'Assessment and treatment of somatization disorders: The high risk model of threat perception', in J.W. Rhue, S.J. Lynn and I. Kirsch (eds), *Handbook of Clinical Hypnosis* (pp. 587–621), Washington, DC: American Psychological Association.

Wilson, S.C. and Barber, T.X. (1981) 'Vivid fantasy and hallucinatory abilities in the life histories of excellent hypnotic subjects ("somnambules"): Preliminary report with female subjects', in E. Klinger (ed.), *Imagery: Concepts, Results, and Applications* (pp. 133–49), New York: Plenum.

—— and Barber, T.X. (1983) 'The fantasy-prone personality: Implications for understanding imagery, hypnosis, and parapsychological phenomena', in A.A. Sheikh (ed.), *Imagery: Current Theory, Research, and Applications* (pp. 340–87) New York: John Wiley.

Wybraniec, A. and Oakley, D. (1996) 'Dietary restraint, hypnotizability and body image', *Contemporary Hypnosis*, 13:150–5.

Yapko, M.D. (1996) 'A brief therapy approach to the use of hypnosis in treating depression', in S.J. Lynn, I. Kirsch and J.W. Rhue (eds), *Casebook of Clinical Hypnosis* (pp. 75–98), Washington, DC: American Psychological Association.

Chapter 9

Enhancing hypnotizability

Donald R. Gorassini

Introduction

One of the central questions of hypnosis research is whether or not hypnotic responsiveness is resistant to change (Lynn and Rhue, 1991). Some researchers argue that it can be enhanced only a small amount (e.g. Benham et al., 1998) whereas others propose that large average increases can be reliably produced (e.g. Spanos, 1986). All investigators agree that hypnotic responsiveness can be increased at least to some degree (e.g. Bates et al., 1988). This chapter describes a number of methods that have been used to enhance hypnotic responsiveness and reviews research on the effectiveness of each procedure. In agreement with Diamond (1974), it is argued that enhancement can be produced using any of a number of methods. Evidence also now makes it clear that some methods are more effective than others and that large gains in hypnotic responsiveness can be generated reliably using some techniques.

Measuring hypnotic responsiveness enhancement

Hypnotic responses consist of cued distortions of perception or memory (e.g. Orne, 1977). The fact that a cluster of such phenomena occurs when suggested says nothing in and of itself about why it occurs. The cluster might represent a manifestation of an underlying hypnotic condition (Hilgard, 1991; Woody and Bowers, 1994) or it might represent a custom or ritual arising for no other reason than that it is asked for (Spanos and Chaves, 1991; Wagstaff, 1981). For the most part, the modification research reviewed below used standardized scales to assess hypnotic responsiveness. Scores on these scales have been found to correlate highly with more informal evaluations of responsiveness (O'Connell et al., 1966; Van Der Does et al., 1989).

Researchers have proposed several criteria of hypnotic responsiveness enhancement (e.g. Perry, 1977; Spanos, 1986):

1   Changes that take place in the context of an enhancement procedure should be compared to no-enhancement controls to distinguish change due to the enhancement procedure from change that would have occurred without the intervention.

2   Owing to the ubiquitous presence of cues in hypnotic situations illustrating how a hypnotically responsive person would act, procedures for ruling out the possibility of faking changes in responsiveness should be applied.

3   To show that a change actually involves learning of the skills necessary for generating increases in responsiveness, researchers should demonstrate transfer of learning to novel suggestions and a persistence of enhancement over time. In summary, enhancement involves increases in behavioural and experiential aspects of hypnotic responsiveness that generalize to novel suggestions, persist over time, and exceed changes that occur when no treatment is given.

The stability of hypnotic responsiveness

Hypnotic responsiveness is stable when tested repeatedly under constant conditions. This is true when the interval between tests is relatively short, consisting of days or a few weeks (e.g. Gfeller et al., 1987), and it is also true of intervals of many years (Piccione et al., 1989). Piccione et al. (1989) present data collected over a 25-year period that show high levels of stability of hypnotic responsiveness. In itself, stability says little about the modifiability of hypnotic responsiveness. Researchers agree that hypnotic responsiveness is highly stable if no attempts at change are made, but will responsiveness change once such attempts are made?

Methods of enhancing hypnotic responsiveness

Attempts to enhance hypnotic responsiveness fall under three broad categories: methods for reducing sensations and activity, methods for enhancing alertness, and methods for instilling direct management of hypnotic responses. (For further information, also see Chapter 1.)

Methods for reducing sensation and activity

The traditional 'induction'

The procedure most commonly used for purposes of optimizing hypnotic responsiveness, and what I shall refer to as 'the traditional induction', can be traced to the early days of hypnosis (Wells, 1924). The traditional induction consists of attempts to produce an unusual co-occurrence in the participant: an increased depth of relaxation or sleep on the one hand and a clear awareness of what the hypnotist is saying on the other. This attempt precedes the administration of test or therapeutic suggestions and usually takes the form of interrelated instructions and suggestions that take several minutes to communicate. Induction procedures usually come packaged with other components, including techniques for establishing rapport and correcting misconceptions about hypnosis. With participants who show responsiveness to these sorts of inductions and test or therapeutic suggestions, the time taken during subsequent hypnotic sessions to give an induction can be substantially reduced, in some cases to a point where the participant will appear to become hypnotically responsive instantly in response to a prearranged cue.

Some researchers speculate that a hypnotic induction prepares the individual to respond hypnotically by producing muscular relaxation, providing a metaphor of sleep, and instructing the individual to *let* suggested responses happen (Hilgard, 1991). That is, relaxation produces disorientation and an experience of detachment from one's actions; suggestions of sleep keep the individual from critically evaluating the hypnotist's message; and instructions to let responses happen prevent the person from voluntarily making the responses. Hence, deep relaxation, behavioural passivity, and reduced critical thinking result in an impairment of memory and reduction in reality testing, so that 'response to the stimulation provided by the hypnotist takes precedence over planned or self-initiated action, and the voice of the hypnotist becomes unusually persuasive' (Hilgard, 1986, p. 227). In this condition, suggested responses occur automatically by ideomotor action, which itself is said to operate behind an amnesic barrier (Hilgard, 1986). The individual lets dissociated cognitive subsystems autonomously transform suggested responses into actual responses.

Effectiveness of the traditional hypnotic induction

In the first experimental evaluation of hypnotic induction effects, Hull (1933) found that participants in no-induction conditions were capable of responding to suggestions, but to a degree slightly less than was exhibited by participants who received a traditional induction. Hull also found that responsiveness in no-induction and induction conditions correlated highly and that great individual variability existed in levels of responsiveness within each context. Since then, researchers have found a similar pattern. When a difference between induction and no-induction conditions has been found – a less-than-universal result – the difference has been quite small (Barber, 1969; Braffman and Kirsch, 1999; Hilgard and Tart, 1966). The effect is more reliably produced using within-subjects than between-subjects designs, and more commonly manifested in the induction followed by no-induction sequence than the no-induction followed by induction sequence (e.g. Braffman and Kirsch, 1999). These findings have been interpreted in two different ways. In one, the mechanisms of hypnotic and non-hypnotic responding are considered different. The responding of waking controls is compliance with task requirements whereas responding in hypnotic conditions arises from ideomotor action and dissociation (Hilgard, 1965, 1986; Woody and Bowers, 1994). According to the other interpretation, the process of responding in waking and hypnotic conditions is the same: compliance with task requirements (Barber, 1969; Sarbin and Coe, 1972; Spanos, 1991; Wagstaff, 1981).

Deepening techniques

Verbal methods

Various traditional induction techniques of a primarily verbal nature have been used in attempts to deepen the states thought to underlie hypnotic responding. Deepening techniques have included reliance on the clinical skills of trained hypnotists who attempt to increase the level of hypnosis of initially low-scoring individuals (Ås et al., 1963; Cooper, et al., 1967) and use of standardized procedures that involve various combinations of suggestions for sleep and relaxation (Leva, 1974a; Mitchell and Lundy, 1986; Page and Handley, 1991, 1992; Reilley et al., 1980; Spanos et al., 1986a; Springer et al., 1977). While such techniques enhance responsiveness slightly compared to untreated controls, a variety of waking procedures enhance responsiveness as much as does deepening. Task-motivational instructions routinely enhance responsiveness as much as do traditional inductions (Barber, 1969), as does the provision of information designed to demystify hypnosis (Coe et al., 1995; Hawkins and Bartsch, 2000; Reilley et al., 1980).

Technological aids

The idea that conditions such as relaxation, partial sleep, focused attention, quieting of the mind, or dissociation are instrumental in hypnotic responsiveness gives rise to the idea that certain forms of technology might be used to produce the states in question and hence raise responsiveness. Such application has met with limited success. Wickramasekera (1973), for instance, proposed that a reduction in muscle tension produced by electromyographic (EMG) biofeedback from the frontalis muscles would reduce internally produced stimulation and improve attention to suggestions. Initial optimism regarding this technique (Simon and Salzberg, 1981; Wickramasekera, 1973) has been tempered by failures to confirm (Radtke et al., 1983; Spanos and Bertrand, 1985) and *positive* correlations (0.55 to 0.59) between muscle tension and hypnotic responsiveness (Spanos and Bertrand, 1985). This latter finding runs opposite to the notion that lower tension is associated with higher responsiveness. Another biofeedback method that has been used is learning to produce more alpha EEG activity. This has led to small gains in responsiveness in one study (London et al., 1974).

Reducing environmental stimulation has enhanced responsiveness in some instances. Talone et al. (1975) found that 10 minutes of sitting still produced a slight increase but 10 minutes of listening to music failed to generate any increase. Prolonged sensory deprivation of 6 to 8 hours produced increases in some studies (Barabasz, 1982; Barabasz and Barabasz, 1989; Sanders and Rehyer, 1969) but not in others (Leva, 1974b; Levitt et al., 1962). When enhancement did occur, hypothesized changes in hypnotic processes (e.g. dissociation) were accompanied by aversive experiences, some intrinsic to sensory deprivation (e.g. stress). Compliance arising from the desire to justify suffering could have fuelled the observed increases in responsiveness (e.g. Aronson and Mills, 1959).

Conclusions

Numerous and varied attempts to deepen hypnosis have proved limited in their effectiveness on responsiveness to suggestions. Although traditional methods produce small increases in responsiveness, one class of waking techniques is as effective: methods that motivate participants to perform suggested tasks well produce the small increases in responsiveness that researchers have come to expect from the gamut of traditional inductions.

Methods for increasing alertness

The research programmes of Hull (1933) and Barber (1969) demonstrated just how hypnotically responsive no-hypnosis control groups could be. Methods known as 'alertness inductions' represent a family of waking procedures that differ from the Hull and Barber applications in that they seek an increased state of alertness. Ludwig and Lyle (1964) studied the effects of what they called a 'tension induction' (p. 71), which was 'designed to increase tension, alertness, sensory and motor stimulation, ideational activity, hostility, and to diminish comfort, focused attention and concentration' (p. 71) and included pronouncements that participants were becoming 'nervous, uncomfortable, and frozen in fear' (p. 72). These outcomes are opposite to those sought by traditional hypnotic induction. The authors examined several impacts of their tension induction on nine 'postaddict' (p. 71) patients in an initial session. In subsequent sessions, hypnotic responsiveness was again tested, first following a traditional induction and then under no induction. The phenomena that were requested and suggested in the context of the tension induction occurred; for example, high emotionality, body rigidity, and reports of a racing mind. Responsiveness to test suggestions was high in all conditions, although slightly higher in the tension and traditional conditions than in the control. Ludwig and Lyle (1964) concluded that their tension induction produced a 'hyperalert trance state' (pp. 73–4), and because of the presence of this 'trance', the state was distinguishable from Barber's 'waking', task-motivational condition. However, on inspection, the data of Ludwig and Lyle (1964) do not rule out a task-motivational explanation. Their participants appeared to do everything that they were directed to do.

Several different alertness inductions – some with and some without concomitant physical activity – have been tested. Bányai and

Hilgard (1976) used what they referred to as an 'active–alert' induction. In this procedure, participants rode a stationary bicycle and were given instructions and suggestions for alertness, heightened and focused attention, and feelings of freshness. Responsiveness to suggestions in the active–alert condition did not differ from responsiveness in a traditional induction condition (Bányai and Hilgard, 1976; Malot, 1984). Passive–alert methods involve procedures designed to increase alertness while requiring little or no physical activity. Usually, passive–alert conditions produce responsiveness levels similar to those found in traditional induction conditions (Cardeña et al., 1998; Vingoe, 1973), but one study showed a slightly higher level of responsiveness under passive–alert induction than traditional induction (Gibbons, 1976). In research assessing phenomenology produced by alert and traditional inductions, it is apparent that there is little to differentiate the methods save for the experience of relaxation itself (Fellows and Richardson, 1993).

Conclusions

Alert methods of induction are as effective as their traditional counterparts at enhancing responsiveness. The fact that such different techniques as traditional and alert inductions have similar effectiveness raises questions about the mechanism responsible for the (small) observed responsiveness gains in the two instances. If a hypnotic process is responsible for the gains observed in alert conditions, as is proposed by some researchers (e.g. Bányai and Hilgard, 1976), then it must be a very different kind of hypnotic condition than the one traditionally proposed (e.g. Hilgard, 1986). As research in the area involves virtually no assessment of mediating processes, there is little to justify the assertion that some sort of hypnosis is involved. The more parsimonious explanation for the available data on enhancement under conditions of alert inductions is that participants are carrying out task requirements (e.g. Fellows and Richardson, 1993).

Influence of suggestion

It has long been assumed that the use of *suggestion* is necessary for eliciting a hypnotic response as opposed to any other kind of response (e.g. Orne, 1977). Yet there is reason to question this assumption. Researchers working within a social–cognitive orientation propose that the clarity of task specification is an important factor in hypnotic responsiveness and that suggestions are not without ambiguity in specifying what participants are expected to do in a hypnotic session (Lynn and Sivec, 1992; Spanos, 1982, 1991). This implies that the very use of suggestions might not be the only or even the best way to elicit hypnotic responding. In this section, I take a closer look at the suggestion concept, examine alternative methods for eliciting hypnotic responding, and evaluate the role in hypnotic responsiveness of the level of clarity of task definition.

The nature of suggestion

A suggestion describes an *occurrence*, that is, something that happens to the person by way of external agency (Hilgard, 1965; Spanos, 1982). 'Your arm is rising' or 'You cannot remember' are suggestions (see also Chapter 1). Suggestions differ from the kinds of influence communications usually used to elicit behaviour in daily life, where instructions such as requests or orders are given. Instructions make it clear that the addressee is the source of the behaviour in question (Hilgard, 1965; Spanos, 1982). Thus, whereas suggestions announce an external-agent-controlled occurrence, instructions seek a self-controlled action.

In hypnosis sessions it is rare for suggestions to be given in simple, one-sentence form and isolated from other messages. It is common for the suggestion to be broken down into component acts, each of which is suggested and repeated ('Your arm is slowly rising. It is rising . . . slowly rising . . . rising. Your arm is rising'). Moreover, several types of instructions accompany suggestions, including requests to use imagery and to perform acts that complement suggested responses (e.g. writing down words you can remember). So, rather than giving a simple, one-phrase suggestion, hypnotists actually convey a complex message made up of interrelated suggestions and instructions. This complex set of messages refers to the concurrent operation of two different classes of conduct, instructed and hence self-controlled, and suggested and hence external-agent-controlled. Participants know that they are required to make the instructed responses. Participants also know that suggested responses are external-agent-controlled, and so should be allowed to *happen* (Hilgard, 1991). It is here that the ambiguity of suggestion lies: *there are different ways to construe 'letting happen'*.

One method of 'letting happen' is to refrain completely from making an expected response, as when a patient lets the patellar reflex occur completely on its own. However, there are other common interpretations of 'letting happen' – ones that lead the participant to make the suggested response. Consider two examples. In one, 'letting happen' consists of making a response with little attentiveness to the process by which it is controlled. This kind of 'letting happen' occurs when an athlete gets into the flow of a game. Instead of micromanaging his or her conduct, actions are left to occur 'on their own'. In these cases, the person exercises broad control of action – but for his or her intervention, no action whatsoever would occur – yet the behaviour occurs with considerable autonomy. In another example, 'letting happen' comprises the removal of restraints that the participant expects will prevent suggested responses. For instance, in order to remove an impediment to a suggested arm-rising response, the person might make his or her arm so 'light' that it rises. When this happens, the mere act of removing restraints results in a response that is identical to that called for in the suggestion.

Suggestions as response-inhibiting

The foregoing indicates how suggestions could serve to inhibit hypnotic responsiveness. Some participants might refrain completely from responding to suggestions because they interpret their task as waiting for suggested responses to occur entirely on their own. Notice that these individuals are cooperating fully with the hypnotist. As they understand it, cooperation entails abstaining from suggested action. Research that has measured interpretations of suggestions shows that approximately 50 per cent of participants believe that they must wait for suggested responses to occur entirely on their own (Gorassini, 1997). This form of interpretation is negatively related to hypnotic responsiveness whereas more active forms of interpretation are positively related to both behavioural and experiential measures of hypnotic responsiveness (Gorassini, 1997). The inherent ambiguity of suggestion would also help explain the limited effectiveness of Ericksonian indirect suggestion techniques (Lynn et al., 1993).

Compared to suggestions, instructions should be unequivocally interpreted as inviting self-generated action. Therefore, provided that the instructions are reasonable and easy enough to execute, responsiveness should be extremely high, and certainly much higher than responses to suggestions. In testing these ideas, Spanos and Gorassini (1984) sought to elicit ideomotor responses by suggestion as well as by instruction. Half of the study's participants received the messages after hypnotic induction whereas the other half received the messages after task-motivational instructions. The type of induction had no influence on responsiveness. Requested conduct occurred with perfect frequency, whereas suggested conduct occurred slightly less than 50 per cent of the time. Spanos and Gorassini (1984) also found that the frequency of classic hypnotic responding, which consists of the combination of a response occurrence and the experience of that response as automatic (cf. Weitzenhoffer, 1974), occurred with close to the same frequency over suggestion and instruction conditions: 21.5 per cent and 16.2 per cent, respectively. These data indicate, contrary to the traditional view, that classic hypnotic responding can occur when messages other than suggestions are used.

These data also demonstrate what can be called a 'suggestion–instruction trade-off' in the production of hypnotic responding. Compared to the use of instructions, the use of suggestions reduces the rate at which participants exhibit suggested responses but increases the likelihood that those who do exhibit the responses will experience non-volition. Compared to suggestions, instructions lead to increased (indeed perfect) responsiveness but a relatively low per capita rate of experienced non-volition. These trade-offs suggest two strategies for enhancing hypnotic responsiveness. One is to continue to use suggestions to elicit responses but supplement them with instructions designed to encourage the kinds of interpretations of 'letting happen' that entail making, rather than waiting for, suggested responses. Considerable research on this strategy has been conducted (see below). The other approach would be to instruct participants to make suggested responses and supplement this with instructions to use strategies that would help create experienced realism. For example, participants could be told to make responses, such as 'gradually raise your arm', and also be told to 'make the arm feel like it is rising all by itself'. A similar approach could be taken with cognitive suggestions. For example, participants could be told to 'see a kitten on your lap and pet it' and instructed further to 'refrain from questioning the reality of this scenario'. The purely instructional approach has not yet been tested in the modification paradigm.

Conclusions

The foregoing discussion suggests that low hypnotic responsiveness is significantly a matter of how participants in hypnosis sessions interpret suggestions. Even though the practice of using suggestions to elicit hypnotic responding is universal, the approach comes with the cost of holding responsiveness down in willing and able participants. At the root of the problem is the ambiguity of suggestion with respect to its definition of 'letting happen'. If supplementary information could be provided to promote the sorts of interpretations of 'letting happen' that would engage participants' active management of suggested responses, hypnotic responsiveness should rise as a consequence. This would not necessarily result in a 'hollow' form of activity. The momentary adoption of suggestion-related fantasies would help evoke experiences of realism and automaticity (Barber et al., 1974). Indeed, recent work in the neuropsychology of hypnosis suggests that active interpretive and attentional processes underlie suggested experiences (Crawford, 1994; Rainville et al., 1999). Central to the next section is how techniques that change construals of 'letting happen' from passive to active can bring about increases in behavioural as well as subjective aspects of hypnotic responsiveness.

Methods for instilling direct management of suggested responses

In this section, I review cognitive–behavioural training procedures. Methods of this type use as their foundation Barber's task-motivational approach, which is considered a necessary but not sufficient condition for enhancement. Task-motivation provides the energizing component of gain, but to this must be added a directing component. It is this directing component, in the form of training in the use of direct management of suggested responses, that is also contained in cognitive–behavioural techniques (Spanos, 1986). Over the course of two generations of cognitive–behavioural research on hypnotic-responsiveness enhancement, the conceptual and operational definitions of direct management have evolved from a relatively limited form of direct management, consisting of adopting suggested construals, to an encompassing form of direct management, consisting of adopting suggested construals *and behaviours*.

Direct management of suggested construals

The 1960s and 1970s saw the application of a number of cognitive–behavioural packages meant to enhance responsiveness. All these methods consisted of techniques meant to increase motivation to perform well and were designed to instil direct management of conceptual activity. For example, Diamond (1972) sought to raise performance motivation in his participants by correcting misconceptions about hypnosis and casting hypnosis in a positive light. He sought to instil direct management by defining the task as 'refocusing attention and "suspending reality concerns" while letting the imagination take over without comparing the present imagined experience with a "real" one' (p. 176).

Research evaluating techniques of this type showed that responsiveness increased reliably in the presence of training but failed to do so in its absence (Comins et al., 1975; Cronin et al., 1971; Diamond, 1972; Diamond et al., 1975; Gregory and Diamond, 1973; Havens, 1977; Katz, 1979; Kinney and Sachs, 1974; Pascal and Salzberg, 1959; Sachs and Anderson, 1967; Springer et al., 1977). The increases were in some cases robust and occurred as frequently when the measure of responsiveness reflected subjective experience as when it reflected behavioural occurrence. Indeed, subjective reports were maintained in the face of honesty exhortations (Kinney and Sachs, 1974). Training also generalized to novel suggestions (Katz, 1979) and persisted at one-month follow-up (Kinney and Sachs, 1974). In research that implemented manipulations of demonstrative models, effects on hypnotic responsiveness were statistically significant but small, and it was more difficult to increase performance using responsive models than it was to decrease it using unresponsive ones (e.g. Botto et al., 1977). Overall, the approach that combined task-motivation and direct construal brought an increase in responsiveness that exceeded that resulting from either task-motivational instructions alone or trance induction techniques. Further development of cognitive–behavioural methodology in the 1980s resulted in a new technique capable of reliably generating robust gains in responsiveness. This is reviewed in the next section.

The Carleton Skills Training Programme

The Carleton Skills Training Programme (CSTP; Gorassini and Spanos, 1986, 1999; see also Chapter 2) is a 75-minute procedure designed to enhance motivation and teach a direct management strategy. Techniques for increasing motivation include dispelling myths about hypnosis, portraying hypnosis positively, giving positive expectations of success, and establishing rapport with the participant. Techniques for instilling direct management consist of insistence that the participant make suggested responses (not wait for them to happen), instructions to use and become absorbed in the imagery accompanying suggestions, training in tactics for responding to four sample test suggestions, the opportunity to respond to four novel and undemonstrated suggestions, and instructions to apply the acquired skill during any further testing. The standard procedure is designed for individual administration (Gorassini and Spanos, 1986), but has been adapted for group use (Kirkeby et al., 1991). To convey the various informational components, the standard CSTP uses a variety of media, including audiotape, videotape, and direct instruction.

The CSTP is the most studied of cognitive–behavioural procedures. Its success at enhancing responsiveness has been shown in ten different laboratories (Bates, 1992; Bertrand et al., 1993; Burgess et al., 1990–1; Cangas and Perez, 1998; Cross and Spanos, 1988–9; Fellows and Ragg, 1992; Gearan and Kirsch, 1993; Gearan et al., 1995; Gfeller et al., 1987; Gorassini and Spanos, 1986; Kirkeby et al., 1991; Niedzwienska, 2000; Robertson et al., 1992; Spanos and Flynn, 1989; Spanos et al., 1986b, 1987a, 1987b, 1987c, 1988, 1989, 1989–90, 1990, 1991, 1993a, 1993b, 1995, 1996; West and Fellows, 1996).

It is common in this research for 50 per cent of participants who score low in responsiveness prior to training to score high in responsiveness afterward. When behavioural responsiveness scores of individuals who score high after CSTP training (trained highs) are matched with behavioural responsiveness scores of individuals who score high in responsiveness without training (natural highs), subjective measures of the two groups fail to differ from each other but are distinguishable from simulators (Gfeller et al., 1987; Spanos and Flynn, 1989; Spanos et al., 1986b, 1989). Training generalizes to a host of novel, difficult suggestions (Gfeller et al., 1987; Spanos et al., 1987b, 1989) and persists (to 4-month follow-up in Spanos et al., 1991; and 21-month in Spanos et al., 1988). The overall picture is one of a large proportion of CSTP-trained individuals acquiring a generalized and persistent skill that enables them to respond experientially to a wide range of hypnotic tasks. Such training produces much higher responsiveness than any other technique used to date.

Components of change

As it is believed that a particularly effective tactic within the family of methods for increasing motivation is establishing rapport with the trainee, the CSTP in its standard form includes rapport enhancement. Gfeller et al. (1987) used two different forms of the CSTP, the standard version as well as one in which even greater rapport was sought. Responsiveness gains in these two conditions were compared with one another and with a no-treatment condition. Manipulation checks on interpersonal rapport and attraction toward the experimenter did not differ between the rapport-CSTP and standard-CSTP but in both conditions exceeded a practice-only control. Hypnotic responsiveness rose significantly and to equal degrees in the two CSTP conditions but did not rise in the control condition. Gfeller et al. (1987) also found that responsiveness rose more following the rapport-CSTP than following the standard-CSTP for participants scoring low, but not medium, in pre-test responsiveness. In other research (Spanos et al., 1989–90, experiment 2), CSTP training was ineffective when low rapport was induced. Thus high rapport is a necessary but not sufficient condition for the typically large increases induced by CSTP training.

Instilling a direct management strategy is also a necessary element in CSTP effectiveness. Participants who received a CSTP containing all components except for direct management training failed to show improvements in hypnotic responsiveness whereas participants given the standard CSTP, in which such information is included, showed the usual robust gains (Spanos et al., 1986b). Spanos et al. (1989–90) gave low responsive participants the standard CSTP, a high-rapport passive induction, or no training. The high-rapport passive induction consisted of techniques designed to produce high task motivation, increased relaxation, and a passive interpretation of 'letting happen'. Perceived rapport of participants in response to the CSTP and the passive induction failed to differ but exceeded control. Hypnotic responsiveness rose sharply following the CSTP but failed to rise in the passive induction and control groups, which did not differ from each other. Hence, the portion of the CSTP that instils direct management of suggested responses is a key component of training, which works above and beyond task-motivation in affecting responsiveness.

Individual differences

Although the CSTP produces sizeable gains in responsiveness, on average, not everyone benefits equally from the intervention. Research into individual differences thought to moderate the relationship between CSTP training and resulting responsiveness has focused mainly on some of the motivational and ability components deemed important in change. Participants who would be expected to hold back from devoting a full effort to training goals fail to benefit as much from the CSTP as participants who do seem disposed to full effort. Hence, participants with negative pre-test attitudes toward hypnosis show smaller gains than individuals with positive pre-test attitudes (Gorassini and Spanos, 1986; Spanos, et al., 1987a). Participants who lack abilities that are important to hypnotic responding would be expected to benefit less from the CSTP than participants who possess the abilities. Researchers have found a relationship between imagery skills and CSTP gains (Cross and Spanos, 1988–9; Spanos et al., 1987a; but see Lynn and Sivec, 1992).

Possible plateau and regression artifacts

It has been proposed that responsiveness scores might rise from one hypnotic testing session to the next, even when no attempt to enhance responsiveness has been made between the testing occasions (e.g. Perry, 1977). This sort of rise is clearly seen with many different kinds of skills. The classic learning curve reflects a sharp increase in proficiency at first followed by a levelling off of subsequent gain. It was suggested that hypnotic responding might rise naturally at first followed by a plateau (Shor and Cobb, 1968; Shor et al., 1966). If a modification procedure happened to be applied early in participants' learning of hypnotic responsiveness, it might appear that the technique is effective because of the coincidental natural rise in performance.

The influence on hypnotic responsiveness of this ostensible type of improvement has been routinely separated from the influence of CSTP training on hypnotic responsiveness by the inclusion of no-training control groups in research designs. As reported above, the research has shown usually large gains in responsiveness in CSTP groups but stability (or losses) in control groups. Indeed, hypnotic research demonstrates that mean responsiveness values among participants with no previous hypnotic testing remain remarkably stable from one testing occasion to the next (Piccione et al., 1989). Even when strong demands for change are made over many testing occasions, responsiveness either fails to rise or rises marginally (Ås et al., 1963; Cooper et al., 1967; Sachs, 1971; Shor and Cobb, 1968). A related artifact consists of regression toward the mean. Extreme scores tend to moderate. If low-scoring groups comprise extreme scores in this sense, then low scores should rise if assessed a second time. As the data above indicate, scores do not change from initial to subsequent hypnotic responsiveness testing. Moreover, any changes due to regression that do occur can be assessed independently of CSTP-induced gains by using no-treatment control groups.

The issue of faking

One early criticism of CSTP research was that trained participants might be faking gains in hypnotic responsiveness (Bates, 1990). However, there are reasons to believe that CSTP-trained participants frequently experience suggested effects:

1   On its face, the CSTP gives low-responsive participants an attractive alternative to faking by providing an opportunity to generate interesting subjective experiences.
2   Strong pressure alone produces limited or no enhancement in responsiveness (e.g. Sachs, 1971).
3   Participants who receive cognitive–behavioural training respond differently to suggestions than participants who receive instructions to fake hypnotic responsiveness but similarly to participants who score high in responsiveness without training (Gfeller et al., 1987; Spanos and Flynn, 1989; Spanos et al., 1986b, 1989).
4   Trained participants respond the same in private as they do in the presence of an experimenter (Spanos et al., 1993a).
5   Trained highs fake no more than do natural highs, and evidently less. Gearan et al. (1995) asked natural-scoring participants if they faked their responses to suggestions. Some admitted that they did. Burgess et al. (1990–1), using their reporting bias paradigm, found that natural highs showed slightly *more* self-report faking than CSTP-trained participants.

Role of response expectancy

A response expectancy is the subjective probability of successfully exhibiting a response. Within the CSTP framework, raising response expectancies comprises one of the techniques for increasing task-motivation. In an alternative depiction, Kirsch and associates (e.g. Wickless and Kirsch, 1989) consider response expectancies the final common pathway of suggested responding. Hence, any increase in response expectancy would result in an increase in responsiveness, and any increase in hypnotic responsiveness must be the result of an increase in response expectancy. This account proposes that a high subjective probability would result in a suggested response occurring even under a passive strategy, which does not occur (see Cross and Spanos, 1988–9). While other research suggests that response expectancies play a role in hypnotic responding, it casts doubt on the central role accorded the variable by the Kirsch group. Inductions of positive response expectancies have tended to produce small gains in responsiveness. This is the case over a wide variety of manipulations of expectancy, including verbal (e.g. Wickless and Kirsch, 1989), experiential (e.g. Benham et al., 1998; Spanos et al., 1990), and placebo (Council et al., 1983; Glass and Barber, 1961). It is also the case that manipulations of strategy orientation – passive versus active – affect hypnotic responsiveness even when expectancies are held constant (Diamond et al., 1975; Gregory and Diamond, 1973), which contradicts the view that changes in response expectancies are the final common pathway to responsiveness. Finally, in research assessing the relationship between expectancy change and CSTP gain, responsiveness rose substantially from pre- to post-testing even though expectancies failed to change (Gearan et al., 1995). A similar kind of asymmetry occurred in Cronin et al. (1971). Overall, the research does not support the view that response expectancies comprise the final common pathway to responsiveness.

Conclusions

Cognitive–behavioural training stands out from the other techniques reviewed above by reliably producing moderate-to-large increases in responsiveness, generalizing to novel, difficult suggestions, and exerting a lasting impact. The changes encompass subjective as well as behavioural responsiveness. Even though some participants in cognitive-behavioural research fake their performances, they do so at a rate that is no greater than that typifying naturally scoring responsive individuals.

Final conclusions

I began this article by describing a debate in the field of hypnosis modification, one side of which views hypnotic responsiveness as stable and immutable and the other side of which considers hypnotic responsiveness significantly changeable. Based on the research reviewed in this paper, two conclusions can be drawn about the degree of change in hypnotic responsiveness that is possible. One echoes Diamond (1974) in asserting that at least some enhancement of hypnotic responsiveness is possible by any one of a variety of techniques. Traditional hypnotic inductions, task-motivational instructions, information about hypnosis, procedures for enhancing alertness or activity, and cognitive–behavioural methods have all been used successfully to increase responsiveness. A second conclusion echoes Spanos (1986) in declaring that one set of methods produces distinctively large gains in responsiveness: cognitive–behavioural techniques, especially the CSTP, comprise reliable and effective enhancement procedures. Based on the research on modifiability, then, it cannot only be said that hypnotic responsiveness is modifiable. Hypnotic responsiveness is highly modifiable.

Hypnosis enhancement research indicates that the best way to enhance hypnotic responsiveness is by inducing a type of *simulation*. The simulation referred to here is to be distinguished from what could be called the *surface* simulation of hypnosis, a notion introduced by Orne (1959), in which a detached behavioural imitation of a hypnotic performance is requested of the participant; during this kind of performance, the individual does not concurrently think or feel like the character being portrayed. The reference made presently is to a *deep* simulation, a concept introduced by social–cognitive psychologists (e.g. Taylor and Schneider, 1989) in referring to a process that involves a more cognitive than behavioural form of imitation and an emotionally involved rather than detached experience of the character being portrayed. According to Taylor and Schneider (1989), 'simulation is the imitative representation of the functioning or process of some event or series of events. ... We will use the term to mean the cognitive construction of hypothetical scenarios or the reconstruction of real scenarios' (p. 175). Cognitive–behavioural training, then, seeks to induce deep simulations of the events suggested by the hypnotist. Participants are induced to imitate the cognitive processes of someone who faces actual events of the kind the hypnotist describes via his or her suggestions. However, in an extension of Taylor and Schneider's (1989) deep simulation concept, cognitive–behavioural training in hypnosis also encourages behavioural simulation as a complement to conceptual involvement.

Viewing hypnotic responsiveness as the deep simulation of events has both research and clinical implications. On the research side, for investigators who are attempting to demonstrate an aspect of hypnosis that is believed to be distinct from deep simulation, it would be necessary to include a deep-simulation control group in research designs that test for ostensible hypnotic processes. For example, if a researcher proposes a brain process that is unique to hypnosis, and thus distinct from either surface or deep simulation, it would be necessary to show that the brain process is present in the hypnotic condition and absent in either a surface simulation or a deep simulation. Until then, it would be difficult to assert that a unique aspect of hypnosis – its essence – has been discovered. Although surface simulation has been commonly used as a control in hypnotic research, deep simulation has not been used as a control, with the exception of recent research on the CSTP (e.g. Spanos et al., 1989).

On the clinical side, it is thought that deep simulation aids the coping process by providing a realistic but safe environment for experiencing and dealing with events (Taylor and Schneider, 1989). By replicating the real world to at least some extent, the individual is afforded the opportunity to rework responses to past events or rehearse new and adaptive responses to possible future events. The hypnosis modification research, in addition to serving as an example of the fact that mental simulations can produce realistic experiences, contributes knowledge to how training in deep simulations should be conducted. It shows how to paint realistic word pictures and underscores the importance of combining behavioural and conceptual activity in the production of realism.

References

Aronson, E. and Mills, J. (1959) 'The effects of severity of initiation on liking for a group', *Journal of Abnormal and Social Psychology*, 59:177–81.

Ås, A., Hilgard, E.R. and Weitzenhoffer, A.M. (1963) 'An attempt at experimental modification of hypnotizability through repeated individualized hypnotic experience', *Scandinavian Journal of Psychology*, 4:81–9.

Bányai, E.I. and Hilgard, E.A. (1976) 'A comparison of active-alert hypnotic induction with traditional relaxation induction', *Journal of Abnormal Psychology*, 85:218–24.

Barabasz, A. (1982) 'Restricted environmental stimulation and the enhancement of hypnotizability: Pain, EEG alpha, skin conductance and temperature response', *International Journal of Clinical and Experimental Hypnosis*, 30:147–66.

—— and Barabasz, M. (1989) 'Effects of restricted environmental stimulation: Enhancement of hypnotizability for experimental and chronic pain control', *International Journal of Clinical and Experimental Hypnosis*, 37:217–31.

Barber, T.X. (1969) *Hypnosis: A Scientific Approach*, Princeton, NJ: Van Nostrand-Reinhold.

—— Spanos, N.P. and Chaves, J.F. (1974) *Hypnosis, Imagination, and Human Potentialities*, New York: Pergamon.

Bates, B.L. (1990) 'Compliance and the Carleton Skills Training Programme', *British Journal of Experimental and Clinical Hypnosis*, 7:159–64.

—— (1992) 'The effect of demands for honesty on the efficacy of the Carleton Skills Training Programme', *International Journal of Clinical and Experimental Hypnosis*, 40:88–102.

—— Miller, R.J., Cross, H.J. and Brigham, T.A. (1988) 'Modifying hypnotic suggestibility with the Carleton Skills Training Programme', *Journal of Personality and Social Psychology*, 55:120–7.

Benham, G., Bowers, S., Nash, M. and Muenchen, R. (1998) 'Self-fulfilling prophecy and hypnotic response are not the same thing', *Journal of Personality and Social Psychology*, 75:1604–13.

Bertrand, L.D., Stam, H.J. and Radtke, H.L. (1993) 'The Carleton Skills Training Package for modifying hypnotic susceptibility – a replication and extension: A brief communication', *International Journal of Clinical and Experimental Hypnosis*, 41:6–14.

Botto, R.W., Fisher, S. and Soucy, G.P. (1977) 'The effect of a good and a poor model on hypnotic susceptibility in a low demand situation', *International Journal of Clinical and Experimental Hypnosis*, 25:175–83.

Braffman, W. and Kirsch, I. (1999) 'Imaginative suggestibility and hypnotizability: An empirical analysis', *Journal of Personality and Social Psychology*, 77:578–87.

Burgess, C.A., du Breuil, S.C., Jones, B. and Spanos, N.P. (1990–1) 'Compliance and the modification of hypnotizability', *Imagination, Cognition and Personality*, 10:293–304.

Cangas, A.J. and Perez, M. (1998) 'The effect of two procedures on hypnotic susceptibility modification', *Contemporary Hypnosis*, 15:212–18.

Cardeña, E., Alarcón, A., Capafons, A. and Bayot, A. (1998) 'Effects on suggestibility of a new method of active-alert hypnosis: Alert hand', *International Journal of Clinical and Experimental Hypnosis*, 46:280–94.

Coe, W.C., Peterson, P. and Gwynn, M. (1995) 'Expectations and sequelae to hypnosis: Initial findings', *American Journal of Clinical Hypnosis*, 38:3–11.

Comins, J.R., Fullam, F. and Barber, T.X. (1975) 'Effects of experimenter modeling, demands for honesty, and initial level of suggestibility on response to "hypnotic" suggestions', *Journal of Consulting and Clinical Psychology*, 43:668–75.

Cooper, L., Banford, S., Schubot, E. and Tart, C. (1967) 'A further attempt to modify hypnotic susceptibility through repeated, individualized experience', *International Journal of Clinical and Experimental Hypnosis*, 15:118–24.

Council, J.R., Kirsch, I., Vickery, A.R. and Carlson, D. (1983) ' "Trance" versus "skill" hypnotic inductions: The effects of credibility, expectancy, and experimenter modeling', *Journal of Consulting and Clinical Psychology*, 51:432–40.

Crawford, H.J. (1994) 'Brain dynamics and hypnosis: Attentional and disattentional processes', *International Journal of Clinical and Experimental Hypnosis*, 42:204–32.

Cronin, D.M., Spanos, N.P. and Barber, T.X. (1971) 'Augmenting hypnotic suggestibility by providing favorable information about hypnosis', *American Journal of Clinical Hypnosis*, 13:259–64.

Cross, W. and Spanos, N.P. (1988–9) 'The effects of imagery vividness and receptivity on skill training induced enhancement in hypnotic susceptibility', *Imagination, Cognition and Personality*, 8:89–103.

Diamond, M.J. (1972) 'The use of observationally presented information to modify hypnotic susceptibility', *Journal of Abnormal Psychology*, 79:174–80.

—— (1974) 'Modification of hypnotizability: A review', *Psychological Bulletin*, 81:180–98.

—— Steadman, C., Harada, D. and Rosenthal, J. (1975) 'The use of direct instructions to modify hypnotic performance: The effects of programmed learning procedures', *Journal of Abnormal Psychology*, 84:109–13.

Fellows, B.J. and Ragg, L. (1992) 'The Carleton Skills Training Programme: A preliminary British trial', *Contemporary Hypnosis*, 9:169–74.

—— and Richardson, J. (1993) 'Relaxed and alert hypnosis: An experiential comparison', *Contemporary Hypnosis*, 10:49–54.

Gearan, P. and Kirsch, I. (1993) 'Response expectancy as a mediator of hypnotizability modification: A brief communication', *International Journal of Clinical and Experimental Hypnosis*, 41:84–91.

—— Schoenberger, N.E. and Kirsch, I. (1995) 'Modifying hypnotizability: A new component analysis', *International Journal of Clinical and Experimental Hypnosis*, 43:70–89.

Gfeller, J.D., Lynn, S.J. and Pribble, W.E. (1987) 'Enhancing hypnotic susceptibility: Interpersonal and rapport factors', *Journal of Personality and Social Psychology*, 52:586–95.

Gibbons, D.E. (1976) 'Hypnotic vs. hyperempiric induction procedures: An experimental comparison', *Perceptual and Motor Skills*, 42:834.

Glass, L.B. and Barber, T.X. (1961) 'A note on hypnotic behaviour, the definition of the situation and the placebo effect', *Journal of Nervous and Mental Disease*, 132:539–41.

Gorassini, D.R. (1997) 'Strategy selection and hypnotic performance', *Contemporary Hypnosis*, 14:37–47.

—— and Spanos, N.P. (1986) 'A cognitive–social skills approach to the successful modification of hypnotic susceptibility', *Journal of Personality and Social Psychology*, 50:1004–12.

—— and Spanos, N.P. (1999) 'The Carleton Skill Training Programme for modifying hypnotic suggestibility: Original version and variations', in I. Kirsch, A. Capafons, S. Amigó and E. Cardeña-Buelna (eds), *Clinical Hypnosis and Self-regulation Therapy: A Cognitive-behavioural Perspective* (pp. 141–77), Washington, DC: American Psychological Association Books.

Gregory, J. and Diamond, M.J. (1973) 'Increasing hypnotic susceptibility by means of positive expectancies and written instructions', *Journal of Abnormal Psychology*, 82:363–7.

Havens, R.A. (1977) 'Using modeling and information to modify hypnotizability', *International Journal of Clinical and Experimental Hypnosis*, 25:167–74.

Hawkins, R. and Bartsch, J. (2000) 'The effects of an educational lecture about hypnosis'. *Australian Journal of Clinical and Experimental Hypnosis*, 28:82–99.

Hilgard, E.R. (1965) *Hypnotic Susceptibility*, New York: Harcourt, Brace and World.

—— (1986) *Divided Consciousness: Multiple Controls in Human Thought and Action (Expanded Edition)*, New York: Wiley.

—— (1991) 'A neodissociation interpretation of hypnosis', in S.J. Lynn and J.W. Rhue (eds), *Theories of Hypnosis: Current Models and Perspectives* (pp. 83–104), New York: Guilford Press.

—— and Tart, C.T. (1966) 'Responsiveness to suggestions following waking and imagination instructions and follow induction of hypnosis', *Journal of Abnormal Psychology*, 71:196–208.

Hull, C.L. (1933) *Hypnosis and Suggestibility: A Scientific Approach*, New York: Appleton-Century.

Katz, N.W. (1979) 'Comparative efficacy of behavioural training, training plus relaxation, and sleep/trance hypnotic induction in increasing hypnotic susceptibility', *Journal of Consulting and Clinical Psychology*, 47:119–27.

Kinney, J.M. and Sachs, L.B. (1974) 'Increasing hypnotic susceptibility', *Journal of Abnormal Psychology*, 83:145–50.

Kirkeby, J.L., Payne, P.A., Hovanitz, C. and Moser, S. (1991) 'Increasing hypnotizability: A comparison of a multimedia form of the Carleton Skills Training Programme with a self-administered written form', *Contemporary Hypnosis*, 8:161–5.

Leva, R.A. (1974a) 'Modification of hypnotic susceptibility through audio-tape relaxation training: Preliminary report', *Perceptual and Motor Skills*, 39:872–4.

—— (1974b) 'Performance of low-susceptible *S*s on Stanford Profile Scales after sensory deprivation', *Psychological Reports*, 34:835–8.

Levitt, E.E., Brady, J.P, Ottinger, D. and Hinesley, R. (1962) 'Effects of sensory restriction on hypnotizability', *Archives of General Psychiatry*, 7:343–5.

London, P., Cooper, L.M. and Engstrom, D.R. (1974) 'Increasing hypnotic susceptibility by brain wave feedback', *Journal of Abnormal Psychology*, 83:554–60.

Ludwig, A.M. and Lyle, W.H., Jr. (1964) 'Tension induction and the hyperalert trance', *Journal of Abnormal and Social Psychology*, 69:70–6.

Lynn, S.J. and Rhue, J.W. (1991) 'Hypnosis theories: Themes, variations, and research directions', in S.J. Lynn and J.W. Rhue (eds), *Theories of Hypnosis: Current Models and Perspectives* (pp. 601–26), New York: Guilford Press.

—— and Sivec, H. (1992) 'The hypnotizable subject as a creative problem solving agent', in E. Fromm and M.R. Nash (eds), *Contemporary Hypnosis Research* (pp. 292–333), New York: Guilford Press.

—— Neufeld, V. and Maré, C. (1993) 'Direct versus indirect suggestions: A conceptual and methodological review', *International Journal of Clinical and Experimental Hypnosis*, 41:124–52.

Malott, J.M. (1984) 'Active-alert hypnosis: Replication and extension of previous research', *Journal of Abnormal Psychology*, 93:246–9.

Mitchell, G.P. Jr. and Lundy, R.M. (1986) 'The effects of relaxation and imagery inductions on responses to suggestions', *International Journal of Clinical and Experimental Hypnosis*, 34:98–109.

Niedzwienska, A. (2000) 'Goal-directed fantasy does not explain the training effect of the Carleton Skills Training Package', *International Journal of Clinical and Experimental Hypnosis*, 48:404–17.

O'Connell, D.N., Orne, M.T. and Shor, R.E. (1966) 'A comparison of hypnotic susceptibility as assessed by diagnostic ratings and initial standardized test scores', *International Journal of Clinical and Experimental Hypnosis*, 14:324–32.

Orne, M.T. (1959) 'The nature of hypnosis: Artifact and essence', *Journal of Abnormal and Social Psychology*, 58:277–99.

—— (1977) 'The construct of hypnosis: Implications of the definition for research and practice', *Annals of the New York Academy of Sciences*, 296:14–33.

Page, R.A. and Handley, G.W. (1991) 'A comparison of the effects of standardized chiasson and eye-closure inductions on susceptibility scores', *American Journal of Clinical Hypnosis*, 34:46–50.

—— and Handley, G.W. (1992) 'Effects of "deepening" techniques on hypnotic depth and responding', *International Journal of Clinical and Experimental Hypnosis*, 40:157–68.

Pascal, G.R. and Salzberg, H.C. (1959) 'A systematic approach to inducing hypnotic behaviour', *International Journal of Clinical and Experimental Hypnosis*, 7:161–7.

Perry, C. (1977) 'Is hypnotizability modifiable?', *International Journal of Clinical and Experimental Hypnosis*, 25:125–46.

Piccione, C., Hilgard, E.R. and Zimbardo, P.G. (1989) 'On the degree of stability of measured hypnotizability over a 25-year period', *Journal of Personality and Social Psychology*, 56:289–95.

Radtke, H.L., Spanos, N.P., Armstrong, L.A., Dillman, N. and Bosvenue, M.E. (1983) 'Effects of electromyographic feedback and progressive relaxation training on hypnotic susceptibility: Disconfirming results', *International Journal of Clinical and Experimental Hypnosis*, 31:98–106.

Rainville, P., Hofbauer, R.K., Paus, T., Duncan, G.H., Bushnell, M.C. and Price, D.D. (1999) 'Cerebral mechanisms of hypnotic induction and suggestion', *Journal of Cognitive Neuroscience*, 11:110–25.

Reilley, R.R., Parisher, D.W., Carona, A. and Dobrovolsky, N.W. (1980) 'Modifying hypnotic susceptibility by practice and instruction', *International Journal of Clinical and Experimental Hypnosis*, 28:39–45.

Robertson, L., McInnis, K. and St Jean, R. (1992) 'Modifying hypnotic susceptibility with the Carleton Skills Training Programme: A replication', *Contemporary Hypnosis*, 9:97–103.

Sachs, L.B. (1971) 'Construing hypnosis as modifiable behaviour', in A.B. Jacobs and L.B. Sachs (eds), *Psychology of Private Events* (pp. 61–75), New York: Academic Press.

—— and Anderson, W.L. (1967) 'Modification of hypnotic susceptibility', *International Journal of Clinical and Experimental Hypnosis*, 15:172–80.

Sanders, R.S. Jr. and Reyher, J. (1969) 'Sensory deprivation and the enhancement of hypnotic susceptibility', *Journal of Abnormal Psychology*, 74:375–81.

Sarbin, T.R. and Coe, W.C. (1972) *Hypnosis: A Social Psychological Analysis of Influence Communication*, New York: Holt, Rinehart and Winston.

Shor, R.E. and Cobb, J.C. (1968) 'An exploratory study of hypnotic training using the concept of plateau responsiveness as a referent', *American Journal of Clinical Hypnosis*, 10:178–97.

—— Orne, M.T. and O'Connell, D.N. (1966) 'Psychological correlates of plateau hypnotizability in a special volunteer sample', *Journal of Personality and Social Psychology*, 3:80–95.

Simon, M.J. and Salzberg, H. (1981) 'Electromyographic feedback and taped relaxation instructions to modify hypnotic susceptibility and amnesia', *American Journal of Clinical Hypnosis*, 24:14–21.

Spanos, N.P. (1982) 'Hypnotic behaviour: A cognitive, social psychological perspective', *Research Communications in Psychology, Psychiatry, and Behavior*, 7:199–213.

—— (1986) 'Hypnosis and the modification of hypnotic susceptibility: A social psychological perspective', in P. Naish (ed.), *What Is Hypnosis?* (pp. 85–120), Philadelphia: Open University Press.

—— (1991) 'A sociocognitive approach to hypnosis', in S.J. Lynn and J.W. Rhue (eds), *Theories of Hypnosis: Current Models and Perspectives* (pp. 324–61), New York: Guilford Press.

—— and Bertrand, L.D. (1985) 'EMG biofeedback, attained relaxation and hypnotic susceptibility: Is there a relationship?' *American Journal of Clinical Hypnosis*, 27:219–25.

—— and Chaves, J.F. (1991) 'History and historiography of hypnosis', in S.J. Lynn and J.W. Rhue (eds), *Theories of Hypnosis: Current Models and Perspectives* (pp. 43–78), New York: Guilford Press.

—— and Flynn, D.M. (1989) 'Simulation, compliance and skill training in the enhancement of hypnotizability', *British Journal of Experimental and Clinical Hypnosis*, 6:1–8.

—— and Gorassini, D.R. (1984) 'Structure of hypnotic test suggestions and attributions of responding involuntarily', *Journal of Personality and Social Psychology*, 46:688–96.

—— Lush, N.I., Smith, J.E. and de Groh, M.M. (1986a) 'Effects of two hypnotic induction procedures on overt and subjective response to two measures of hypnotic susceptibility', *Psychological Reports*, 59:1127–30.

—— Robertson, L.A., Menary, E.P. and Brett, P.J. (1986b) 'Component analysis of cognitive skill training for the enhancement of hypnotic susceptibility', *Journal of Abnormal Psychology*, 95:350–7.

—— Cross, W.P., Menary, E.P., Brett, P.J. and de Groh, M. (1987a) 'Attitudinal and imaginal ability predictors of social cognitive-skill training enhancements in hypnotic susceptibility', *Personality and Social Psychology Bulletin*, 13:379–98.

—— de Groh, M. and de Groot, H. (1987b) 'Skill training for enhancing hypnotic susceptibility and word list amnesia', *British Journal of Experimental and Clinical Hypnosis*, 4:15–23.

—— Robertson, L.A., Menary, E.P., Brett, P.J. and Smith, J. (1987c) 'Effects of repeated baseline testing on cognitive skill training induced increments in hypnotic susceptibility', *Journal of Personality and Social Psychology*, 52:1230–5.

—— Cross, W.F., Menary, E. and Smith, J. (1988) 'Long term effects of cognitive-skill training for the enhancement of hypnotic susceptibility', *British Journal of Experimental and Clinical Hypnosis*, 5:73–8.

Spanos, N.P., Lush, N.I. and Gwynn, M.I. (1989) 'Cognitive skill-training enhancement of hypnotizability: Generalization effects and trance logic responding', *Journal of Personality and Social Psychology*, 56:795–804.

—— Flynn, D.M. and Niles, J. (1989–90) 'Rapport and cognitive skill training in the enhancement of hypnotizability', *Imagination, Cognition and Personality*, 9:245–62.

—— Warnock, S. and de Groot, H.P. (1990) 'Cognitive skill training, confirming sensory stimuli, and responsiveness to suggestions in subjects unselected for hypnotizability', *Journal of Research in Personality*, 24:133–44.

—— DuBreuil, S.C. and Gabora, N.J. (1991) 'Four-month follow-up of skill-training-induced enhancements in hypnotizability', *Contemporary Hypnosis*, 8:25–32.

—— Burgess, C.A., Roncon, V., Wallace-Capretta, S. and Cross, P. (1993a) 'Surreptitiously observed hypnotic responding in simulators and in skill-trained and untrained high hypnotizables', *Journal of Personality and Social Psychology*, 65: 391–8.

—— Flynn, D.M. and Gabora, N.J. (1993b) 'The effects of cognitive skills training on the Stanford Profile Scale: Form I', *Contemporary Hypnosis*, 10:29–33.

—— Burgess, C.A., DuBreuil, S.C., Liddy, S., Bowman, K. and Perlini, A.H. (1995) 'The effects of stimulation and expectancy instructions on responses to cognitive skill training for enhancing hypnotizability', *Contemporary Hypnosis*, 12:1–11.

—— Burgess, C.A., Wallace-Capretta, S., Quaida, N., Streich, T. and Cross, P. (1996) 'Simulation, surreptitious observation and the modification of hypnotizability: Two tests of the compliance hypothesis', *Contemporary Hypnosis*, 13:161–76.

Springer, C.J., Sachs, L.B. and Morrow, J.E. (1977) 'Group methods of increasing hypnotic susceptibility', *International Journal of Clinical and Experimental Hypnosis*, 25:184–91.

Talone, J.M., Diamond, M.J. and Steadman, C. (1975) 'Modifying hypnotic performance by means of brief sensory experiences', *International Journal of Clinical and Experimental Hypnosis*, 23:190–9.

Taylor, S.E. and Schneider, S.K. (1989) 'Coping and the simulation of events', *Social Cognition*, 7:174–94.

Van Der Does, A.J.W., Van Dyck, R., Spinhoven, P. and Kloosman, A. (1989) 'The effectiveness of standardized versus individualized hypnotic suggestions: A brief communication', *International Journal of Clinical and Experimental Hypnosis*, 37:1–5.

Vingoe, F.J. (1973) 'Comparison of the Harvard Group Scale of Hypnotic Susceptibility, Form A and the Group Alert Trance Scale in a university population', *International Journal of Clinical and Experimental Hypnosis*, 21:169–79.

Wagstaff, G.F. (1981) *Hypnosis, Compliance, and Belief*, New York: St. Martin's.

Weitzenhoffer, A.M. (1974) 'When is an "instruction" an "instruction"?', *International Journal of Clinical and Experimental Hypnosis*, 22:258–69.

Wells, W.R. (1924) 'Experiments in waking hypnosis for instructional purposes', *Journal of Abnormal and Social Psychology*, 18:389–404.

West, V. and Fellows, B. (1996) 'How to be a "good" hypnotic subject!', *Contemporary Hypnosis*, 13:143–9.

Wickless, C. and Kirsch, I. (1989) 'Effects of verbal and experiential expectancy manipulations on hypnotic susceptibility', *Journal of Personality and Social Psychology*, 57:762–8.

Wickramasekera, I. (1973) 'Effects of electromyographic feedback on hypnotic susceptibility: More preliminary data', *Journal of Abnormal Psychology*, 82:74–7.

Woody, E.Z. and Bowers, K.S. (1994) 'A frontal assault on dissociated control', in S.J. Lynn and J.W. Rhue (eds), *Dissociation: Clinical and Theoretical Perspectives* (pp. 52–79), New York: Guilford Press.

Chapter 10

High hypnotizability
Relevance and utility to cognitive and clinical psychology?

Graham Turpin

Introduction

Hypnosis has been a feature of western society for some two hundred and fifty years or so, and predates the development of psychology as a scientific discipline. Nevertheless, hypnosis and psychology have tended to run parallel existences. Whereas hypnosis and psychotherapy are perceived by the general public as being very similar activities, undertaken by therapists within consulting rooms, usually for payment, and having the purpose of curing or alleviating some physical or psychological condition, the status afforded to hypnosis by psychology as a discipline has been inconsistent, to say the least, and characterized by deep scepticism for most of the time. Hypnosis is rarely taught or discussed on undergraduate programmes and, especially within the UK, is seldom included in applied psychology postgraduate programmes for the professional training of clinical or health psychology practitioners. This apparent lack of interest is despite a sizeable body of psychological literature, which has explored the phenomenology and processes said to underlie this unusual state. For example, a recent report from the British Psychological Society concludes that 'hypnosis is a valid subject for scientific study and research and a proven therapeutic medium' (Heap et al., 2001, p. 2). Why are psychologists so reluctant to be associated with this area of psychological enquiry or therapeutic endeavour?

Science or pseudoscience?

A possible explanation lies in the juxtaposition of what Lilienfield et al. (2003) have termed within the psychotherapy literature: 'pseudoscience and science'. They draw attention to the expanding activities of innovative and complementary therapies, which, they assert, frequently have no scientific basis or independent evidence on which to substantiate their claimed therapeutic effectiveness. Why should clinicians adopt such pseudoscientific therapies in the absence of objective and confirmatory evidence of therapeutic effectiveness? These authors refer to the 'scientist–practitioner gap': clinicians who were once trained to be critical of therapeutic claims and to expect them to be rigorously tested, are now subjected, along with their clients and the public at large, to an unrelenting multi-media barrage of therapeutic techniques and claims, which are published within the therapeutic and self-help literatures without any adequate standards of proof or peer review. In contrast, within the public care sector the pendulum has perhaps swung in the opposite direction; now the obsession with therapeutic evidence derived from randomized controlled trials reflects the supremacy of philosophies such as 'evidence-based practice' (Stevens et al., 2001) and 'managed care' (Morgan and Morgan, 2001). Psychologists involved in psychological treatments, therefore, ought to require a high burden of proof prior to embarking on the application of innovative or complementary therapies. Perhaps the longstanding association of hypnosis with ideas and practices outside the traditional boundaries of both psychology and medicine has deterred its extensive and in-depth study by psychologists.

A second reason may be that the two disciplines have effectively grown apart. Much psychological research into hypnosis is published not in mainstream journals but in specialist journals within the hypnosis field (e.g. the *International Journal of Clinical and Experimental Hypnosis*, the *American Journal of Clinical Hypnosis*, and *Contemporary Hypnosis*). There are few exceptions to this rule and these tend to relate to clinical applications of hypnosis and their evaluation within the clinical literature (e.g. Kirsch et al., 1995). The existence of different literatures reduces the opportunities for the interchange of new ideas and research between the two disciplines and, to a degree, impacts on the notion of 'peer review' since many ideas within hypnosis are not directly tested within mainstream psychology publications. It must also serve to preserve the level of ignorance around hypnosis research displayed by most psychologists.

I must confess to being one of those cautious and perhaps ignorant psychologists who has managed to study and practise for twenty-five years or so without any meaningful exposure to hypnosis. Despite working as an academic clinical psychologist and responsible, at one time, for both accrediting and running professional psychology courses, my only real exposure and interest has been to relate hypnosis to other therapeutically related 'altered states' such as relaxation and meditation (Turpin and Heap, 1998). Why, therefore, should I have been invited to contribute a chapter to this text on: 'The Highly Hypnotizable Person'?

The implicit question posed above is whether modern hypnosis and the serious scientific study of hypnosis, as exemplified by the chapters making up this book, can successfully live up to the 'pseudoscience versus science' challenge of Lilienfield et al. (2003). How do the chapters within this book stand up to the criteria of 'good' and 'pseudo' science identified by Lilienfield et al.? These criteria include adherence to Popperian principles of falsifiability and refutation, operationalism, reliance on peer review, adequate burden of empirical proof, and continuity with other areas within the discipline. What would my own peers from psychophysiology, clinical psychology or cognitive psychology make of these chapters? What is the relevance of hypnosis to contemporary theories and approaches in these fields? Would it prompt me to reappraise whether more undergraduates or professional trainees ought to be exposed and trained in hypnotic induction procedures? These are some of the questions that I will attempt to touch upon in my review of this book, although a detailed and critical systematic review of the area is beyond both my capabilities and my resources.

Hypnosis and contemporary psychology

It appears to me that there are several areas of overlap or continuity between psychology and hypnosis. First, there is the phenomenological study of the state itself and attempts to observe, assess and measure its characteristics, and whether they are similar to or different from other psychological states or phenomena. Such an enterprise need not be restricted to psychology but may also encompass physiological aspects of hypnotic states or functioning and these involve psychophysiological and neuroscientific investigations. Second, there is the study of the process and procedures of hypnotic induction whereby the hypnotist and subject interact, and through the use of these and suggestion, the subject's behaviour or perception is modified or altered. Social psychologists, in particular, have been interested in the rather unique interaction between hypnotist and subject, and have used a variety of explanations to account for

the demand characteristics said to exist within the experimental setting. These have evolved into what have been termed 'sociocognitive'
accounts of hypnosis. Third, it is acknowledged from various perspectives that individuals differ in the way that they respond to
demands placed upon them as a result of hypnotic induction procedures. This is frequently termed 'hypnotic suggestibility' or 'susceptibility' and various accounts of individual differences in these
attributes have been elaborated. Finally, there is the use of hypnosis
as a therapeutic technique and the degree to which its efficacy can be
proven and the therapeutic mechanisms identified and explained.

Most of these disparate approaches have been expertly dealt with
within this volume. Indeed Heap, Brown and Oakley within their
introductory chapter, provide a concise procedural introduction to
hypnosis for the naive reader and go on to review and describe the
major scientific theories existing currently within the field. In particular, they emphasize the differences between hypnotic state or
trance theories and non-state theories. The latter associate hypnotic
induction with the creation of a separate and distinctive psychological state or hypnotic trance, and then attempt to account
for it in relation to known psychodynamic, psychological or neuropsychological processes. For example, they identify ego-psychological
theory, which suggests that within the trance state the subject loses
the distinction between imagination and reality, and, from a Freudian perspective, primary processes are said to predominate over secondary processes. This is contrasted with several cognitive models of
hypnosis, which emphasize altered processing at the level of the central executive or consciousness: dissociated control theory and
neodissociation theory. A final state model is reviewed, based on
Gruzelier's neuropsychological theory.

The non-state models constitute the sociocognitive theories that
have stressed the role of imagination and expectancy in accounting
for suggestibility. The hypnotic induction, therefore, does not result
in the creation of an altered state or trance, but instead is a procedure
for establishing expectancies and engaging motivation, in order that
the subject comply with the hypnotist's suggestions. Various theories
account for whether the subject is aware of this compliance, whether
the actions are automatic or involuntary, and the degree of hypnotic
amnesia.

From the above perspectives, hypnosis is interesting in that it has
always encouraged an amalgam of psychodynamic and contemporary
psychology, involving cognitive processes such as the supervisory

attention system, unconscious and conscious executive systems, and dissociative psychopathology. However, current models of psychopathology also have re-considered the appropriateness of psychodynamic processes that had once firmly been left behind by mainstream psychology. For example, models of attentional bias said to underlie anxiety disorders have indicated that such biases might operate at a preconscious stage and outside the immediate awareness of the client (Mogg and Bradley, 1998). Neuropsychological models of fear responding have also suggested the existence of parallel pathways that allow the rapid processing of fear information within the amygdala without the necessity of cortical or conscious involvement (Damasio, 2003; Le Doux, 1996). Such ideas have also been adopted by Brewin (2001, 2003) to account for different memory systems implicated in the processing of traumatic events, which might account for the development in some individuals of persistent intrusions and flashbacks, frequently diagnosed as post-traumatic stress disorder (PTSD).

Interestingly, the importance of dissociative states is a major area of focus for acute stress disorder and also for the understanding of recovery from trauma (see Bryant and Harvey, 1997). Further parallels between trauma processing and hypnosis exist in the form of a controversial therapy, eye movement desensitization and reprocessing (EMDR), which bears a striking similarity to some aspects of hypnotic induction (see Harvey et al., 2003).

Finally, many therapeutic interventions now focus on the importance of imagery and re-experiencing as a means of therapy. Explanations of the effectiveness of these procedures range from habituation through to changing narrative contexts and attributions. Hence, whereas hypnosis might have invoked a language of dissociation, primary processes and the unconscious, which would have once been unpalatable to most psychologists, advances in cognitive psychology, neuroscience and psychopathology have required a re-examination of the relevance of some of these defunct Freudian concepts. It may be that contemporary models of hypnosis now have far more in common with contemporary psychology than at any other time in the field's recent development.

The two chapters by Barnier and McConkey (Chapters 2 and 3) provide an in-depth and authoritative treatment of measurement and assessment issues within hypnosis. First, the range of scales and methods with which to measure hypnotizability is reviewed in detail by Barnier and McConkey who critically appraise their theoretical basis, psychometric properties (including reliability and cross-cultural comparisons), and contemporary research areas. From a clinical perspective the notion of modifying hypnotizability via training programmes is particularly interesting both in enhancing the specific efficacy of hypnosis but also in understanding therapeutic change generally. I wonder whether there are any overlaps in techniques with other 'mental state' training experiences such as meditation or mindfulness training (e.g. Kabat-Zinn, 1994; Segal et al., 2002). A brief section in Chapter 2 deals with the correlates of hypnotizability, including Tellegen's 'absorption dimension' and measures of fantasy proneness and dissociation. I am left wondering whether any research has been conducted looking at psychosis-proneness or psychoticism scales, given the renewed interest in these personality measures as indices of vulnerability to psychosis and psychological trauma (e.g. Morrison et al., 2003).

The second chapter by McConkey and Barnier goes on to assess in greater depth means and measures to discriminate between the high hypnotizable and the low hypnotizable individual. This involves a detailed appraisal of the different theoretical approaches to hypnotizability and their implications for assessment and measurement. I suspect that this chapter will be of most interest to hypnosis researchers in the field than the curious psychologist, such as myself. I was still left with some uncertainties as to how I might measure or assess hypnotic susceptibility or induction, if ever I was sufficiently intrigued to follow up my curiosity empirically.

Wagstaff (Chapter 4) sets out to challenge the more traditional model of hypnosis as an altered state of consciousness or trance state. Although he acknowledges that the state model has always been implicit in accounts of hypnosis since the days of Mesmer, and indeed has recently been given added credibility by neuropsychological theories (e.g. Gruzelier, 1998), he emphasizes instead sociocognitive explanations that have sought to explain hypnosis using a variety of 'ordinary' concepts derived from social and cognitive psychology. From the outset, I must admit that to a clinical psychologist I find this approach less appealing since it is the promise of 'abnormal states and processes' that perhaps appeals most in the search for parallels or applications to psychopathology. Nevertheless, the goal set by sociocognitive models to account for the apparently 'unusual' using ordinary models of psychology is an identical philosophy to that which pervades contemporary psychopathology research. That is, many researchers have rejected diagnostic or pathological explanations of psychological disorders (e.g. Bentall, 2003; Persons, 1986); instead they have emphasized dimensional models whereby continuity in behaviours between individuals experiencing psychological dysfunction and 'normal' populations has been emphasized. For example, using contemporary social cognition models, Bentall attempts to account for psychotic experiences such as hallucinations and delusions, which traditionally are viewed as abnormal and lacking contact with reality. From this perspective sociocognitive models of hypnosis have much in common with social cognition models of psychopathology.

Some other interesting parallels emerge from Wagstaff's chapter. The careful deconstruction of hypnotic induction procedures also parallels some of the dismantling approaches used to evaluate psychotherapy. In particular, the comparison of the subjective experience of hypnotizable subjects with those of clients undergoing relaxation or imagery therapies is worthy of further exploration. A striking parallel also emerged between cognitive theories of hypnosis, which have evolved from working memory models and dual-task studies, and recent analogue studies of EMDR by Andrade and colleagues (Andrade et al., 1997). As has already been mentioned, EMDR bears some resemblance to hypnotic induction and would appear to have beneficial effects on imagery exposure interventions for clients with PTSD. According to Andrade and colleagues, the involvement of dual tasks, such as eye movements, within therapy leads to more effective exposure and subsequent habituation and reprocessing of traumatic images. However, an alternative explanation emerges independently from this chapter and concerns clients' expectancies. Wagstaff draws attention to the importance of expectancy within hypnotic therapy and cites work by Kirsch et al. (1995) that suggests that the inclusion of hypnotic induction or even the label 'hypnosis' may enhance therapeutic effectiveness of cognitive–behavioural interventions. It may also be the case that the EMDR procedures also lead to the induction of positive expectancies as regards therapeutic outcomes. Finally, Wagstaff takes a critical view of recent neuropsychological theories of hypnotic states and especially Gruzelier's (1998) frontal dysfunction model. He attempts to employ the strategic enactment account developed from the sociocognitive perspective to explain the different patterns of psychophysiological responding observed between low and high hypnotizable subjects. Essentially, highly susceptible subjects comply with the hypnotic induction procedures; this subsequently results in psychophysiological correlates of hypnotic responding, and these are distinguished psychophysiologically from low susceptible subjects who fail to comply with the induction demands.

Rhue (Chapter 5) concisely summarizes the literature surrounding the developmental aspects of hypnosis and its clinical application in children. She examines the relationship between fantasy-proneness in young children and the further development of hypnotic suscepti-bility in later childhood. She also reviews practical issues around the assessment and application of hypnosis with children. One interest-ing finding is the reported relationship between fantasy-proneness in individuals using the Inventory of Childhood Memories and Imagin-ings (Wilson and Barber, 1981) and reports of childhood adversity, including punishment and physical abuse. Such a relationship would be consistent with current ideas relating vulnerability for psychosis with dissociation and experience of childhood abuse and trauma (Mollon, 2002; Morrison, in press).

Chapter 6 by Horton and Crawford is essentially a rejoinder to the sociocognitive position elaborated by Wagstaff and his implicit critique of neuropsychological state models. These authors review a wide range of literature that relates biological processes to hypnosis and includes genetic mapping and functional imaging. Interesting questions such as the inheritance of hypnotic susceptibility are raised, together with neurophysiological studies of attention and frontal brain functioning. A particular focus is the therapeutic role of hypnosis in acting analgesically to control pain, in relation to either surgery or chronic pain disorders. Essentially Horton and Crawford argue that the highly hypnotizable individual is character-ized by a more effective attentional system that is more flexible, has greater resources and capacity, and may operate faster than that of the low hypnotizable individual. They also describe electroencepha-logic studies (EEG), which associate such attentional advantages with asymmetrical activation of theta rhythm. However, their chap-ter is largely descriptive and argues well for neurophysiological and psychological correlates of high hypnotizability, which are associ-ated with individual differences. It does not address directly ques-tions of mechanism or process, and therefore fails to provide an adequate rebuff to the challenge issued by Wagstaff that neuro-physiological differences are merely correlates of strategic enactment as posited by sociocognitive theorists.

In Chapter 7 Brown and Oakley assist in contributing further to the emerging cognitive model of hypnosis based on the complex interaction of different attentional systems. They first review the major cognitive theories put forward to account for hypnosis and automaticity, and examine critically the empirical evidence. They argue that the experimental studies conducted to test cognitive theories of hypnosis, involving studies of dual-task paradigms and resource allocation, have not only contributed to our understanding of hypnosis but have also made significant advances in our understanding generally of the cognitive architecture subsuming attention. Indeed, they go on to provide a detailed account of their own 'integrative theory of hypnosis' which constitutes an in-depth heuristic model based on contemporary cognitive psychology. Although working within the principles of a sociocognitive framework, they suggest that 'state variables' including information processing may heavily influence the outcome of suggested phenomena, as well as 'non-state' variables such as expectancies, context, and motivation. Oakley has previously termed this a 'neo-state view' of hypnosis (Oakley, 1998). The model describes how suggested expectancies are selected by the 'primary attentional system' (PAS), which results in self-evidently valid (i.e. real) perceptual distortions since the supervisory attentional system (SAS) has no direct access to this process. Such distortions ought to account for suggested phenomena such as analgesia and negative hallucinations, which are frequently demonstrated in highly hypnotizable subjects. Interestingly the different attentional systems might be implicated to differing degrees and this may result in cognitive dissociations between systems. Factors that influence the process are identified and these include deliberate SAS strategies such as 'thinking with', the hypnotic context and previous associations, and the notion of absorption. It is suggested that these factors may work together in order to achieve an 'absorbed state' whereby higher-level attentional functions (e.g. SAS) have become dissociated from more primary attentional systems.

The above theory is attractive since it is essentially an extension of existing cognitive models to account for the phenomenon of hypnosis. Accordingly, it does provide a useful interface for mainstream cognitive researchers to understand and become involved in hypnosis studies. It is perhaps a shame that more is not published in mainstream journals, as opposed to specialist hypnosis journals. The theory also attempts to explain some of the basic sensory processes implicated in therapeutic applications of hypnosis, together with a sophisticated account of factors that might influence their operation. I can't help drawing parallels between Brown and Oakley's model and some of the concepts (e.g. situationally and verbally accessible memory systems) and innovative interventions (e.g. narrative approaches to changing trauma contexts and memories) discussed within the trauma literature by researchers such as Brewin (Brewin, 2001; Brewin and Holmes, 2003).

Chapters 8 and 9 both perhaps interested me, as a clinician, the most. They examine the relationship between individual differences in susceptibility and clinical disorders and treatment, and attempts to enhance hypnotic responsiveness. It should also be mentioned at this point that the editors had planned to include a final clinical chapter reviewing the efficacy of clinical hypnosis in psychosomatic disorders but this had to be omitted at a late stage owing to unforeseen circumstances. It is unfortunate that no systematic review of clinical efficacy exists within the book, since the interested clinician is only exposed via the remaining chapters to some promising therapeutic indications for a growing list of conditions. However, most studies are underpowered statistically and are largely poorly controlled. If clinical hypnosis is to move into the mainstream of psychological therapies greater attention needs to be placed on systematic reviews and evidence based practice (Stevens et al., 2001)

Lynn, Meyer and Shindler's chapter examines the clinical correlates of high hypnotic susceptibility and starts from T.X. Barber's influential work which suggests three main categories of highly susceptible individuals: fantasy-prone, positively set and amnesia-prone. They review rather inconclusively the evidence for the basis of these claims and examine the suggestion that amnesia-prone individuals may reflect conversion hysteria and the possible influences of dissociative disorders and early child abuse. They discuss how these distinct groups might be of interest to clinicians and might affect the outcomes both for clinical hypnosis and more mainstream cognitive–behavioural therapies involving procedures such as relaxation or imaginal desensitization.

The final chapter by Gorassini deals with the question as to whether and how susceptibility may be modified. Although citing research to endorse the position that hypnotic responsiveness is remarkably stable, he reviews the evidence and techniques devised to enhance susceptibility, particularly within therapeutic situations. Essentially these techniques have focused on enhancing traditional induction procedures that seek to reduce sensation and activity, paradoxical alertness-increasing procedures, and methods for influencing suggestion and instructions. Perhaps unsurprisingly, at least to a clinician, one of the factors that appears to determine the success of these susceptibility enhancing methods is a focus on therapeutic engagement and the establishment of rapport with the client.

Conclusions

This has been a stimulating and knowledgeable book to read. Its strengths lie in the detail and the seriousness of the scientific approach with which the subject is approached. It helps to analyse and explain a complex and sometimes controversial phenomenon with clarity and authority. The detailed discussion of conceptual and methodological issues currently influencing the direction and outcome of research in this area will be invaluable for researchers interested in the highly hypnotizable person. Hopefully it will also open out a fascinating and sophisticated research area to mainstream academic psychologists. The treatment of theory and theoretical developments within this area is a particular strength of the book. For the clinician, it helps to provide a scientific foundation for a therapeutic technique; this is often ignored owing to a perceived lack of a scientific basis. Unfortunately, the text tantalizingly omits a systematic review of the status of the efficacy of clinical hypnosis and rarely addresses the mechanisms of change that might underlie any therapeutic gains. Nevertheless, I recommend this text wholeheartedly and trust that subsequent readers will learn even more about hypnosis during their exploration of the book than I have done.

References

Andrade, J., Kavanagh, D. and Baddeley, A. (1997) 'Eye-movements and visual imagery: A working memory approach to the treatment of post-traumatic stress disorder', *British Journal of Clinical Psychology*, 36:209–23.

Bentall, R.P. (2003) *Madness Explained: Psychosis and Human Nature*, London: Penguin and Allen Lane.

Brewin, C.R. (2001) 'A cognitive neuroscience account of posttraumatic stress disorder and its treatment', *Behaviour Research and Therapy*, 39:373–93.

—— (2003) *Post-traumatic Stress Disorder: Malady or Myth?*, New Haven, CT: Yale University Press.

—— and Holmes, E.A. (2003) 'Psychological theories of posttraumatic stress disorder', *Clinical Psychology Review*, 23:339–76.

Bryant, R.A. and Harvey, A.G. (1997) 'Acute stress disorder: A critical review of diagnostic issues', *Clinical Psychology Review*, 17:757–73.

Damasio, A. (2003) *Looking for Spinoza: Joy, Sorrow and the Feeling Brain*, New York: Heinemann.

Gruzelier, J. (1998) 'A working model of the neurophysiology of hypnosis: a review of the evidence', *Contemporary Hypnosis*, 15:3–21.

Harvey, A.G., Bryant, R.A. and Tarrier, N. (2003) 'Cognitive behaviour therapy for posttraumatic stress disorder', *Clinical Psychology Review*, 23:501–22.

Heap, M., Alden, P., Brown, R.J., Naish, P.L.N., Oakley, D.A., Wagstaff, G.F. and Walker, L.J. (2001) 'The nature of hypnosis: Report prepared by a working party at the request of the Professional Affairs Board of the British Psychological Society', Leicester: British Psychological Society.

Kabat-Zinn, J. (1994) *Wherever You Go, There You Are: Mindfulness Meditation in Everyday Life*, New York: Hyperion.

Kirsch, I., Montgomery, G. and Sapirstein, G. (1995) 'Hypnosis as an adjunct to cognitive-behavioral psychotherapy: A meta-analysis', *Journal of Consulting and Clinical Psychology*, 63:214–20.

Le Doux, J.E. (1996) *The Emotional Brain*, New York: Simon and Schuster.

Lilienfield, S.O., Lynn, S.J. and Lohr, J.M. (2003) *Science and Pseudoscience in Clinical Psychology*, New York: Guilford Press.

Mogg, K. and Bradley, B.P. (1998) 'A cognitive–motivational analysis of anxiety', *Behaviour Research and Therapy*, 36:809–48.

Mollon, P. (2002) *Remembering Trauma: A Psychotherapist's Guide to Memory and Illusion*, 2nd edn, London: Whurr.

Morgan, D.L. and Morgan, R.K. (2001) 'Single-participant research design: Bringing science to managed care', *American Psychologist*, 56:119–27.

Morrison, A.P., Frame, L. and Larkin, W. (2003) 'Relationships between trauma and psychosis: A review and integration', *British Journal of Clinical Psychology*, 42:331–54.

Oakley, D.A. (1998) 'Editorial commentary', *Contemporary Hypnosis*, 15:1–2.

Persons, J.B. (1986) 'The advantages of studying psychological phenomena rather than psychiatric diagnoses', *American Psychologist*, 41:1252–60.

Segal, Z.V., Williams, J.M.G. and Teasdale, J.D. (2002) *Mindfulness-based Cognitive Therapy for Depression*, New York: Guilford Press.

Stevens, A., Abrams, K., Brazier, J., Fitzpatrick, R. and Lilford, R. (2001) *The Advanced Handbook of Methods in Evidence Based Healthcare*, London: Sage.

Turpin, G.M. and Heap, M. (1998) 'Arousal reduction methods: relaxation, biofeedback, meditation, and hypnosis', in A.S. Bellack and M. Hersen (eds), *Comprehensive Clinical Psychology*, New York: Elsevier Science.

Wilson, S.C. and Barber, T.X. (1981) 'Vivid fantasy and hallucinatory

abilities in the life histories of excellent hypnotic subjects ("somnam-
bules"): Preliminary report with female subjects', in E. Klinger (ed.),
Imagery (Vol. 2): Concepts, Results, and Applications (pp. 133–49), New
York: Plenum.

Index

Page numbers referring to figures and tables appear in **bold** type

empirical evidence 155–8;
heuristic model 158, **159**;
high-level behavioural control
162–3; pre-attentive processing
158, 160, 161; secondary
representations 162–3; subjective
experience 158, 163–5; willed
actions 152, 153, 158, 164 *see also*
cognitive model of hypnosis
colour blindness, hypnotic 72
complementary therapy 241
compliance 10, 20, 45, 243, 246;
sociocognitive perspective 88,
92–6, 97–100 *see also* faking;
role-theory approach;
simulation
compulsions, posthypnotic 67, 187
computer administrated scales 44
COMT (catechol
O-methyltransferase) evaluation
135, 139
concentrative style of suggestion
170, 171, 172, 175–8
conscious awareness 136, 138, 157
see also experience, subjective
consciousness: altered states *see*
trance/s; first-person 163, 165;
nature of 152, 163–5; primary
164; secondary 163, 165
constructive style of suggestion 169,
170, 171, 172, 175–8
contention scheduling 14
context, hypnotic 40, 86, 172–3, 248
conversion disorder/hysteria 152,
187, 188, 202–3, 249
correlates of hypnotizability *see*
neurophysiological correlates;
personality profiles
counter-expectational experience 10
Crawford, Helen J. 133–51, 247
Creative Imagination Scale (CIS)
33, **34, 35**, 38, 39
criminal behaviour 97
CSTP *see* Carleton Skills Training
Program
cultural differences, hypnotizability
43–4, 51

Davis-Husband Scale 63

daydreaming, young children 115,
118
deepening methods 6, 216–18;
technological aids 217; verbal
216–17
delusions 246
Denmark 43
depression 203
depth of hypnosis *see* hypnotic
depth
detachment *see* absorption
developmental factors in hypnosis 3,
115–32, 247; adolescence 119,
120, 121, 124; adulthood 120;
fantasy-proneness 115, 124–7,
247; infancy 122; preadolescence
119, 120, 121; preschool 119–20,
124; reality-based behaviour 117,
121
developmental-interactive theory of
hypnosis 67
Diagnostic Rating Scale (DRS) 33,
34, 35, 38; role in assessing
diversity 63–4
Differential Attentional Processes
Inventory 137
difficulty/pass rates of hypnotic
tasks 9, 14, 37–8, 39, 40, 41, 42
disattention 176
dissociated control theory 13–15,
92, 153–4, 174, 177, 243 *see also*
executive functioning inhibition;
neodissociation theory
dissociation 9, 39, 48, 96, 97, 123,
245; and amnesia 152, 194;
cognitive model 167–8, 215, 216;
pathological 16, 190, 193–4, 199,
244; play 123 *see also* dissociated
control theory; neodissociation
theory
Dissociative Experiences Scale
(DES) 16, 48
distortion: cognitive 67; cued 213;
perceptual 167, 204, 248
diversity *see* hypnotic
responsiveness, variation
dopamine metabolism studies 139
dreams 67
DRS *see* Diagnostic Rating Scale

responsiveness; measurement scales
hypnotic experience *see* experience of hypnosis
hypnotic induction *see* induction
Hypnotic Induction Profile (HIP) 33, **34**, **35**, 36, 37, 38, 42
hypnotic profiles *see* personality profiles
hypnotic responsiveness: assessment 62–6, 140; children 118, 119–20; cultural differences 43–4, 51; fluctuation 49; measurement scales 62–6, 140; performance patterns 70–4; population percentages 187; profiles 66–70; and relaxation 217–18; stability over time 1, 2, 3, 9, 16, 20, 40, 43, 44, 86, 120, 134, 214, 249; true 134, 142; types/phases 74–6; variation 1, 8–10, 20–2, 30, 32, 40–1, 61–6, 76–9, 140, 243, 245 *see also* highly hypnotizable people; personality profiles; suggestion/suggestibility; three-dimensional theory; virtuosos
hypnotic responsiveness, training *see* Carleton Skills Training Program; enhancement of hypnotizability; training for hypnotizability
hypnotic role 173 *see also* role-theory approach
hypnotic susceptibility *see* highly hypnotizable people; hypnotic responsiveness; measurement scales
hypnotizability *see* highly hypnotizable people; hypnotic responsiveness
hysteria 188

ideomotor suggestion 6, 88, 215; population levels 9; tests 39, 41, 75–6
ideosensory suggestion 6
illusions, visual 137
imagery 30, 38, 246; and

responsiveness 227; therapeutic use 192, 244
imagination 19, 20, 22, 30, 243; active 195
imaginative play: persistence into adulthood 117; young children 115–16
imaginative suggestibility 21–2
implementation intention 155
implosion 192
induction 2, 6, 246, 249; absence in tests 38, 39; active-alert 218–19, 249; brain hemisphere activation 100–3; and dissociated control 154; passive 226; relaxation 17, 215, 226; standardized 31, 32; traditional 215–16
infants, inter-subjectivity 122–3
information processing: automatic 30; heuristic model 158, **159**
inherited hypnotizability 122–3, 247 *see also* genetic determinants of high hypnotizability
inhibition: high level cognitive *see* supervisory attentional system; *see also* dissociated control theory; frontal cortex; response 221–2
insight therapy 201
insomnia 202
instructions, hypnotic 221–2, 249
intention 157 *see also* automatic behaviour/processes; involuntary behaviour; willed actions
interference, task *see* dual-task paradigm
International Journal of Clinical and Experimental Hypnosis 33, **35**
intuitive experience 164
Inventory of Creative/Childhood Memories and Imaginings (ICMI) 48, 189, 247
involuntary behaviour, hypnotic 13–14, 15, 19, 37, 89, 91, 106; cognitive theory 153–4, 157, 158, 164; movement 187; understanding 158 *see also* automatic behaviour; willed actions